Public Policy and Politics

Series Editors: Colin Fudge and Robin Hambleton

Public policy-making in western democracies is confronted by new pressures. Central values relating to the role of the state, the role of markets and the role of citizenship are now all contested and the consensus built up around the Keynesian welfare state is under challenge. New social movements are entering the political arena: electronic technologies are transforming the nature of employment; changes in demographic structure are creating heightened demands for public services; unforeseen social and health problems are emerging; and, most disturbing, social and economic inequalities are increasing in many countries.

How governments – at international, national and local levels – respond to this developing agenda is the central focus of the Public Policy and Politics series. Aimed at a student, professional, practitioner and academic readership, it aims to provide up-to-date, comprehensive and authoritative analyses of public policy-making in practice.

The series is international and interdisciplinary in scope, and bridges theory and practice by relating the substance of policy to the politics of the policy-making process.

D0230457

Public Policy and Politics

Series Editors: Colin Fudge and Robin Hambleton

PUBLISHED

Kate Ascher, *The Politics of Privatisation: Contracting Out Public Services*
Rob Atkinson and Graham Moon, *Urban Politics in Britain: The City, the State and the Market*
Jacqueline Barron, Gerald Crawley and Tony Wood, *Councillors in Crisis: The Public and Private Worlds of Local Councillors*
Danny Burns, Robin Hambleton and Paul Hoggett, *The Politics of Decentralisation: Revitalising Local Democracy*
Aram Eisenschitz and Jamie Gough, *The Politics of Local Economic Policy: The Problems and Possibilities of Local Initiative*
Stephen Glaister, June Burnham, Handley Stevens and Tony Travers, *Transport Policy in Britain*
Christopher Ham, *Health Policy in Britain: The Politics and Organisation of the National Health Service* (third edition)
Ian Henry, *The Politics of Leisure Policy*
Peter Malpass and Alan Murie, *Housing Policy and Practice* (fifth edition)
Robin Means and Randall Smith, *Community Care: Policy and Practice* (second edition)
Gerry Stoker, *The Politics of Local Government* (second edition)
Kieron Walsh, *Public Services and Market Mechanisms: Competition, Contracting and the New Public Management*

FORTHCOMING

Tony Green and Geoff Whitty, *The Changing Politics of Education: Education Policy in Contemporary Britain*
Robin Hambleton, *An Introduction to Local Policy-Making*
John Solomos, *Racial Inequality and Public Policy*

Public Policy and Politics
Series Standing Order
ISBN 0–333–71705–8 hardcover
ISBN 0–333–69349–3 paperback
(outside North America only)

You can receive future titles in this series as they are published. To place a standing order please contact your bookseller or, in the case of difficulty, write to us at the address below with your name and address, the title of the series and the ISBN quoted above.

Customer Services Department, Macmillan Distribution Ltd
Houndmills, Basingstoke, Hampshire RG21 6XS, England

Transport Policy in Britain

Stephen Glaister

June Burnham

Handley Stevens

and

Tony Travers

MACMILLAN

First published 1998 by
MACMILLAN PRESS LTD
Houndmills, Basingstoke, Hampshire RG21 6XS
and London
Companies and representatives
throughout the world

ISBN 0–333–66123–0 hardcover
ISBN 0–333–66124–9 paperback

A catalogue record for this book is available
from the British Library.

This book is printed on paper suitable for recycling and
made from fully managed and sustained forest sources.

10   9   8   7   6   5   4   3   2   1
07 06 05 04 03 02 01 00 99 98

Printed in Hong Kong

Contents

List of Tables

List of Figures

Preface

This book has its origin in a report on *Transport Policy-Making in Britain*, which was commissioned from the Greater London Group of the London School of Economics by the Rees Jeffreys Road Fund. The research undertaken for that report has been extended and widened to provide a more comprehensive text. We owe a considerable debt to the Trustees of the Road Fund for having stimulated our joint approach to transport policy across a range of disciplines and expertise. The authors would like to thank all those who helped them in the collection of material, ideas and opinions, including David Bayliss, June Bridgeman, Peter Bryant, Mike Cottell, Tony Ridley and all the practitioners who commented on drafts and debated the issues with us in meetings of the Greater London Group and other fora.

STEPHEN GLAISTER
JUNE BURNHAM
HANDLEY STEVENS
TONY TRAVERS

Part I

The Context

1 Introduction

The operation of a modern economy and the enjoyment of a modern lifestyle depend heavily on the smooth running of efficient transport systems, but there has until recently been remarkably little sustained and comprehensive debate about transport policy in Britain. Even among politicians it has received only limited attention. A measure of shrewd political judgment might be needed to make the best choice of road and public transport schemes within the inevitable constraint of limited resources, but by and large transport policy was regarded as a rather unglamorous technical portfolio to be given to someone at the far end of the Cabinet table.

This situation is changing. The closing years of the twentieth century may well prove to be a critical period in British transport policy for two reasons. The first has to do with the framework of economic regulation within which decisions have to be made by the users and providers of transport services; the second concerns the adjustments which transport policy must make in the light of growing understanding and concern about the impact of transport on the environment. In both respects major changes have taken place over the past decade or so, in the first case as a result of deliberate government policies, in the second as a result of increasing public awareness of environmental issues generally and their relevance to transport policy in particular.

This book sets out the background to transport policy in Britain in the context of both these changes at a time when a new government has signalled its intention to develop an integrated transport policy which must also be environmentally sustainable and yet affordable. At what appears to be a turning point in the history of transport policy in Britain, an analysis of the major issues confronting policy-makers in the closing years of the twentieth century should facilitate an informed assessment of the

3

legislation and practical decisions through which the concept of an integrated transport policy will have to be defined and elaborated as Britain moves into the twenty-first century.

The framework of economic regulation

Eighteen years of Conservative governments between 1979 and 1997 have resulted in the return to private ownership of nearly all transport services and a substantial proportion of transport infrastructure. In the private sector the transport industries are subject to market disciplines within a framework of government regulation designed to ensure fair competition as well as high standards of public safety. The profit motive acts as a spur to technological advance as well as lower costs and keener prices. However, aggressive competition can make it difficult to use more than one company in the course of a single journey. Yet it is essential that such transfers should be easy, even effortless, if journeys by public transport are to compete effectively with the seamless experience of travel by car.

There is therefore a continual tension between the commercial freedom which competition demands and the degree of regulation which may be needed in order to ensure public convenience in terms of easily accessible, unbiased information about competing services, through-ticketing and convenient connections. The 1997 Labour government has adopted the concept of an integrated transport policy, which it regards as a more rational way to resolve these tensions than market disciplines and freedom of choice, that underpinned the regulatory structures for a privatized and deregulated transport system. The pendulum is swinging back towards more regulation, but the lessons of the past (Chapter 2) stand as a clear warning against the consequences of too much government intervention. It will be of considerable interest to see where the new balance between competition and regulation is struck as an integrated transport policy takes shape.

Transport and the environment

If Labour and Conservative politicians tend to start from rather different ideological positions in relation to the economic regulation of the transport industries, there is much less difference between them when it comes to the second set of issues which makes transport policy of such critical importance on the threshold of a new millennium. Over the past decade or so, it is the growing concern about the impact of transport on the environment which has done more than anything else to bring transport policy into the forefront of political debate. Since 1991, when environmental activists became prominent in seeking to frustrate or at least delay construction of the M3 motorway through Twyford Down to the east of Winchester, there has almost always been at least one transport project, usually a road scheme, which has been the focus of active resistance with the attendant media coverage. It is a mark of the importance now attached to issues involving transport and the environment that in the Labour government of 1997 the Department of the Environment, Transport and the Regions was headed by the Deputy Prime Minister, John Prescott.

It is difficult to say who first crystallized this growing sense of public concern about transport policy into a coherent policy debate, but the trustees of the Rees Jeffreys Fund can take some credit for being among the first to identify the issues which were coming to the fore when in 1988 they commissioned a research project on 'Transport and Society' with a brief which stated:

The insatiable demand for personal travel and the movement of goods has to be balanced with the inevitable limitations of land space and the environmental desires of people – as travellers, dwellers and pedestrians.

In April 1989 the scale of the problem was confirmed when the Department of Transport published a new national road traffic forecast which suggested that traffic flows would double by about 2025. As the practical implications of these forecasts were absorbed, particularly for road-building, they heightened the already growing concern for the environment. Another key event was the Earth Summit at Rio de Janeiro in June 1992 which focused attention on the large contribution which transport makes to air pollution with its links to global warming and climate change. Transport was now seen as putting at risk not merely the physical environment of town and countryside, but even our climate and with it our whole way of life. Increasing air pollution also raised concerns about public health, as evidence linked the rising incidence of asthma and other respiratory diseases to increasing levels of vehicle exhaust emissions.

The transport debate

Since 1992 transport policy, and particularly its impact on the environment, has been more or less continuously in the news (see Chapter 10 for a fuller analysis). In 1995 Brian Mawhinney, then Secretary of State for Transport, tried to reclaim the initiative for government by launching what he called a national transport debate. He made and published a series of speeches in which he explored all the main issues – urban transport, freight, the international dimension, transport and the economy, transport and the environment, and not least transport choices. The well documented, but for the most part indecisive Green Paper, *Transport: The Way Forward*, which followed in 1996, took its inconclusive cue from the speech on transport choice which concluded 'it is not the role of ... a Conservative government to limit people's choices unnecessarily'.

As the Conservative government concentrated its remaining energies on completing the controversial privatization of British Rail, it was left to the Labour Party to take up the wider debate with their policy paper *Consensus for Change*, which promised a return to the concept of an integrated transport policy. The election of a Labour government in May 1997 on a manifesto which included a commitment to an environmentally sustainable integrated transport policy precipitated the commissioning of yet more reviews – of roads, of buses, of rail regulation – leading to a White Paper, which in turn is likely to fuel a continuing debate about the measures required to implement the new policy. Over the years the intensity of the debate will vary as newsworthy stories come and go, but the chances are that it will remain a topic of both technical and political contention, because the issues

FIGURE 1.1   Motor vehicle traffic growth and GDP, 1965–94

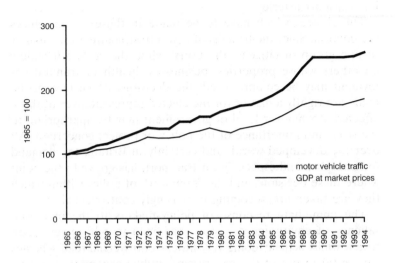

Sources: Transport Statistics (various years) and other sources.

which have been raised but not resolved are likely to become
more rather than less acute.

Responding to the transport debate

The core of the problem can be stated in a few words. Over a
long period of time vehicle traffic has tended to grow at least as
fast and often faster than GDP (see Figure 1.1).

As incomes rise people are prepared to spend more on transport, which lends powerful support to those who insist that the
demand should be met. However, there is increasing resistance
to the social costs of other people's transport, not only the burden of increased taxation to pay for infrastructure built in the
public sector, but also the reduced amenity – the damage done
to both urban and rural neighbourhoods, and the increased pollution and associated health risks which arise from more exhaust
gases, more noise and even from the perpetual glow of lighted
highways which have banished darkness and starlight as well as

peace and quiet from broad strips of countryside along the major transport arteries.

The choices which have to be made in these circumstances are political. Since the benefits of new infrastructure accrue mainly to one group of citizens, the users, while the costs fall mainly on others whose properties, businesses, health or tranquil enjoyment may be compromised, the decisions which have to be made are rightly a matter for the elected representatives of those affected at whatever level of government may be appropriate to the scale and importance of the policy or project concerned. All over the developed world, and certainly in Britain, the demand for transport, and especially car transport, has grown to the point where these decisions and the framework of policy within which they are taken are becoming increasingly controversial.

The immediate response of policy-makers to the increased salience of environmental issues has been to pile review upon review whilst actually doing very little. Controversial road schemes can be taken out of the programme, public expenditure can be cut, environmental protest is denied a focus, and there are no more dramatic confrontations for the media to report. However, as the pressures arising from economic growth put the transport system under increasing strain, it is not the contested building of new infrastructure which hits the news but the symptoms of ever greater transport congestion. Journey times lengthen, cities choke on the smog created by exhaust from vehicles caught in huge traffic jams, and conditions become intolerable on overcrowded trains and buses. When he was Secretary of State for Transport, Cecil Parkinson 'liked to say that he was the only minister who had to offer rather than accept apologies when his visitors were late for a meeting. Rightly or wrongly the government collects some share of the blame for every delay and more seriously for every accident on crowded roads or railways which can be put down to inadequate provision for investment. Eventually the pressure builds up again to the point where new proposals have to be rushed forward.

There is an element of caricature in this description of the way transport policy responds to changes in the economic and political environment, but all effective caricature has a basis of truth. And short-term changes in policy, responding first to the threat of congestion, then to the opposite threat of environmental damage, are no substitute for a steady policy. The forces which shape transport policy – the inexorable growth in mobility, the changes in the patterns of economic and social activity which go with it, the gradual erosion of environmental amenities – are all longer-term developments which need to be addressed by the steady application of well-conceived longer term policies.

Following publication of the Conservative government's 1996 Green Paper as well as the Labour Party's policy document, *Consensus for Change*, the range of options was already well documented, even before publication of the new Labour government's White Paper on an integrated transport policy. Unless provision is made for some increased capacity to meet the projected growth in demand, then either that growth will have to be eliminated, which is hard to envisage in a free society, or existing capacity will have to be ever more tightly rationed by congestion, by price or by regulation. None of these approaches is likely to be popular, and finding the right balance among them will require the exercise of a high degree of political skill. The terms of the debate have been changed with the election of a Labour government in 1997, but since the issues remain as intractable as ever, it seems likely that the debate over the practical means to implement an environmentally sustainable integrated transport policy will have to be engaged at every level of government from Cabinet to parish council for many years to come.

Policy and policy-making

The initial research on 'Transport and Society' which was undertaken for the Rees Jeffreys Fund pointed to the need for policies which would strike a better balance between the demand for mobility and an acceptable impact on the environment, and for institutional arrangements within which such policies could be worked out. The present book has its origins in a further study of transport policy-making in Britain, published in 1994, which the Rees Jeffreys Fund commissioned to explore those arrangements. For the purposes of this book the coverage of that study has been extended from roads to all forms of transport, though we have retained a strong emphasis on roads and the main modes of UK domestic public transport (rail and bus services) since these are much more significant in volume terms than air and sea transport. The latter are also – with the exception of airports and aircraft noise – less controversial.

The emphasis on policy-making has also been retained for the sound practical reason that anyone with an interest in transport policy who wants to exercise an effective influence in that process needs to understand who the actors are, how they relate to one another, what powers they exercise and what constraints they face. But the importance of the policy-making structures is not merely practical. They also shape the terms of the debate itself. A structure which keeps oversight of road and rail spending separate is liable to find that it has applied different criteria to the approval of road and rail projects, or at the very least that it has applied similar criteria in a different way. Likewise, an organization which has direct responsibility for the construction and maintenance of the trunk road network but stands at one remove from the construction and maintenance of the railway network and the operation of its services is likely to have a roads emphasis in its policy-making simply because that is what most of its staff spend most of their time doing. This situation was beginning to change in the last year of the Conservative government (1996) as more than 10 per cent of the trunk road network was transferred to the private sector to manage and maintain under wide-ranging contracts to design, build, finance and operate (DBFO) substantial segments of the network, with more to follow (see Chapter 8); but it remains to be seen whether the financial and economic benefits of this rolling privatization programme will be enough to induce a Labour government to pursue the progressive transfer of responsibility for the national road network to the new road operating industry in the private sector of the economy which the Conservative government were seeking to create.

Part I: the context

Just as current institutional arrangements for policy-making have an important bearing on the policy which emerges, so too do they in their turn bear the imprint of past events which led to their development. We therefore begin with a historical survey of the events which have shaped both the physical networks and the organizations responsible for administering and developing transport policy, transport infrastructure and transport services. Chapter 2 recalls how most of Britain's transport infrastructure was created by the entrepreneurial vigour of the private sector. The dominance of the public sector in the decades following the Second World War may have been the accidental consequence of adverse economic circumstances, but it also suited the policy inclinations of the Labour governments of that time who believed they should control the commanding heights of the economy and be directly responsible for the provision of public services. Boards were appointed by ministers, wages, fares and service levels were subject to bureaucratic intervention, and capital investment required Treasury approval. The Conservative governments of the 1950s and 1960s also accepted the need for a large public sector.

The extent of the change brought about by Conservative administrations between 1979 and 1997 can scarcely be exaggerated. Driven by a policy stance which favoured privatization and deregulation as a means of rolling back the frontiers of the state in order to secure the greater economic efficiency which could be delivered by a competitive market for transport as for other goods and services, 18 years of Conservative government succeeded in returning to private ownership road freight and coach services, airlines and airports, buses and trains. By 1997 the London Underground was the only major provider of transport services still in public ownership, and this too would have been privatized if a Conservative government had been re-elected in 1997. As government has withdrawn from the board room, it has had to rethink all the mechanisms required to oversee companies providing a public service in the private sector. We describe the new regulatory arrangements which were put in place to maintain the stimulus of competition wherever possible, and to safeguard the public interest against abuses of market power where local or national monopolies emerged.

Part II: the decision-makers

Part II identifies the decision-makers, explaining how they work and how they relate to one another. Chapter 3 sets out the position in central and local government and in the main transport industries including the complex structures devised to regulate the privatized railways, whilst Chapter 4 adds the European dimension. We show how the structures have been adapted under the Labour government of 1997 to recreate a united Department of the Environment, Transport and the Regions (DETR), and how British policy-makers are well placed to influence the transport policies of the European Union under a government whose European policies are no longer paralysed, as were those of the Conservative government in its last years, by fears of the Eurosceptic opposition within its own ranks. These explanations are complemented by four case studies (Chapter 5) illustrating the ability of a range of interest groups to influence the policy-making process at every level of government.

Part III: the planning framework

Part III examines in more depth the planning framework within which the key decisions are taken about the transport infrastructure and services which are the immediate focus of so much controversy. It is essential to understand how these arrangements work at both local and national levels of government. During the 1980s, as a consequence of the struggle to establish more effective central government control over local government spending, there was a marked shift of power from town hall to Whitehall, which affected transport as much as any other policy sector. In the 1990s the pendulum has begun to swing back towards the town halls as it is increasingly recognised in Whitehall and Westminster that local authorities have a major contribution to make to the solution of local problems, not least in the application of transport and planning policies. Chapter 6 explains how even the Conservative government used its controls over planning frameworks and local authority expenditure to encourage the integration of transport and land-use planning at local and regional levels. At the national level (Chapter 7) ideological objections to planning by government made it impossible for Conservative ministers to acknowledge any need for a national strategy beyond exercising the Secretary of State's functions within the planning regime, and operating the regulatory structures required to maintain the competitive market in privatized transport services which they had created. However, we show how in practice government decisions on major projects filled the gap. A Labour government may feel the need to put some new structures in place to signal its intentions for an integrated transport policy, but in practice many of the powers and structures which might be needed are in place already.

Part IV: the economic framework

Nothing can be built or operated without the money to pay for it, and Part IV turns to the all-important economic framework that has changed so much with the transfer of many transport industries to the private sector. The balance between public expenditure and private investment is shifting, not just as a consequence of privatization, though that has a significant effect, but as both Conservative and Labour governments make increasing use of the Private Finance Initiative (what Labour have called Public–Private Partnerships) to involve the private sector in investments which would previously have been carried out within the public sector. Chapter 8 describes both the traditional and the new sources of finance, and the implications of the shift which has taken place, whilst Chapter 9 examines the economic issues which arise, particularly in relation to competition and regulation of public transport in the private sector, and in the criteria which determine the allocation of the limited resources available for public sector investments.

Part V: Conclusions

Since the early 1980s central government has fashioned a powerful new range of administrative and financial tools for the oversight of the transport industries in the post-privatization era, but they are capable of being used to achieve a wide range of differing political objectives. The concluding chapter follows the development of the transport debate which has gathered momentum since the late 1980s, and explores the issues which will have to be addressed and the range of policy instruments which are available to implement an integrated, affordable and environmentally sustainable transport policy for the twenty-first century.

2 The Evolution of Transport Policy

From canals and turnpikes to state-regulated private railways

The crowds which gathered in October 1829 to watch the Rainhill trials, which resulted in the choice of Stephenson's 'Rocket' for the Liverpool and Manchester railway when it opened a year later, would have been proud of the tremendous advances in transport which had already been made within their lifetime. As children some might have watched the construction of the Bridgewater Canal in the 1760s, in the same transport corridor between Manchester and Liverpool, signalling the start of the great era of canal building which by the end of the century had linked the Mersey first with the Trent and then with Thames and Severn in a network which laid down the essential transport infrastructure for Britain's industrial revolution. Over the past decade or so the appalling state of the roads had been much improved by John Loudon Macadam's better surfaces and Thomas Telford's engineering on the London–Holyhead road, which together had reduced coach journey times between London and Manchester from four-and-a-half days with the first 'Flying Coaches' in 1754 to a mere eighteen hours and eighteen minutes by the 'Manchester Telegraph' in 1830 (Savage, 1966: 30). The canals and turnpikes were transporting goods and passengers more speedily and efficiently than before, but their monopoly position enabled them to charge excessive prices.

The new railway between Manchester and Liverpool promised vigorous competition, reducing the transit time from 36 hours to only five or six and cutting charges by a third. It was a huge success, both for goods and passenger traffic, soon carrying nearly half a million passengers in a year. However, far from stimulating competition, it would not be long before the traders who applauded Stephenson's 'Rocket' would find they had exchanged one monopoly for another. The economic advantages of railways over canals and turnpikes were so great that within twenty-five years the railway network had grown to nearly 10 000 miles and had very largely overwhelmed any competition there might have been at first from the canal companies and the turnpike trusts.

Given the success of private enterprise in so radically improving transport provision by water, by road and now by rail, it is not at all surprising that the liberal politicians of the nineteenth century were content to 'leave it to the market' to choose how and where to invest in service-provision whilst using state intervention to limit monopoly profits and protect rights to life, liberty and property. They thought these rights should be defended, where necessary, by state regulation against large or monopoly enterprises. Thus one of the earliest pieces of rail legislation was the Railway Regulation Act 1840 empowering the Board of Trade to appoint railway inspectors to check new passenger lines and receive information about rail accidents. The Whigs (or Liberals) were more willing to intervene in a 'utilitarian' search for efficiency, and to defend rail users, especially small businesses. The Tories (or Conservatives) were more protective of property-owners' rights. But all were 'free market' when contrasted with the Labour Party of the following century, which expected to plan and coordinate transport through centralization and nationalization (Morrison, 1933). With these principles in mind it is easier to understand the route transport policy took.

Once the steam locomotive was developed, high canal charges stimulated the rapid construction of commercial rail lines, though opposition from canal-owners and landowners demanding high compensation made the passage of private bills difficult or at least expensive. Rail companies needed parliamentary approval to come into being, but Parliament took only limited interest in the 'network' which was being created, ad hoc, from local lines. In 1844, the growing pressure of private rail bills encouraged MPs to set up a select committee on railways, chaired by William Gladstone, then a 'Peelite' (liberal Tory) and President of the Board of Trade. The committee wanted the construction of lines to be more rational. It thought the duplication of lines would take trade from existing companies without necessarily keeping prices down. Gladstone set up a railways board within the Trade department to oversee railway promotion, but the railway interest groups opposed it. Peel abolished it in 1845 after Gladstone left the department, and between 1845 and 1847 Parliament approved 425 Acts covering more than 8500 miles of railway.

The oligopolistic competition of the early 1840s soon gave way to a process of consolidation which progressively limited competition as moves towards the creation of a more coherent rail network were taken by the rail companies themselves. The Railway Clearing House had already been established voluntarily by companies to facilitate through-traffic across company boundaries when it was made statutory in 1846. The same year also saw the passage of 18 Acts sanctioning railway company amalgamations, including the London and North Western Railway, the major trunk route between London and Manchester/Liverpool via Birmingham. The taking over of weaker companies by successful ones from the 1840s improved coordination and efficiency without government having to act. From the mid-1850s until after the First World War the railways enjoyed an almost complete monopoly of inland passenger and freight transport. Few British canals remained prosperous after the 1840s and by 1850 stage coaches had been all but driven off the road. Parliament worried about the establishment of monopolies in certain regions, but in 1872 a select committee concluded that railway amalgamations were inevitable and perhaps desirable. Product emulation, such as the copying by all railways of Midland Railways third-class carriages, had improved and standardized service quality. In 1909, following another wave of amalgamations, a Departmental Committee on Railway Agreements and Amalgamations concluded that some regulation of cooperation would be to the advantage of the public as well as the railway companies.

In these circumstances the main role of government, exercised through the Board of Trade, was to defend the trading community against the monopoly power of the railway companies. Gladstone's 1844 Railway Regulation Act gave the government the option of revising prices downwards if a company paid dividends of 10 per cent or more, and the right of compulsory purchase after 21 years, though these options were never exercised. The so-called 'Parliamentary' train, under the same Act, was an early instance of consumer protection. All companies were required to provide one return passenger train a day at a reasonable speed (at least 12 mph) and maximum fare (1d or 0.4p a mile). In 1854, under a coalition government, Parliament passed the Railway and Canal Traffic Act which required each railway company to take all trade offered (to be 'a common carrier'). They had to set and publish the same levels of fares and charges to all for any particular service (not give 'undue preference'). Though the state did not intervene directly in rail provision, neither did it allow rail companies to set tariffs flexibly on strictly commercial criteria, or pick and choose between the types of traffic they would carry.

Even so, under the multitude of private Acts of Parliament the railway companies retained extensive scope to exploit their monopoly position, and as the process of railway amalgamations proceeded, the trading community, often powerless in the face of a monopoly carrier, became increasingly agitated. The Railway and Canal Traffic Act of 1873 compelled the publication of all rates in force, broken down into their component elements, and set up a Railway Commission to enforce the legislation requiring the railways to offer the same rate to all their customers, but the legal situation was complex and the Commission lacked teeth. Eventually the Railway and Canal Traffic Acts of 1888 and 1894 required companies to set maximum rates which could not be raised without the permission of the Railway and Canal Commission (a Board of Trade-appointed quango). This Act was to prove all too effective in constraining the commercial flexibility of the railway companies. They could not raise their rates without permission, which was hard to obtain, and they dared not lower them, even to attract new business, for fear that they would be unable to raise them again if the lower rate proved uneconomic. The combined effect of more than half a century of monopoly domination of the transport market, together with a degree of government regulation that tended to stifle any commercial initiative which might have survived, left the railways ill-prepared to face effective competition from road transport when that began to emerge after the First World War.

FIGURE 2.1   Transport policy 1555–1914: early development

1555   Highways Act: parishes to maintain roads using their own labour and equipment.

1663   First Turnpike Trust established under private Act of Parliament. Creation of about 1 000 Trusts administering some 22 000 miles of road by 1830. Acts allowed companies to charge tolls to finance improvements and repairs.

1767   Bridgewater Canal opened, linking Manchester and Liverpool.

1791–4   Height of canal investment boom, with 81 canal bills in parliament.
         Main network in place by about 1800.

1820   Macadam pioneered improved road surfaces.
        Telford improved road engineering, for example on London–Holyhead road.

1830   Opening of Liverpool and Manchester Railway.

1835   General Highway Act replaced statute labour for parish roads with power to levy a rate.

1840   Railway Regulation Act: Board of Trade could appoint railway inspectors.

1846   Rail gauge standardized at four foot eight-and-a-half inches. 219 private bills in Parliament at height of railways investment boom: mileage increased trom 2000 miles in 1843 to nearly 10 000 miles by 1854. Mileage reached 15 000 in 1870, 23 000 in 1910, falling back to 15 000 in 1960 and 10 000 today.

1854   Railway and Canal Traffic Act prohibited undue or unreasonable preference in setting fares and required the provision of convenient interchange.

1873   Railway Commission – from 1888 Railway and Canal Commision – established as regulator at arm's length from Board of Trade.

1894   Railway and Canal Traffic Act froze rail freight rates for a generation by giving traders a right of appeal to Railway and Canal Commision against any increase.

1910   Lloyd George introduced Road Fund and Road Board. All revenue from vehicle licences and fuel duty put into Road Fund. Raided for other purposes trom 1926, subsumed into general budget from 1937.

From local to national roads: the creation of the Road Board

Before the canals were built in the closing years of the eighteenth century, navigable waterways were used to bring goods as far inland as possible, and then they had to be carried by pack horses. Since 1555 road maintenance had been a parish responsibility relying on local labour and equipment which had to be supplied gratis for up to six consecutive days in a year. It was not till 1835 that the statutory labour requirement was replaced by the right to levy a rate, and even then the control of the work was left in the often ill-qualified hands of locally appointed surveyors. The development of Turnpike Trusts after 1663, and especially in the second half of the eighteenth century, created about 20 000 miles of better roads, particularly once their administration and surfacing was improved after 1810 under the influence of Macadam. But even the improved road surfaces could not tolerate the heavy loads which might have been conveyed by steam-driven road vehicles, and the condition of the turnpikes deteriorated when they became uneconomic in the face of railway competition. The Trusts themselves were gradually abolished by Parliament between 1870 and 1890, the burden of maintenance being thrown back on the parish authorities who could not afford to maintain roads to suitable standards for faster, long-distance traffic, or did not see why they should do so. From 1876 they had some help from a government grant, and after 1878 there were contributions from county funds. But it was only with the Local Government Act of 1888 that the parishes were relieved of part of their ancient responsibility, the maintenance of main roads being transferred to the county councils with additional aid from the government exchequer.

Part of the impetus for this important change seems to have come from the touring cyclists of the 1880s. In 1886 the Cyclists' Tourist Club and the National Cyclists' Union set up a joint body, the Road Improvement Association (RIA), to campaign to improve road surfaces. The transfer of highways maintenance to the new county councils and county boroughs created in 1888 was said to be as a result of RIA pressure (Hamer, 1987: 23). However, the roads were not much improved, and the RIA itself soon ran out of funds. When the (Royal) Automobile Club (RAC) was set up in 1897 as a 'gentlemen's club' for motorists it joined the RIA, whose honorary secretary from 1901 was William Rees Jeffreys, then a civil servant at the Board of Trade. The motorists revived the RIA. There was little opposition to motor vehicles from the railway lobby until the 1920s; it thought they would act as 'feeders' for rail, bringing goods and passengers to stations. The anti-motor lobby was made up of horsebreeders, and residents of rural areas who worried about accidents, and thought motorists should pay for road maintenance. County magistrates imposed high speeding fines because until 1920 the money subsidized the rates (Plowden, 1971: 64).

In 1901 the RIA sent a delegation to the Local Government Board (the forerunner of the Department of Environment) proposing a single-purpose, national body should be set up to control and develop the road system. The LGB recommended setting-up county road boards, to be given grants in proportion to the class of road. The government appointed a Royal Commission to look at possible legislation on speed limits and roads finance. The Commission decided motorists not ratepayers should pay, probably through vehicle taxation. However, the LGB was unwilling to administer it. The RAC suggested a Road Fund, administered by a central highways department and financed by taxation on vehicles. But the government found it difficult to implement the Commission's report on road finance because the conflict over speed limits had not been settled (ibid. 75–8).

Both the anti-motorist campaign and the roads lobby became increasingly active. In 1908 the Chancellor, David Lloyd George, told RAC members he wanted to increase revenue from vehicles through a tax on petrol; in return he would do what he could for roads. He argued the amount raised would not justify a special roads board. However, the Treasury did not want money raised and spent from this special tax to form part of the general budget, because it might lead to further hypothecation (earmarking) of the budget (ibid. 88–9). In the 1909 budget Lloyd George introduced the Road Fund, to be administered by a public body, the Road Board. The revenue from vehicle and fuel taxes would be spent on roads.

Rees Jeffreys was appointed secretary of the Road Board; it was chaired by a railway director. William Plowden criticized the Road Board for building no new roads, allocating nearly all grants to small-scale improvements, and failing to spend its income. He said Rees Jeffreys blamed opposition from the Treasury, landowners and the railways, but a civil service inquiry found the board was badly administered and had insufficient technical expertise (ibid. 101). During its short life, 1910–20, the Road Board received £16m, committed £13m and spent only £7m (Savage, 1966: 149). But from 1914 the local authorities, because of wartime restrictions and increases in costs of labour and materials, were unable to take on the reconstruction or improvement of roads, even though vehicle use multiplied.

Road versus rail, 1919–39

In 1918–19 the government took a series of steps to remedy the problems of roads and road transport made apparent by the war. In 1919 the newly created Ministry of Transport took over the powers and functions of the Road Board, and the duties of the Local Government Board in regulating traffic, road design and road vehicles. The ministry co-financed the highways work of local authorities from the Road Fund, the grant depending on the class of road. It employed a divisional road engineer in nine regions in England and Wales from 1919 (the origin of its modern regional offices) to advise it on road funding priorities. Partly as a consequence of RIA pressure the Local Government Act 1929 transferred most of the important roads from districts to counties (Hamer, 1987: 32). County boroughs, small in area but with a county's powers, remained responsible for all roads within their boundaries, in return for central government taking over their Poor Law (social welfare) duties in 1929 – an arrangement whose consequences still linger since main road improvements often halted at their boundaries until county boroughs were abolished in 1974. Under the Trunk Roads Act 1936 the Ministry of Transport took over from counties full financial liability for 4500 miles of roads of national importance. The Road Fund had been 'raided' by Churchill and other Chancellors from 1926, and was wound up in 1937 (though the name lingered on), vehicle receipts becoming part of general exchequer funds.

During the First World War the railways had been controlled by the government and run by an executive committee of rail company managers. In 1919 a decision had to be made on how the railways should be returned to the private sector. Coordinating and pooling arrangements during the war had saved costs, suggesting there should not be a return to the pre-war network of more than 130 separate lines and 21 major companies (Savage, 1966: 98–9). Four regional groupings were created.

Thus the four 'historic' railway companies (LNER, LMS, Southern, and Great Western) were less the product of private enterprise than of the rationalizing efforts of government, Parliament and the Ministry of Transport, as promulgated in the Railways Act 1921. Brunner refers to the 'partial nationalization' of the railways because the charges set by these railways, each given a virtual monopoly, were in government hands (Brunner, 1929: 89). The Railway Rates Tribunal, whose members were appointed by the Minister of Transport, the President of the Board of Trade and the Lord Chancellor, replaced the Railway and Canal Commission. The Act gave little incentive for rail companies to increase efficiency or improve services. Rules on revenue and prices meant companies would retain only a small proportion of any economies made. Employees could not be given a worse post in a new company than they held in a pre-war company, which resulted in over-manning at senior levels compared with firms in other sectors, according to Brunner, who campaigned against the railways, 'the proud monopolists of the transport world' (ibid. 48, 26). Though it proved easier than expected to get the approval of the Railway Rates Tribunal to increase charges, if only because the railways never reached the target revenues based on their 1913 results which they were not to exceed, the heavy hand of price regulation nevertheless seriously handicapped the rail companies in competing with road transport. Rates had to be published and were determined on a value-for-weight basis, which implied high charges for carrying valuable manufactured goods, and low charges for bulky heavy commodities like coal. The charges had to be the same right across the network and could not show undue preference to any particular customer over another. Customers could demand the disaggregation of the rate charged into its component elements (such as collection, transit and delivery) and choose which parts of the service they would take from the railway and which they would do themselves or offer to road freight carriers who were not subject to price or quantity regulation (until 1933) and would take goods at any price that covered their costs (Savage, 1966: 141–6) Between 1919 and 1938 rail freight tonnage for general merchandise declined by a third (Gwilliam, 1964: 90). The regulatory arrangements, made on the assumption the rail industry was a monopolistic predator, made it difficult for rail to compete effectively with road transport.

By the end of the 1920s the railway's effective monopoly was reduced to 'very long-distance express passenger traffic, outer-suburban business traffic . . . coals and minerals, and the coarsest and lowest classes of goods traffic' (Brunner, 1929: 32). There had been an increase not only in road haulage contractors but in firms distributing their own goods. There were commercial advantages for companies in being able to ensure the delivery of goods to time and securely in vehicles that advertised the firm's name. Rail's advantages over road on freight were mainly in heavy, bulky goods and over long-distances – but heavy industries were in decline and British industrial geography was relatively compact. In passenger transport, rail was already losing first-class fares in the late 1920s because that section of the population could afford cars. Rail had chosen to compete on speed of journey, but not on costs or quality of service; and it was nearly always at a disadvantage on ease of access compared with lorries, cars or buses. Whereas at the beginning of the century it had seemed that road and rail transport would be complementary (operating in different markets), they were now competing for the same goods or travellers.

Brunner argues that the demand for 'coordination' of road and rail in the 1920s came from the railway companies, worried about the trade they were losing to road traffic (ibid. 88–9). The road transport lobby's suspicions were fuelled by the rail companies' campaign to run road services, culminating in the Railway (Road Transport) Act of 1928. Rail companies were seen as trying to change 'from railway companies to general operators of transport services' (ibid. 71). Rail companies said their users, unlike road users, had to pay the full cost of transport, including track costs – a continuing and familiar complaint. Road transport interests said they were unfairly taxed. Figures produced by Christopher Savage (1966: 174) show that motor taxation receipts (fuel tax, vehicle and licence duties) exceeded road expenditure (by local and central government) until 1932, but after that date the inverse was true. Social and environmental costs, from coal-fired engines as well as motor vehicles, did not at that time figure much in transport or any other calculations.

In response to such disputes, and concern about the large number of road accidents (killing about 3000 pedestrians a year; see Hamer, 1987: 31), Baldwin's Conservative government in 1928 appointed a Royal Commission on Transport to consider road traffic control and safety, how best to review the deployment of transport resources 'to the greatest public advantage', and to propose how they should be better regulated and controlled in the public interest 'to promote their co-ordinated working and development' (Cmnd 3751, 1930: vii). The Commission's recommendations on the licensing of motor vehicles and drivers, and on the regulation of passenger services, were implemented in the Road Traffic Act 1930 introduced by Herbert Morrison, transport minister in MacDonald's Labour minority government.

Until 1930 the licensing of buses and coaches was the responsibility of local authorities but not always taken seriously. During the depression bus operators and owner-drivers were more likely to work long hours at low capacity and little profit. The Road Traffic Act 1930 put in place a series of Area Traffic Commissioners, appointed by the Minister of Transport, who worked as quasi-judicial bodies, examining applications for licences from bus and coach operators. They were expected to 'introduce stability into an industry where competition was resulting in chronic instability'. The Commissioners restricted entry to the road passenger industry by requiring applicants for licences to show the public need for the additional service. Existing operators on a route were protected from newer applicants. Local buses and regular train services were protected from long-distance coaches; long-distance coaches were protected from tour operators. Tramways were given some protection from buses. The Commissioners' work was somewhat contradictory in that one of their purposes was to weed out those operators working unprofitably, yet they had to look too at the overall needs of the area, including the provision of unremunerative services. Licence applicants felt they had to provide some services on unrewarding routes or at unrewarding hours as evidence of a 'public service' commitment. The Commissioners had powers to ensure fares were not 'unreasonable', and could fix them 'so as to prevent wasteful competition', yet their deliberate use of cross-subsidy as a condition of granting licences made it difficult for them to determine what was a reasonable fare. Stability was introduced 'in the public interest' by protecting existing operators from new enterprises and from the market discipline of route profitability, but such a policy was not necessarily in the public interest (Savage, 1966: 154–62).

Despite their terms of reference (see above) the Commission's 1930 Report said little on 'coordination'. The government therefore asked a conference of road and rail interests to find a fair regulatory system for road haulage. The result was the Road and Rail Traffic Act 1933, which required the Area Traffic Commissioners to regulate road haulage under a system of quantity licensing like that introduced for buses. Applicants for road freight licences had to prove a need for new licences, and incumbents, including the railways, could object. The principle used in granting licences was again that 'wasteful competition' was against the public interest. Licences were often refused on the grounds that new services would abstract revenues from the railways. The system caused distortions, leading to a few, over-large firms, though traders carrying their own goods were less severely constrained than hauliers carrying goods on contract. 'The effects of the Act of 1933 were therefore to check the growth of a highly competitive industry' (ibid. 171). Chester expressed the 'liberal' aims of the legislation in a classic formula. The 'legislation concerning railways and tramways . . . was designed to obtain some of the benefits of competition in an industry mainly monopolistic, whilst the [Road Traffic Act 1930] was introduced to secure the benefits of monopoly in an industry mainly competitive' (1936: 198). Savage summed up in the 1960s the balance of advantages of a regulated passenger transport industry in terms that would be used again in the 1980s when deregulation became the transport policy in vogue. The 1930 system had produced safer, more reliable services. But protecting the 'little monopolies' by barring the entry to newcomers, and not relying on the normal economic criterion of profitability, had overemphasized stability at the cost of enterprise (1966: 162).

The most significant move towards transport coordination through structural integration before the Second World War was the creation of the London Passenger Transport Board. It was

expected to solve the particularly acute problems in the capital
caused by the growth of traffic, road congestion and bus competition, especially through developing the Underground. The prime
movers were Lord Ashfield, who chaired London Underground,
and Herbert Morrison, Minister of Transport and former Labour leader of the London County Council. The private and
municipal transport companies in the London area were transferred to the LPTB in 1933. Mainline railway companies were
excluded but they and the LPTB were required to share receipts
from services provided by joint lines and within the London area
– Ashfield had organized a similar agreement on a voluntary
basis since 1929. The London Passenger Transport Act 1933 made
LPTB a monopoly provider of road passenger transport in London. The performance of the new system proved difficult to judge,
partly because it had only six years to establish itself before the
impact of the Second World War. Operating costs increased,
for which growing traffic congestion – which it was supposed to
reduce – was held to blame (ibid. 164). However, its success in
administering a coordinated transport service appeared to provide a good model for full-scale nationalization of transport services after the war.

Postwar nationalization and the switch to roads

During the Second World War the government took overall control
of rail transport. Road transport was more difficult to organize
because of the multiplicity of small operators, and in 1943 the
government set up a fleet of lorries hired from their owners.
For the postwar Labour government there was no question of
returning the controlled enterprises to the private sector. The
Transport Act 1947 created the British Transport Commission,
operating through separate executives dealing with rail, canals,
road transport, and London transport. The main exception was
in road freight, since licensed short-distance hauliers were left
out of the BTC, and firms could still transport their own goods.

   Because the purpose of the BTC was to provide an integrated
system, financial control was given to the BTC, not the separate
executives. This arrangement perpetuated the accounting practices of the railway companies by allowing cross-subsidy between

FIGURE 2.2 Transport policy 1914–50: coordination and control

1914–18 First World War. Railways controlled by government.

1919 Creation of Ministry of Transport, which subsumes Road Board.

1921 Railways Act moved towards state control. Railways amalgamated into four regional groups, maximum rates under 1894 Act replaced from 1928 by standard rates, which could be varied to achieve net revenue equivalent to that earned in 1913.

1928 Royal Commission on Transport (Final Report 1930) established to improve regulation and control of the available means of transport and 'to promote their coordinated working and development'.

1930 Road Traffic Act established licensing system for bus services under Area Traffic Commissioners responsible for licensing both vehicles and services.

1933 Road and Rail Traffic Act established licensing system for goods vehicles, also under the Area Traffic Commissioners. Licences to be granted only on basis of proof of public need.

1933 London Passenger Transport Act established Board to own all Underground railways and bus companies serving London.

1936 Trunk Roads Act transferred responsibility for 4500 miles of trunk roads to Ministry of Transport.

1939 Amalgamation of Imperial Airways and British Airways to form state corporation: granted monopoly of scheduled air services from 1946.

1939–45 Second World War. Most transport under government control.

1947 Transport Act nationalized railways, long-distance road haulage, parts of road passenger transport, London Transport, canals, all to be run by the British Transport Commission, charged with providing a 'properly integrated system of public inland transport'.

different parts of the operation, and between different financial years. It hid changes in rail use and allowed the postponement of difficult decisions. BTC's charges were regulated by a Transport Tribunal and ministerial directives, and both the Tribunal and ministers used their powers to limit BTC's proposed fare increases even where it would worsen deficits (Gwilliam, 1964: 96–8). Manufacturers exploited rail's value-based pricing structures and obligation to take all trade, by sending 'expensive' loads in their own lorries, and 'difficult' loads by rail. Changes were in any case taking place in the relative popularity of the two modes of transport.

The changing preferences in transport from rail to road for both goods and people had been masked in the 1940s by wartime and postwar fuel rationing and by the need to increase vehicle exports. Savage gives some comparative figures (1966: 178–81) which show clearly the difficulties facing the rail executive. In 1963 there were almost four times as many motor vehicles as in 1939, and about two-and-a-half times as many as in 1951. The number of goods vehicles had risen by over 300 per cent between 1939 and 1963, and these vehicles were likely to be larger than before. The number of buses and coaches had risen from about 50 000 to about 80 000, though growth had ceased by the early 1960s as passenger journeys started to fall. Rail freight traffic increased enormously during the war but fell back to prewar levels after 1948. Rail passenger traffic was fairly stable but was thought to have combined decline on some, especially rural, lines with increased demand on others. However, rail was not sharing in the general increase in people's expenditure in the same way car travel did. Between 1950 and 1960 expenditure on cars (including running costs) rose 400 per cent; expenditure on travel by public transport was unchanged.

The growth of road traffic was seriously underestimated by the Ministry of Transport in the 1950s and later decades, and indeed there is some doubt about the actual figures for road passenger transport and car mileage in the 1950s and 1960s (ibid. 180–2), a problem that was bound to affect the drawing up of realistic policies for both rail and roads. The Ministry's permanent secretary in the early 1960s expressed his regret that British governments had not been able to improve run-down or inadequate infrastructure in the 1950s and 1960s.

There was naturally considerable enthusiasm both at headquarters and among local authorities to get on with things, many of which had been planned in detail before the war started ... When, then, decisions were taken which made it clear that nearly all schemes would have to go back into the pigeon hole the result was, to say the least of it, discouraging (Dunnett, 1962: 259).

There is reason to believe the Treasury would not have entertained the idea of an increase in roads spending even had transport forecasts been more realistic – in 1952 the Treasury said it was satisfied if the ministry continued its roads spending at about 70 per cent of the 1938 figure (Savage, 1966: 199–200). But the debate about spending priorities might have been conducted in different terms if the growth in traffic had been recognized earlier.

Coordination and control

The British Transport Commission established under the Transport Act 1947 was the high-water mark of Government control and coordination of the transport industries. During the nineteenth century the public demand for coordination, articulated by Gladstone and others, had been largely met by voluntary cooperation among the railway companies themselves, within a framework of government control designed to control any abuse of their monopoly power. Coordination with other modes of transport was not an issue after 1850 because there was no other mode of transport which needed to be coordinated with rail in the public interest. Canal transport had been largely superseded. Coastal shipping remained important but was not in direct competition, and such horse-drawn road services as there were concentrated on local business which included feeder services to the railway. Each mode had its own clearly defined market and so far as coordination was required, it was in the interests of both parties to cooperate in ensuring it.

The experience of transport coordination during the First World War, and thereafter the growth of competition between road and rail, prompted a more active approach to coordination. In 1919 the most urgent task of the new Ministry of Transport was to put the railways back on a commercial footing, but when financial problems persisted and seemed to be exacerbated by growing competition from commercial road transport, the response of the Royal Commission of 1928–30 and the government of the day, embodied in the Acts of 1930 and 1933, was to seek to manage the market through the licensing and control first of road passenger services and then of road freight haulage.

The Second World War again seemed to demonstrate what could be achieved in the national interest when all transport provision was centrally coordinated, and the Transport Act 1947 created a British Transport Commission which was to provide 'an efficient, adequate, economical and properly integrated system of public inland transport'. It is doubtful whether anyone knew then (or now) what was meant by a properly integrated system of transport, but it would certainly have meant coordination under some degree of government control rather than competition. Extensive government ownership failed to deliver the benefits which had been hoped, and over the succeeding fifty years, especially since 1979, most of the transport industries were returned to private ownership with an emphasis on the benefits of commercial disciplines and competition. In the end, however, the zeal with which this process was carried out, and the rough edges of competition which it exposed here and there, reawakened the old concerns for coordination and tougher regulation in the public interest, enhanced by a concern for the effect of transport on the environment, and in 1997 a government was once again elected with a commitment to establish and develop 'an effective and integrated transport policy at national, regional and local level that will provide genuine choice to meet people's transport needs' (Labour Party Manifesto, 1997: 29).

FIGURE 2.3   Transport policy after 1951: rediscovering competition

1953	Transport Act denationalized long-distance road haulage.
1960	Civil Aviation (Licensing) Act creates Air Transport Licensing Board with duty to 'foster the development of British civil aviation'.
1962	Transport Act abolished British Transport Commission, but retains railways, docks, canals, London Transport in separate public ownership. Coordination assigned to an advisory council for nationalized transport.
1963	Beeching Report on the Reshaping of British Railways recommends closure to passenger traffic of 2000 stations and 5000 miles of track.
1963	Buchanan Report on Traffic in Towns suggests more investment to separate vehicles from pedestrians.
1968	Transport Act endeavours to put railways on a commercial footing with subsidies for unremunerative services. Road haulage released from capacity controls.
1969–72	Passenger Transport Authorities created in six major English metropolitan areas.
1971	Civil Aviation Act establishes Civil Aviation Authority leading to the gradual licensing of more competition.
1980	Transport Act deregulates long-distance coach services.
1982	Sale of National Freight Corporation completes the privatization of the road haulage industry.
1984	White Paper on Buses, implemented through Transport Act 1985, leads to deregulation of bus services, break-up and sale of National Bus Company.
1984	White Paper on Airline Competition opens domestic market to competition. British Airways privatized 1987.
1985	White Paper on Airports leads to privatization of British Airports Authority.
1989–91	Dock Work Act abolishes 1940s dock labour scheme, opening market to competition. Ports Act 1991 enables trust ports to become private-sector companies.
1992	White Paper on New Opportunities for the Railways leads to the break-up and privatization of British Rail under the regulatory regime of the Railways Act 1993.

Rediscovering competition

Between 1951 and 1979 the evolution of transport policy was more pragmatic than ideological, with many of the more important developments carried over from one government to the next even when the political direction had changed. Under the Labour governments of 1964–70 there was a brief return to policies favouring coordination through integration and public control, but even in the 1960s recognition of the benefits of competition and a more commercial approach to the provision of transport services continued to gain ground. David Starkie remarked that the continuity in road policy-making from the Second World War to the 1980s showed little sign of party-political influence (Starkie, 1982: 145–8). The motorway building programme reflected a practical response from all sides to a growth in road traffic, at a time when interest in the environment was regarded as eccentric. Road-building was spurred on or held back by financial considerations, but not much by party ideology. Road-building was highly conflictual, but the conflict was mainly between policy-makers and local people who suffered the impact of the new construction.

The gradual relaxation of state control over civil aviation was similarly pragmatic rather than political, although most of the relevant legislation was enacted under Conservative governments in 1960 and 1971. Many of the companies which had pioneered air services in the 1930s, under licences issued by the Air Ministry, were small independent operators (though some were partly owned by the railways), but competition among them gave rise to a rather unstable pattern of services, and in 1938, following the recommendations of the Maybury Committee (Cmnd 5351, 1937), an Air Transport Licensing Authority was established. This was followed by the 1939 amalgamation of Imperial Airways and British Airways, and after the war the state corporation was granted a monopoly of all air services. From 1948 independent companies were allowed to operate complementary services under associateship agreements, but it was not until 1960 that the Air Transport Licensing Board (ATLB) was required to issue licences 'in such a manner as to further the development of British civil aviation' (Civil Aviation (Licensing) Act 1960). This half-open door proved unsatisfactory. The decisions of the ATLB were hard to predict, and in any case a dissatisfied party could appeal to the minister, who might take a different view. There was a gradual growth of scheduled services provided they did not compete too directly with the state corporations (by now British European Airways and British Overseas Airways Corporation), but the private companies found more scope for their initiative and enterprise in the development of charter services for the growing market in inclusive tour holidays.

The Civil Aviation Act of 1971, which established the Civil Aviation Authority (CAA) in place of the ATLB and promoted the recently formed British Caledonian Airways as a second force independent airline, was passed under a Conservative government, but it was based on the recommendations for *British Air Transport in the Seventies* (1969) of the Edwards Committee, set up by Labour. The CAA was itself a nationalized industry, but the guidance it received from government on the licensing of air services was published, fewer decisions were overturned by ministers on appeal, and gradually through the 1970s the CAA fostered the development of a competitive industry, albeit under policy guidelines which continued to give priority in scheduled service provision to British Airways and British Caledonian.

In road haulage liberalization began with the Conservative government's Transport Act 1953 which aimed to denationalize those parts of road haulage which Labour had nationalized. The attempt to privatize the whole of the British Road Service fleet was only abandoned when some vehicles found no buyers. But the 1953 Act left in place the quantity licensing regime in force since 1933 under the Area Traffic Commissioners. The Geddes Committee, appointed by a Conservative government to inquire into the way licensing was working, recommended the abolition of all restrictions on the capacity of the road haulage industry. Its report, *Carrier Licensing* (1965), was received by a Labour government, which passed the Transport Act 1968 abolishing capacity controls on all vehicles under 16 tons, but tightened the safety regulations and proposed to maintain control on heavy lorries. In the event a Conservative government was returned before these latter provisions entered into effect, and capacity controls were abolished completely from December 1970.

As a 'quid pro quo' for road freight privatization in the 1953 Act the government simultaneously removed the requirement on the railways not 'to show undue preference' between traders, in order not to worsen rail's financial position relative to road haulage (Gwilliam, 1964: 100–1). The Railway Executive was replaced by six area boards, whose general managers were told to modernize and compete with other modes of transport. However, in 1960 a Select Committee inquiry showed modernization programmes had been embarked upon with no clear idea of their value, and that the debts incurred would not be balanced by increased traffic. The Committee's report also criticized governments over the years for muddling commercial criteria and social needs in its expectations of the BTC. In 1962 the government abolished the BTC, and reconstituted the British Railways Board, putting an outsider, Dr Beeching, in charge. The railway would no longer have to take all goods as 'a common carrier' or have its charges approved by the Transport Tribunal. While remaining within the public sector, it was promised more commercial freedom.

The reforms broke up what was left of the 'integrated transport' organization which the BTC had been supposed to bring about. Moreover, Beeching's investigations into the rail network broke it up financially so that for the first time the viability of each part became explicit. His 1963 report on *The Reshaping of British Railways* was criticized for its narrow definition of costs, for example not taking account of social or economic development needs, or of savings in urban congestion or environmental damage. His recommendations for widespread closures of loss-making stations and lines horrified many politicians, especially in the Labour government which had to implement his closure programme after winning the 1964 election, and some loss-making lines remained open into the 1990s. But the Beeching exercise was a necessary first step in 'transparency', relating public subsidy to specific lines and services so that decisions about whether to keep them open could be based on accurate information.

In those respects the Buchanan Report on roads, *Traffic in Towns* (1963), performed a similar service in making policy-makers and citizens consider the consequences for the physical and social environment of allowing urban traffic to grow unchecked, except by congestion. The alternative was high expenditure on reconstruction (opponents said destruction), to accommodate traffic but separate it from residential and pedestrian areas. A different approach was offered by the Transport Act 1968, an important piece of Labour legislation, that made provision for government subsidy of unprofitable but socially-necessary public transport. The Act created 'Passenger Transport Authorities' in four of the conurbations outside London (two more were added under the Local Government Act 1972), whose remit was to develop and improve the coordination of services as the London Transport Board was seen to have done. In these areas the British Railway Board did not control rail services but supplied them on contract to the PTAs who specified the terms and recovered any subsidies from the constituent local governments. They coordinated bus and rail services and fares across the modes of transport until the deregulation of bus services (outside London) in the 1985 Transport Act, but the abolition of the county councils in 1986 and the privatization of rail services under the Railways Act 1993 changed the structure within which they worked twice in a decade.

Privatization and deregulation

Between 1979 and 1997 policy was characterized by a much more radical commitment to privatization and deregulation. When Mrs Thatcher's Conservative Party came to office in 1979 a main concern was to remove barriers to competition; to foster the free market in the belief it would encourage efficiency. Norman Fowler had written a pamphlet in 1977 arguing there was no reason for the strict system of quantity regulation in the bus industry to be maintained. He became Secretary of State for Transport in 1979, and one of the new government's first pieces of legislation was the deregulation of long-distance bus services (discussed below). The prime aim was to reduce the involvement of the state to a minimum.

The Conservative government subsequently discovered additional motives for privatization. The sale of British Telecom demonstrated the substantial sums privatization brought to the Exchequer, that counted as negative public expenditure. Income from privatization helped deal with the pressing problem of funding the cost of rapidly-increasing social security claims without increasing taxation. Transport privatizations in the period 1982–4

(National Freight, British Rail Hotels and Sealink, Associated British Ports and Jaguar) yielded about £500m. By contrast, transport privatizations in the years 1987–8 (British Airways, Rolls-Royce aero engines, British Airports and the National Bus Company) yielded about £4bn (Banister, 1994: 73). It was thought too that privatization could be used to introduce the experience of share ownership to a much wider range of people, in the expectation they would continue to hold shares and thus perhaps become more sympathetic to the values espoused by the Conservative Party.

However, there may well be a conflict between the desire to promote competition and the desire to sell public utilities at a good price for the benefit of the Exchequer, as there probably was in the case of the British Airports Authority, which was allowed to retain a virtual monopoly of airports in the London area. In the case of London Buses (see below and Chapter 9), Price Waterhouse was asked to have regard to both competition and proceeds in its advice to the Department of Transport. The number of companies was more or less determined by the existing structure, but there was debate over whether it would be better to sell companies off one-by-one, simultaneously or in a few groups to maximize the proceeds. Yet there was serious consideration too of the terms under which companies would be free to vary their services, for example to compete with a neighbouring company. Ministers wanted them to have more freedom to innovate than had been allowed under LRT in the past, but there were fears that complete deregulation would cause highly public chaos in central London, and would also reduce the potential proceeds of the sale. It was therefore decided that whilst deregulation should remain the long-term policy objective, London Transport Buses would retain a powerful role as regulator for the time being.

Aviation and shipping

The intention to privatize British Airways (BA) was announced in July 1979, within weeks of Mrs Thatcher's first government being elected, and the legislative framework was provided in the Civil Aviation Act 1980. The recession of the early 1980s delayed the privatization of BA until January 1987, but it has since become one of the most successful and profitable airlines in the world. The 1980 Act also required the Civil Aviation Authority (CAA) to give the interests of airline users equal standing in its licensing decisions with those of service providers. As a result British Midland was allowed to open services from London Heathrow to Belfast, Edinburgh and Glasgow in direct competition with BA, whilst Cathay Pacific and British Caledonian were both allowed to start services to Hong Kong, albeit from London Gatwick. In October 1984 a further White Paper on Airline Competition encouraged the CAA to further relax its domestic licensing regime, by allowing airlines to serve any routes within the UK, and removing the requirement for fares to be approved specifically (Cmnd 9366: para. 26). The White Paper also committed the government to a policy of liberalizing the bilateral and multilateral agreements under which international air services are operated, especially within the European Community, and this goal was very largely achieved between 1983 and 1992 (see Chapter 4).

Most of the major British airports have been privatized. In June 1985 the Airports Policy White Paper (Cmnd 9542) paved the way for the British Airports Authority to be privatized as a holding company (BAA plc) for its seven airports, three around London and four in Scotland. Many other British airports are owned by local authorities (for example, Manchester, Birmingham, Luton), who are reluctant to privatize them, and the government has stopped short of requiring them to do so, but they have been encouraged to involve the private sector to the maximum extent possible, especially in the provision of capital facilities, such as the Eurohub air terminal at Birmingham, which is owned by BA.

The Civil Aviation Authority, which has the status of a nationalized industry, is the regulator. In 1996, in preparation for the eventual privatization of air traffic control services, these functions were established as a public limited company within the CAA. As a regulator the CAA's main functions are now safety-related, though it does also retain some economic functions, for example in advising the government on the need for airport expansion, licensing airlines for specific international routes and approving international fares where these functions are required by international agreements.

There was less need to liberalize and deregulate the shipping industry, since the principal companies have never been in the public sector, and economic regulation has long been liberal. The only significant privatizations have been the sale of British Rail's ferry operator, Sealink, and of the Scottish ferry operator, Caledonian MacBrayne. There was more need to open up the ports industry to market forces. The Dock Labour Scheme, that required the registration of dockworkers and the licensing of their employers, was abolished by the Dock Work Act 1989. It opened the labour market to competition, and provided substantial compensation to those dockers (a high proportion of those registered) who were made redundant within three years. The Ports Act 1991 enabled the major trading trust ports, which are autonomous statutory corporations, to become private-sector companies, and several of the larger ports have taken advantage of this opportunity to move into the private sector. Well over half British national port capacity is now owned or run by private-sector companies (DoT, 1993a: 125).

With the exception of a few local authority ports and airports, the aviation and shipping industries and their infrastructure are now very largely in private ownership. The result is an industry which is considerably more competitive than it was in the 1970s, and provides a more responsive service to its customers.

Road freight

The road haulage sector was already virtually deregulated when Mrs Thatcher took over. The remainder of the state holding, the National Freight Consortium, was sold in a management buy-out in 1982, and has subsequently proved to be a profitable business. Operators must hold a licence from the Area Traffic Commissioners and meet various regulations on vehicle safety and drivers' hours, including requirements agreed with other European Community states, as shown in Chapter 4. Road haulage now has many of the classic characteristics of a free entry, competitive industry; that is, low profits, a substantial turn-over of firms entering and leaving the industry, and widely varying firm sizes. A large proportion of output is produced by single-vehicle, owner-driver firms. Distance travelled per vehicle increased from 60 000 km to 75 000 km a year during the 1980s. Real operating costs decreased by an average of 2.5 per cent a year followed closely by haulage prices to users. There have been policy reviews of the sector but in recent years no strong arguments have been advanced for making further changes to the economic regulation of the system.

Long-distance (express) coaches

Norman Fowler's Transport Act of 1980, deregulating coach services, referred to long-distance 'express' coaches (as distinct from local services), which were previously defined as services with a minimum passenger journey length of 30 miles. In the legislation the criterion was adjusted to 15 miles, bringing more services into the deregulation provision. Most services were then being operated by the state-owned National Bus Company. Outside the major conurbations NBC ran the majority of local services, too, under the oversight of the Traffic Commissioners in place since 1930, who restricted quantity and controlled fares. In the new legislation all quantity and price restrictions were removed – the residual regulations related, as in road freight, to relatively uncontroversial safety requirements. However, the NBC itself was not privatized at that time.

Initially there was large-scale competitive entry to the business. Fares fell markedly and the volume of service increased. Other attributes of service quality also changed – product differentiation emerged with the introduction of luxury vehicles with TV and steward services on board. Nevertheless, the competition was fairly quickly defeated by the NBC who re-emerged as the dominant operator because of three factors: first, the NBC was a good, experienced bus operator which was able to respond to the spur of competition by improving its own efficiency. Second, it was allowed to keep exclusive rights to the existing major coach terminals, Victoria in central London in particular, where 25 per cent of passengers transferred to other routes. Third, it was alleged it used profits earned in some of its local businesses to cross-subsidize the long-distance business.

These last two features were clear failings of the deregulation process. The government did not recognize that if competitive forces are relied upon to police a market then it must ensure there are no substantial barriers to competition. The failings were corrected in the 1985 Transport Act: the NBC was broken into a large number of distinct companies and all hidden cross-subsidy was prevented. Equal access was granted to terminal facilities, and the Victoria coach station was transferred to London Transport. Since then the benefits of the deregulation of express coaching seem to have stabilized. Fares are generally lower and service levels have improved relative to the period just before deregulation, as illustrated in the graphs in Thompson and Whitfield (in Bishop, Kay and Mayer (ed.), 1995).

British Rail responded to coach competition by aggressive fares cutting, especially on services where it had spare capacity, and by sales promotions in those markets in which coach travel is particularly strong: young and elderly passengers. The deregulation and privatization of long-distance bus services can be counted as a success. As in the case of freight, it was achieved by promoting the free market in both the market for passengers and in the markets in which inputs are procured by the bus companies.

Bus deregulation

The impetus for bus deregulation did not result only from a desire on the part of the Thatcher government to introduce competition into markets as a matter of principle. The government's determination to reduce overall public expenditure – by both central and local authorities – was probably just as important. Nor was it primarily to increase private ownership of public-sector assets through privatization, nor to secure government income by non-tax means. Most of the controversy about the merits and demerits of bus deregulation and much of the subsequent evaluation has concerned the effects on passengers. Although the government expressed hopes of increased patronage and lower fares, the prime motivation for the policy was to change the way the industry worked in order to meet the overall goal of reducing subsidy whilst minimizing the damage done to passengers by increases in fares and reductions in service.

The policy was laid out in Nicholas Ridley's White Paper, *Buses*, which contained three main proposals:

(1) *Privatization*. The nationalized National Bus Company was to be broken up into a large number of smaller entities and sold to the private sector. The remaining publicly-owned

operators, in the metropolitan counties and other municipal enterprises, were to be made into regular, 'arms-length' companies, owned by the local authorities but with normal company accounts.

(2) *Deregulation.* Safety regulation would remain essentially unchanged, but the controls over service provision would be swept away. Instead of having to apply for a road-service licence specifying the services to be operated, the bus companies would simply be required to register the routes and timings of their services, and give notice of their intention to commence or withdraw a service, or to make significant changes.

(3) *Subsidies.* Companies were to register only those routes and services they were willing to operate on a commercial basis, without subsidy. It would then be for the local authority to secure any additional, subsidized, routes or services they considered necessary through a competitive tendering process which gave equal access to any operator who cared to bid.

The government believed the publicly owned bus companies (including the National Bus Company), protected from competition and subsidized by local authorities, had become inefficient, and that free competition among private companies was the way to drive down costs, and in consequence the volume of subsidy provided through public expenditure. On the basis of investigations of bus operators' costs and the level of earnings in the industry by comparison with other similar industries such as road haulage, the White Paper concluded that 'the potential exists for cost reductions of up to 30 per cent of total costs of public operators' (DoT, 1984: para. 4.10).

In the public debate that followed, many of those involved in the industry advocated an alternative approach based on some system of requiring authorities to put routes out to tender, but disallowing free competition on the road. This option, which was later adopted in London, became summarized as competition *for* the route rather than competition *on* the route. Gwilliam, Nash and Mackie give good contemporary statements of the arguments (1985a; 1985b). Their argument was that tendering would avoid the risks perceived from deregulation, such as bad behaviour on the road in the attempt to win passengers; and that it would allow local authorities to keep control of fares and to plan an integrated set of services with cross-subsidy, perhaps optimally adjusted according to the principles of the second best familiar to economists. At the same time competition for tenders would provide the required pressure on costs. Glaister and Beesley gave counter-arguments and responses (Glaister, 1985; Beesley, 1985).

The government went ahead with its proposals in the Transport Act 1985. All the former NBC companies were sold within a couple of years and the new deregulated regime took effect, after a short transitional period, on 1 January 1987. The consequences for competition are discussed in Chapter 9; it is sufficient to note here that a far higher proportion of routes were registered as commercial than anyone had predicted – over 80 per cent – and the cost to public expenditure fell dramatically. Although some of the municipal bus companies remain under local authority ownership, a considerable number have been sold since 1987, so that by the mid-1990s the industry was substantially in private hands.

Railways

By 1988 the Thatcher government had considered rail privatization in sufficient detail to identify five options – the sixth was the status quo (see *The Times*, 29 June 1989).

(1) Privatization of BR as one railway and one company – the option favoured by the British Rail Board.

(2) Privatization of BR as a single holding company with a range of subsidiaries – a decentralized version of the previous option.

(3) Establishment of a track authority or company to own infrastructure [Railtrack] with separate private companies operating the services – put forward by the Adam Smith Institute, and the option eventually enacted and implemented.

(4) Division of BR into parts based on geography – similar to the arrangements 1923–47; favoured by the Centre for Policy Studies and by the Prime Minister, John Major.

(5) Division of BR into business sectors on the basis of the existing management structure: InterCity, freight, parcels, Network SouthEast, Regional Railways.

(6) Retain BR in public ownership – favoured by a majority of the public, and a large minority of MPs.

The government could not come to an immediate agreement on any option, but the debate was reopened when John Major's government was drawing up its manifesto for the 1992 election. The government's view, in the words of Secretary of State for Transport John MacGregor, introducing the bill to MPs, was that: 'As an organization, BR combines the classic shortcomings of the traditional nationalized industry. It is an entrenched monopoly. That means too little responsiveness to customers' needs, whether passenger or freight; no real competition; and too little diversity and innovation' (*HC Debs*, 2 February 1993: 124).

Rail privatization was introduced in the White Paper, *New Opportunities for the Railways,* in July 1992, two days before the Commons rose for its summer recess. Legislation was promised for the following parliamentary session, with the first franchise to be awarded in 1994. There was no Green Paper or formal consultation process examining the issue of rail privatization, or its place in a transport policy, or why some options had been rejected in favour of the one chosen. The government was still issuing separate consultation papers on particular items for instance, rail franchising, BR pensions, while Parliament was conducting its initial examination (see Chapter 5). The Commons Transport Select Committee complained loudly about the absence of full details, and the insufficient time for informed public debate (Transport Committee, 1993: para. 6). Details were modified but in November 1993 the main thrust of the Bill passed as the government had planned. The organizational changes proceeded more smoothly than opponents had expected, and almost immediately, with the sale of Railtrack, went further than envisaged. The post-privatization organization is described in Chapter 3. Some of the issues that remained are discussed in Chapters 5 and 9.

The last frontiers

By 1997, when John Major's government was defeated after nearly 18 years of Conservative rule, the frontiers of the state had been rolled back a long way in the transport industries, though there were still some surviving monuments to the old orthodoxy of public ownership and control. At the Civil Aviation Authority the air traffic control services were being prepared for privatization but there were no plans to privatize safety regulation. At London Transport the bus companies had been privatized, but LT remained the bus regulator. The Underground was still a traditional nationalized industry, but ministers were reviewing a range of options for its privatization in the course of the next parliament. Even the network of national trunk roads was beginning to be privatized piecemeal as substantial stretches of road were mortgaged to the private sector under the new Design Build Finance and Operate (DBFO) contracts. The Labour government which took office in May 1997 has its own plans for injecting private finance into the London Underground, and although it is reviewing the roads programme in the context of its plans for an integrated transport policy, its review of the first dozen urgent cases led to the confirmation of at least one further major DBFO contract. The terms may differ from those which might have been negotiated under a Conservative government, but it looks as if the last frontiers of the public sector in the transport industries will continue to crumble under Labour, who have long seen the advantage of using public–private partnerships to get more investment into public transport than could be afforded under the traditional public expenditure regime.

Conclusion

Although there has been much talk since 1979 of 'the lack of a national transport policy' the discussion in this chapter shows that the Conservative governments after 1979 followed policies of privatization, competition and deregulation that have transformed the essentially public-sector transport industries which they inherited. By 1996, of all the major transport service industries, only London Underground remained in the public sector. Government and Parliament have always intervened actively in the framework of transport provision, and if the period since 1979 has been unusual it has been on account of the concentration on strategic goals. Transport ministers and parliamentary select committees have more often been criticized, especially since the Second World War, for taking too great an interest in the fine detail of transport services instead of setting out the main structures and long-term regulations and letting both nationalized and privatized industries work unhindered within them. The history of freight and passenger transport shows the ability of some companies or sectors to perform well, almost despite the arrangements under which they are required to work. The view that transport policy has been lacking since 1979 seems rather to express dissatisfaction with part or all of the prevailing transport programme: cuts in public spending; the deregulation or tendering of bus services; the 'lack of coordination' of transport, which has various meanings from the absence of central direction to the loss of a uniform fleet of red London buses; or the absence of a precise map of infrastructure projects.

For many critics a 'transport policy' is assumed to be a high public-spending policy and a highly regulated transport system, probably directed by a central corporation, typified by Labour Party policy of the 1930s and 1940s. Perhaps because transport is 'technical', long-associated with engineering achievements and quantified design standards, it is easy to forget that as a policy it is as ideological as social welfare provision or the reform of prisons. The history of transport legislation shows that the different parties often had different goals. Moreover, even if different parties say they want 'coordination', they can give the word different meanings or have diametrically-opposed views on the way it could be achieved, by central direction or through the market. Set in the context of 150 years of history, the transport policy of Conservative governments after 1979 may have been unwelcome to some, but it does not seem so unusual, or a 'non-policy'. The Conservatives carried out in practice the *laisser-faire* principles that Victorian governments are often thought to have promoted. Until the 1950s, transport undertakings were subjected in the name of competition to government-imposed regulations that controlled a potential monopoly. Those regulations appear now to have worked against the railways when they had to compete with the development of road freight transport. But they probably only hastened the date when rail would be beaten by road transport in an era when environmental and social factors were not included in calculations about the comparative costs to society of road and rail, or of private and public transport.

But policy decisions that appear to diverge from the general policy goals may not always have such a rational explanation as regulations under a liberal regime. Overlaid on the ideological influences on policy are electoral considerations, such as satisfying economically significant or politically sympathetic interest groups, or finding ways to reduce, or appear to reduce, the burden of taxation. Furthermore, all governments have to work within parameters set by others that may not chime very well with their own aims, such as the cutbacks in public expenditure imposed by the International Monetary Fund, or the regulations increasing road freight maximum weight and dimensions, agreed between European Community states.

Yet beyond the institutional changes that express the different priorities of each government are changes in society that produce changes in perceptions of the crucial factors in transport. Some changes may be outside the competence of any individual government in office. Examples include the enormous growth of and desire for individual road transport, difficult to predict even in the 1950s; and the popular surge in environmental awareness in the 1980s. But Beeching and Buchanan in the 1960s educated citizens as much as did the Houghton Report on Environmental Pollution in the 1990s by alerting people to the costs of different policy choices, and the conflicts within those choices. Transport policy is not a technical issue which can be debated and decided between experts. It has been and remains a political decision.

Part II

The Decision-Makers

3 Making Transport Policy in Britain

One of the strengths of the British system of governance is the collective responsibility of ministers for all aspects of the government's policy; but this collective strength carries with it the consequence that the minister responsible for transport is by no means a free agent. Other ministers, especially the Chancellor of the Exchequer, the Chief Secretary (Treasury) and the ministers responsible for planning and local government, for environmental protection and for industrial competitiveness all have a major impact on the shaping of transport policies. Implementation is in the hands of a very wide range of agents in both the public and the private sector, and although the Department of Transport controls some of them directly, its ability to influence others is more limited, particularly after 18 years of Conservative governments committed to 'rolling back the frontiers of the State'. Between 1979 and 1997 governments turned increasingly to the market to provide competitive transport services subject to a minimum of regulation in the public interest, rejecting coordination by politicians and bureaucrats in departments, councils and corporations. The Labour government elected in May 1997 inherited a structure of government that allows the transport industries more freedom from government control than at any time since at least 1930 and probably since before the First World War. To implement their commitment to an 'integrated transport policy' may require the creation or re-creation of structures designed to facilitate greater coordination.

This chapter explains how the responsibility for transport policy is shared between government departments and local authorities, as well as the increasing number of regulatory and other public bodies with major transport functions, and the arrangements for coordination. The machinery of government is subject to continual change as ministerial responsibilities are shaped and reshaped around the personalities and policy priorities of the day, but there is also a considerable measure of stability and continuity about the major elements of the structure, however much they may be rearranged. There is in addition a European dimension to policy-making, which is described in Chapter 4; it is sufficient to note here that the conduct of transport policy has to be consistent with Britain's international obligations, including those arising from membership of the European Union.

Central government responsibilities

The Department of the Environment, Transport and the Regions (DETR)

Since May 1997 the Department of Transport has been united with the Department of the Environment under a single Secretary of State, who is supported by ministers for Transport and for the Environment. The main functions of the department and its related organizations and agencies are identified in Figure 3.1. Within the united department the Secretary of State carries ultimate responsibility for all that is done in his or her name; the most important decisions will be referred up to this senior minister. However, although some functions have been merged and in other cases the Secretary of State receives coordinated advice (see below under 'Coordination within DETR'), most of the Department's policy directorates retain a functional identity which is recognizably either Transport or Environment. For the purposes of this book it will therefore be convenient to describe the Transport and Environment functions of DETR separately, and to continue to refer to the former Departments of Transport (DoT) and Environment (DoE) where that is appropriate for historical reasons or to maintain the continuity of data series.

FIGURE 3.1 The Structure of the Department of the Environment, Transport and the Regions (DETR), 1997

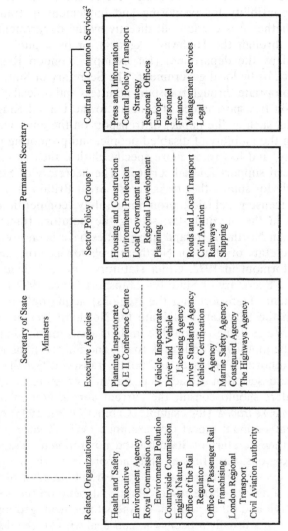

Secretary of State ———— Permanent Secretary

Ministers

Related Organizations

Health and Safety Executive
Environment Agency
Royal Commission on Environmental Pollution
Countryside Commission
English Nature
Office of the Rail Regulator
Office of Passenger Rail Franchising
London Regional Transport
Civil Aviation Authority

Executive Agencies

Planning Inspectorate
Q E II Conference Centre

Vehicle Inspectorate
Driver and Vehicle Licensing Agency
Driver Standards Agency
Vehicle Certification Agency
Marine Safety Agency
Coastguard Agency
The Highways Agency

Sector Policy Groups[1]

Housing and Construction
Environment Protection
Local Government and Regional Development
Planning

Roads and Local Transport
Civil Aviation
Railways
Shipping

Central and Common Services[2]

Press and Information
Central Policy / Transport Strategy
Regional Offices
Europe
Personnel
Finance
Management Services
Legal

Notes:
[1] The major building blocks of policy remain constant, but the linkages vary. For example, shipping is often linked to aviation, and local transport has sometimes been linked with railways rather than roads.
[2] These services were provided separately within the former Departments of the Environment and Transport.

Transport

The powers vested in ministers by legislation are invariably attributed to 'The Secretary of State'. He or she carries the primary responsibility for proposing and implementing transport policy, whether it is carried out directly by the department (for example, through the Highways Agency), or by a public body sponsored by the department (for example, London Regional Transport), or by local government. The Secretary of State (acting as appropriate through transport ministers and officials) takes the lead on transport issues of concern to the United Kingdom as a whole, such as the impact of transport on the environment, improving the mobility of disabled people, and promoting transport safety, and has some more specific duties, such as providing financial support for rail services. The Secretary of State is responsible for some other tasks across Great Britain only: testing and licensing vehicles; promoting safety, competition and reliability in the bus industry; setting the statutory framework for ports. In Northern Ireland these duties have been exercised by the Secretary of State for Northern Ireland since the suspension of Stormont in 1972. Other statutory tasks are divided by region; the Secretary of State for Transport (since 1997 for the Environment, Transport and the Regions) acting only in England, with the Secretaries of State for Northern Ireland, Scotland and Wales being responsible in their areas for building and maintaining motorways and trunk roads, and for providing grants to local authorities for roads and public transport. For the most up-to-date description of each department's structure and functions readers should consult the current annual edition of the *Civil Service Yearbook* (for example, Cabinet Office, 1996) or the department's annual report (for example, DoT, 1996a).

Under the Secretary of State for the Environment, Transport and the Regions, the Minister of Transport deals with all transport business. He or she is assisted by a variable number of other transport ministers whose responsibilities depend on the volume of legislation and other political business to be managed; one of the ministers is usually a peer, who can deal with all the department's business in the House of Lords. There are usually ministers responsible for roads and for public transport, and since 1992, responding to demands for better coordination of traffic

and transport policy in the capital following the earlier abolition of the Greater London Council (Travers *et al.*, 1991: 36),
there has been a Minister for Transport in London.

At official level, the constant elements within the organization include policy directorates dealing with railways, roads, urban and public transport, road and vehicle safety, aviation and
shipping, ports and airports; a range of executive agencies to
administer such services as the testing and licensing of both drivers
and vehicles, the construction and maintenance of national roads,
maritime safety and the coastguards; a network of regional offices
which bring together staff from transport, environment, trade,
education and employment departments; and central services such
as finance, personnel, statistics, legal services and information.

The policy directorates are subject to continual reorganization, partly in response to changing political priorities, which
can have a dramatic effect on workloads and consequently on
the staff and organization required (for instance, rail privatization), and partly in response to the continual pressure to econo-
mize in the use of staff and resources. These changes also reflect
a continual search for the ideal structure. Transport is a set of
interlocking networks, with the interfaces between them presenting
problems to which answers may sometimes be found by bringing
the relevant policy divisions together. For example it seemed
sensible in the mid-1980s for the department to link its oversight of British Rail's London rail services with those of London
Regional Transport (LRT) in order to facilitate the search for
joint solutions to meet complaints about the lack of a coherent
transport policy for London; later, when BR was being privatized but LRT was retained in public ownership, the two groups
were separated again. Another example, on a grand scale, was
the attempt made in 1994–5 to divide all the policy directorates
between infrastructure and operations in order to break down
the barriers between modal cultures (roads, public transport,
aviation and shipping) and demonstrate a determination to deal
even-handedly with road and rail infrastructure.

The benefits claimed for such reorganizations are debatable.
As well as signalling a political intention, they may give a fresh
perspective to policy-making by bringing together topics which
had previously been kept apart, but they may also separate other
topics which had usefully been held together. Fortunately, their

main impact is on senior managers who are accustomed to ad-justing quickly to changing circumstances and priorities. Much of the department's more routine work continues more or less undisturbed, but the constant upheaval in response to the latest pressure could well contribute to the culture of the short-term political fix, which some commentators find to be characteristic of British policy-making, and not only in regard to transport.

Although the structure of the department's policy directorates is predominantly modal, there are some important exceptions. The most significant of these is the transport strategy directo-rate. The small transport policy unit which Conservative minis-ters inherited from their Labour predecessors in 1979 was abolished in the early 1980s, and although useful work contin-ued to be done under the aegis of the department's chief economist until this post was also cut, a policy unit was not re-established until a decade later to work with DoE on a joint submission to the Royal Commission on Environmental Pollution (DoE and DoT, 1992), to provide support to ministers for 'the Great De-bate' in 1994–5, and to prepare the Green Paper *Transport: The Way Forward* which set out their response (DoT, 1995b; 1996b). Raised to the status of a full directorate in 1997, it occupies a key position within the united DETR, dealing with a range of intermodal issues, including safety, transport and the environ-ment, and transport taxation, and preparing the White Paper setting out the environmentally sustainable integrated transport policy which was promised in the Labour Party's election manifesto.

Another small division with cross-modal responsibilities is the Mobility Unit, which considers the impact of all traffic and trans-port polices on disabled people and on others who may have particular transport needs, such as elderly people, women trav-elling alone or passengers with young children. A third group with cross-modal responsibilities is the division which acts as a coordinating point for the department's relations with the Euro-pean Union (see Chapter 4). The remaining divisions of the core department provide the usual central services, such as person-nel, finance and legal advice. Since these functions are repli-cated on the environment side of the united department, they may well be amalgamated.

Transport executive agencies

About 80 per cent of the department's staff work in seven executive agencies. They are, in the order in which they were created between 1988 and 1994:

   Vehicle Inspectorate Executive Agency
   Driver and Vehicle Licensing Agency
   Vehicle Certification Agency
   Driving Standards Agency
   Marine Safety Agency
   Coastguard Agency
   Highways Agency

The Marine Safety Agency and Coastguard Agency were to form a single Marine Agency in April 1998. The Department of Transport was in the forefront of the Next Steps administrative reform programme, the Vehicle Inspectorate being the first executive agency to be set up by any department. Executive agencies remain part of the department. Their financial and policy objectives are set by the Secretary of State, but the agencies' chief executives are given day-to-day managerial freedom in how they achieve those objectives. For example, both the Vehicle Inspectorate and the Driving Standards Agency operate within the commercial disciplines of a trading fund regime, which is more flexible but no less demanding than the Treasury control of running costs (a rigid limit) which applies to government departments.

Relations between departments and their agencies work best where they are able to reflect a clear distinction between the formulation of policy and the delivery of a service. Difficulties arise where the delivery of a service is itself so sensitive and controversial that ministers cannot or will not refrain from intervening personally in the day-to-day operations of the agency. This consideration was an important criterion in deciding which sections of the department would form the Highways Agency. The agency has been given responsibility for the operational side of motorway and trunk road construction and maintenance, but ministers remain responsible for the politically sensitive decisions about which schemes should go ahead.

An eighth agency, the Transport Research Laboratory (TRL), was privatized in 1996. The department continues to sponsor research to a value of approximately £36m a year, much of it conducted under contracts with TRL. Privatization was a natural evolution of the customer–contractor relationship which had been established for several years. There is a risk that resources may be squeezed further, and some expertise lost when paying customers cannot be found, but the disciplines associated with financial provision are expected to ensure that research is more effectively and economically focused on topics to which the department attaches priority.

Environment

The Environment wing of DETR is inevitably linked into transport policy. Land-use planning, oversight and support of the construction industry, housing, local authority spending and environmental controls are all issues that link Environment with Transport. Road schemes have required the approval of both Transport and Environment ministers since the departments were first united in 1970.

The department's planning directorate looks at 'coordination of planning and transport issues' within the planning system as a whole. In 1992 it produced for the Royal Commission on Environmental Pollution a joint memorandum with the then separate Department of Transport on the effects of transport on the environment. Though the department's policy under Conservative governments was to work through the market rather than through regulation, there was a noticeable shift in emphasis after the Commission reported. In the late 1980s Nicholas Ridley as Secretary of State seldom ruled against out-of-town hypermarkets, whereas in the early 1990s his successor John Gummer made known his opposition to them (see Chapter 6).

Transport provision can play an important part in major development programmes. For example, the route of the Channel Tunnel Rail Link, and especially the decision to have an international station at Stratford in East London, was an important factor in Michael Heseltine's plans for the development of the East Thames corridor when he was Secretary of State for the Environment and later as Deputy Prime Minister. Planning and development considerations affecting the same area were also an important factor in the government's 1992 decision to transfer ownership of the Docklands Light Railway from London

Regional Transport, which had supervised its construction and initial operation, to the London Docklands Development Corporation.

Road construction as an industry is fostered by Environment through its promotion of 'the construction market' including contractors, professions and building materials, and its collection and publication of tender price indices for large road construction projects and road maintenance among other construction data. The environmental impact of transport is examined by the environmental protection group, which liaises with a wide range of autonomous organizations within the UK and with international organizations including the EU. The department's stated priority is to protect the environment and to see environmental concerns are reflected in all areas of policy. The environment directorate provides economic advice on environmental policy. Technical advice on pollution control, transport and the effects of fuel on air pollution is given by the air quality division.

Spending by local authorities on highways and transport is heavily influenced by decisions on local government finance. The department estimates standard spending assessments by service (central government's estimate of how much each local authority should spend), including on highway maintenance and capital financing. It pays transport-specific grants to highway authorities for capital projects, but all local authorities use part of the non-hypothecated revenue support grant allocated by central government, or their own resources within limits set by ministers, on road maintenance or to subsidize transport services.

Coordination within DETR

There has long been some degree of coordination between the Departments of Transport and the Environment, though it is more strongly emphasized when the two departments are together than when they are apart. Although the first marriage was dissolved in 1976, staff retained 'common citizenship' until 1989 and shared the same headquarters building in the Marsham Street towers until 1995, when DoT (and later DoE) began moving out to allow the towers to be pulled down. For 25 years they used the same library and the same staff canteen, as well as the same enormous underground car park, so that an unusually dense network of informal relationships persisted throughout the years of formal separation.

Coordination is closest within the nine regional offices which were established in 1971 under the first united department. When DoT and DoE separated again in 1976 the shared regional offices were retained (except in London), and both Secretaries of State had to approve recommendations for road schemes. In 1994 creation of the Highways Agency removed from regional offices their responsibility for oversight of road maintenance, but they continue to work closely with regional and local authorities on their development plans, including both road construction and public transport. They receive the annual transport policy and programme submissions from local authorities and recommend to the department what action should be taken on them. In 1993 the regional offices were given additional responsibilities for the coordination of urban regeneration programmes, and extended accordingly to include the regional staff of the Department of Employment and the Department of Trade and Industry, and one representative each from the Home Office and Education. They remain the key focus for the coordination of land-use planning and transport at the regional level.

At the headquarters of the two departments there was little incentive to coordinate national policies during the 1980s. Environment ministers were preoccupied with sales of council houses and the reform of local government finance, whilst transport ministers were busy privatising and deregulating the transport industries. However, coordination gradually strengthened during the 1990s as it became increasingly urgent to reconcile policies for transport and the environment, bearing fruit particularly in joint planning guidance to local authorities (see Chapter 6). The London regional office (the Government Office for London) served both departments, but the oversight of public transport provision through British Rail and London Regional Transport was handled separately by transport ministers, and not integrated with the regional office. The reunited department will be able to build on these foundations. It has a joint management board which includes the directors of all the major sectoral policy groups, and although much effort will doubtless have to be invested in re-establishing joint arrangements for the management of the department's common resources, the board is

serviced by a central policy unit, and the commitment to develop an environmentally sustainable integrated transport policy
should act as a catalyst for coordinated policy thinking.

Department of Trade and Industry (DTI)

Sponsorship of the vehicle manufacturing industry lies with DTI.
One of DTI's Industry branches considers the role of the vehicles industry together with various other more-or-less related
industries, including steel and mechanical engineering. Its 'sponsorship of manufacturers' division looks at the effect of environment and transport polices on the vehicles industry. The inclusion
since 1992 of the Department of Energy into DTI may in future
integrate vehicles and energy policies; it does not appear to have
done so yet.

The implications for vehicle safety, environmental pollution
and taxation revenue (including VAT) give DETR, Inland Revenue and Customs & Excise a greater interest than DTI in vehicle
design (for instance on engine size, consumption, fuel emissions).
Transport takes the lead in negotiating and implementing in UK
law most of the relevant EU legislation which now governs vehicle design. The DTI's intervention in transport focuses more
on transport infrastructure and vehicles as a potential export
commodity. Roads, bridges, tunnels, rail and urban transport
systems, road and railway vehicles together with their air and
sea equivalents form a 'project sector' in its Overseas Trade branch.

The Office of Fair Trading (OFT), which is attached to DTI,
plays an important part in trying to ensure fair competition in
the transport market and especially in those parts which are not
otherwise subject to economic regulation, notably the deregulated
bus industry. OFT has concurrent jurisdiction with the Office of
the Rail Regulator over competition issues in the privatized rail
industry. (See Chapter 9 for a discussion of fair competition in
the bus and rail industries.) The OFT also determines whether
mergers in the privatized transport industries should be allowed
to go ahead. For example, P&O were not allowed to merge with
Stena Sealink, the other major ferry company at Dover, until
the OFT was satisfied that Le Shuttle would provide effective
competition via the Channel Tunnel. Where there is concern
that companies might operate against the public interest, mergers

can be referred to the Monopolies and Mergers Commission, which also has a role in the periodic review of organizations still within the public sector such as London Regional Transport and the Civil Aviation Authority.

The Home Office

In the Home Office, 'road traffic' is grouped with public order, firearms and other offensive weapons in a division of the Police department. If the police could be persuaded to put more resources into controlling illegal parking in bus lanes, or checking overloaded freight lorries or the parking on pavements which causes most of the structural damage to roads and pavements, costs would be saved and there might even be some effect on the balance between road and rail use, and between public and private transport. But for the Home Office these questions are peripheral to its main concerns. In the meetings of the 'Tapwork' central–local government committee on parking, the Home Office 'retained observer status' only – a device that enables a department to take no responsibility for any decisions or recommendations made (DoT, 1987a).

The Home Office is the Metropolitan Police Authority. Because the Home Office and the Metropolitan Police were unable to devote the resources LRT would have liked to keeping bus routes unobstructed, the DoT introduced a measure in the Road Traffic Act 1991 allowing local government officials to control street parking in London (Burnham, Jones, Travers, 1992: 14–17).

HM Treasury

The Treasury is more important than any other Whitehall department because it draws up national economic and fiscal policies, and controls public expenditure. This gives Treasury ministers and officials enormous influence over transport which is both a significant source of revenue and a major area of public expenditure.

Responsibility for different aspects of transport policy is divided between the Treasury, and its associated, semi-autonomous departments: the Inland Revenue and Customs & Excise. The Chief Secretary oversees public expenditure, which includes central government spending on trunk roads, local authorities' spending on roads and public transport, and grants to support railway services and investment. The Financial Secretary oversees the Inland Revenue and taxation policy, together with privatization and deregulation – major facets of transport policy since at least 1983. The Paymaster-General oversees Customs & Excise which levies duties and taxes (fuel taxes, VAT on fuel and cars, and road vehicle tax).

The Treasury was reorganized in 1994 following a fundamental review of its running costs. The senior management structure was simplified, and its activities in overseeing other departments were to be limited to strategic control. Severe staff cuts followed, but it is difficult to separate strategic control from day-to-day management, and in practice there has been no perceptible relaxation of Treasury control. With the creation of DETR, Treasury oversight of all transport and environment expenditure programmes has been brought together in one division of the Spending Directorate, with the exception of any expenditure related to privatization proposals or public–private partnerships (the Labour name for what had previously been the Private Finance Initiative) which are considered within the Finance, Regulations and Industry directorate. Advice to Treasury ministers on taxation policies is given by a third unit within the Treasury, the Fiscal Policy division.

Criticisms of the Treasury were almost universal among the people interviewed by the authors for this book. The first criticism, voiced by a Treasury official but widely shared, is that it does not consult. For example, the Treasury consulted neither the Department of Transport nor the Department of Environment before increasing fuel duties in the spring 1993 budget (Potter, 1993:42), and although Kenneth Clarke as Chancellor of the Exchequer made an environmental virtue of his commitment to raising such taxes by 5 per cent per annum more than the rate of inflation, there can be no certainty that anyone will be consulted before any different policy is announced. Indeed, there was no consultation before Gordon Brown increased the margin to 6 per cent in 1997. Nor was there any consultation in 1994 when Treasury ministers suspended publication of the formula by which the road maintenance costs of heavy goods vehicles (track costs) had for some years been linked to the level of vehicle excise duty. The linkage had been regarded by the Department of Transport as an important economic signal to the road haulage industry, but it was abandoned when the implications for competitiveness became too uncomfortable.

Treasury officials may well discuss specific issues with officials in other departments from time to time, and there is an annual round robin seeking proposals for changes in advance of each year's budget; but it suits the Treasury well enough to spread the cloak of budget secrecy over all the key decisions on both spending and taxation, which obliges the Chancellor to take many important decisions within a very small circle of Treasury officials. Such an absence of properly informed debate, even behind closed doors, would be a matter of concern in any circumstances. It is particularly serious when prices (heavily influenced by taxation) are a key component of any transport strategy. Yet the Chancellor's decisions are taken in a context where the implications for the national economy are his first priority, whilst the consequences for transport policy and for the environment, if indeed they are properly understood, are a secondary consideration – used as additional arguments for the budget speech, to be adduced where convenient, ignored if they do not fit the case which needs to be made, or even dismissed if they add to administrative costs in the Chancellor's departments.

A second criticism of the Treasury is that it is so reluctant to commit funding or to allow other departments to do so, that it spends inefficiently – for instance, refusing maintenance spending that would save later but more expensive capital replacement. Faced with a critical report on road maintenance from the National Audit Office, backed by the powerful Public Accounts Committee, the Treasury did eventually concede the DoT's case that it is cheaper to spend money on timely resurfacing than to allow roads to deteriorate to the point where structural renewal is unavoidable. LRT claims it could get much keener prices for its track renewal contracts if it could negotiate a steady programme over several years, which it is unable to do because it never knows until four months before the start of each financial year how much grant it will get and experience shows that there can be very large fluctuations (see Chapter 8).

The Treasury has in the past been particularly cautious about longer-term expenditure commitments which would make it difficult for the Chief Secretary to cut expenditure in later years if necessary. This attitude has militated against major public transport investments which often extend over five years or more and cannot easily be stopped once construction has begun. It is a constraint that remains an important obstacle to traditional public expenditure commitments, though it has been eased where private finance has been introduced. Private-sector companies were not prepared to put up large sums of money to invest in transport infrastructure or equipment without suitable financial undertakings from government to cover payback periods which have ranged from seven to 15 years in the case of some rail franchise agreements, and extended to as much as 30 years for design, build, finance and operate (DBFO) contracts on the national road network, and even longer for the Channel Tunnel Rail Link.

The third criticism is that the Treasury sends relatively junior, inexperienced officials to meetings with interdepartmental committees or organizations, with insufficient authority to commit the Treasury. The practice might be explained by the civil service tradition of giving young, promising officials a wide range of experience. However, it can equally be seen as giving the Treasury a chance to delay a decision and better prepare its case against spending. Another frequent Treasury tactic, with the same object of delaying expenditure commitments if they cannot be refused outright, is to call for further studies, as they did repeatedly in the case of Crossrail, a major rail tunnel, first proposed in 1989, which would run east–west under central London to link the rail services either side of the city.

Up to a point such criticisms may reflect the frustration of the specialized transport official, naturally concerned by the needs of the particular policy area or organization with which he or she deals, faced by an official with broader concerns. There are advantages for sound policy-making that the Treasury is neutral between service departments and unlikely to be attracted by special pleading. Yet its narrow focus on resisting public expenditure commitments, and particularly on squeezing capital expenditure even where it could be beneficial, has contributed to the persistent underfunding of transport infrastructure in the public sector.

Customs & Excise and the Inland Revenue

Customs & Excise advises the Chancellor of the Exchequer on indirect taxes, such as excise duties and Value Added Tax. Excise duties on hydrocarbon oils, including petrol substitutes such as liquid propane gas (LPG), and VAT on transport are dealt with by one directorate, and car tax by a division of a different directorate. The Inland Revenue advises the Chancellor of the Exchequer on policy concerning direct taxes, including income tax. The areas of direct tax policy which have an impact on transport are, or could be, personal tax allowances and emoluments including benefits-in-kind on the provision and use of company cars, subsidized fuel, maintenance and parking spaces. (For a discussion of the issues which arise, see Chapter 8.)

Mention has already been made of the difficulty inherent in any discussion with Customs & Excise or Inland Revenue which could have a bearing on the Chancellor's budget. The main responsibility of the two revenue departments is to collect the revenue, so they naturally give advice which lays emphasis on factors which make for the economic and efficient administration of the tax system. Their views are then filtered by the Treasury's own Fiscal Policy division, with its emphasis on the macroeconomic implications of taxation, and the decisions are finally taken under conditions of great secrecy within the Chancellor's small budget team. For example, there would seem to be, as we were told, 'universal agreement across the departments that tax allowances on business cars and free petrol were in principle wrong', and that these tax benefits were declining in value. That is, the technical argument for abolition had been accepted and was being implemented as fast as political imperatives allowed. But political and macroeconomic considerations affecting each successive budget continue to dictate the pace of this reform, and it remains the case that there is little scope for discussion of proposals which do not accord neatly with the Treasury's own priorities.

The finance departments together are in a better position to coordinate transport income and expenditure than those departments most intimately connected with the transport planning process. It is unfortunate that their control seems to be exercised in a negative way; that is, the main aim is to cut back expenditure, not to spend effectively. Income is raised and spent in ways which profoundly influence transport policy, yet without adequate discussion even behind the government's closed doors, much less in an open forum, with the result that key components of transport policy may be irrational from a transport policy perspective.

Cabinet Office

The main function of the Cabinet Office is to support the Cabinet and the Prime Minister in maintaining collective responsibility for government policy. It acts as the clearing house and secretariat for the committees which ensure that the government maintains a coherent policy, determining priorities and resolving differences among departments as necessary. But it may also be entrusted with more specific functions, particularly where these cut across departmental responsibilities. In recent years such functions have included the Deregulation Unit and the Competitiveness Unit which coordinated and spurred on the relevant programmes in all government departments. These policies were of crucial importance in the privatization of the transport industries. In addition, within the Office of Public Service (itself part of the Cabinet Office) the Next Steps Unit drove forward the reforms which led to the creation of the Department of Transport's Executive Agencies, and the Efficiency Unit worked tirelessly for the application within the public service of management practices adopted and adapted from the private sector.

Nationalized industries and other public bodies

A very large number of public bodies with a direct or indirect responsibility for transport policy are sponsored by or attached to DETR, such as the British Waterways Board, the Port of London Authority, the Standing Committee on Trunk Road Asssessment (SACTRA), the Countryside Commission, English Nature. We refer to some of these organizations in other chapters, but here the emphasis is on bodies directly responsible for providing or overseeing transport services, especially the arrangements for the privatized railway companies.

The Secretary of State for the DETR oversees the work of

some nationalized industries and government-owned companies. Their number changed frequently in the 1980s and early 1990s as the government pursued its privatization programme. In 1997 the department still oversaw the work of London Regional Transport, the Civil Aviation Authority (CAA) and what was left of the British Railways Board (all nationalized industries), but a year earlier the list would have included Railtrack (which owned British Rail's former track and other infrastructure, privatized in May 1996), as well as Union Railways and European Passenger Services, which were both sold during the year to London & Continental Railways, the successful bidder for the operation of Eurostar services and the construction of the Channel Tunnel Rail Link.

Nationalized industries as envisaged by Herbert Morrison in the postwar Labour government were to combine the private sector's managerial autonomy with the parliamentary accountability demanded of public enterprises. Government intervention was supposed to be limited to appointing board members and setting broad objectives. The position is spelled out in more detail in the 1978 White Paper, *The Nationalized Industries* (Cmnd 7131), which remains the most recent formal statement of policy. Ministers still insist they are not responsible for LRT's managerial decisions; for instance, refusing to answer parliamentary questions about its expenditure on track maintenance (*HC Debs*, 23 April 1993: 209). But ministers have intervened over the past decade or so to force the pace of privatization and deregulation. These are certainly legitimate strategic issues, though the extent of ministerial involvement in the detail may be more questionable. Ministers also intervene regularly to influence pay negotiations and fare increases, areas in which political sensitivities and management autonomy often collide. Some transport planners argue ministers must intervene if transport policies are to be coordinated and integrated. For example, following the abolition of the Greater London Council in 1986, the Secretary of State for Transport took the initiative in convening meetings of LRT and BR executives which were welcomed by both sides. The joint work which was commissioned led to the Central London Rail Study and the East London Rail Study, which examined the case for complementary upgrading and new construction on both networks.

The CAA has been given two somewhat conflicting roles by government. First it has to promote the growth of the air transport and travel industry through reducing regulation and opening-up airports and routes to greater competition. Second, it must maintain and improve safety standards, mostly through regulation. The CAA used to run National Air Traffic Services (air traffic control) jointly with the Ministry of Defence, but in 1996 NATS was established as a semi-autonomous company within the CAA as a first step towards the privatization of air traffic services. The part played by the CAA in increasing airport capacity is noted in Chapter 5. British Airways and the British Airports Authority (which operates the three London airports and four in Scotland), were privatized in the 1980s. They are regulated by the CAA and thus much more under the direction of central government than the bus and coach industries which were both privatized and deregulated.

The department sponsors some small executive bodies such as the London Regional Passengers Committee and the Traffic Director for London, and the Area Traffic Commissioners who license road haulage and bus operators. The Secretary of State for Transport nominates the people appointed to all these bodies.

The role of the transport inspectorates and quasi-independent watchdogs, such as the Railways Inspectorate of the Health and Safety Executive, should not be underestimated. Safety and service standards have been much enhanced over the decades by official inquiries into accidents, accident investigation reports, and more recently by parliamentary select committees. The inspectorates are given professional independence by a power of direct access to both the minister and the permanent secretary (the top official in the department). While the Marine Accident Investigation Branch and the older Air Accident Investigation Branch deal with 'routine' analyses, the Transport Secretary's response after a major disaster is often to set up an inquiry headed by a senior judge (such as those conducted by Sheen, Fennell, Hidden, Donaldson). These high-profile inquiries have their advantages and their disadvantages. In their favour it can be said that the government is seen to be taking the issue seriously, the inquiry is seen to be independent, the judge can look with a fresh mind at routine procedures, and the Treasury comes under strong pressure to make new money available to pay for full implementation. On the other hand, the effect on policy of the most publicized inquiries may not be wholly rational. Some of the investment made in LRT infrastructure as a direct response to the recommendations of the Fennell report into the King's Cross fire might have been more effective in reducing the risk of fatalities if spent on different safety measures. Some would even argue that greater reforms may be made as a result of media exposure of the circumstances than as a result of the official report (for example, to counteract alcoholism among crews following the loss of the *Herald of Free Enterprise*).

Regulating the privatized railway

Standing slightly outside DETR but working to fulfil objectives for mainline rail services set by the Secretary of State are the Office of Passenger Rail Franchising and the Office of the Rail Regulator. The post-privatization railway organization, described below and in Figure 3.2, is a mix of private- and public-sector bodies (Glaister, 1995).

Railtrack owns the signalling and fixed infrastructure, including the land and stations. Railtrack recovers its costs through charging users for access to its facilities, except that the Secretary of State retains the power to give direct capital grants for freight facilities if justified on public interest grounds. Railtrack 'buys in' most of its services – such as track maintenance engineering – through competitive tender. It is responsible for central timetabling and coordination of all train movements, signalling, and planning investment in infrastructure and ensuring it is carried out. It is responsible for safe operation of the network under the supervision of the Health and Safety Executive. Railtrack's property portfolio includes stations, railway land, buildings, installations and light maintenance depots, many of which will be leased to train operators. However, 14 large mainline stations remain under Railtrack's direct control.

The *Franchising Director* heads the Office of Passenger Rail Franchising. Financial support to the railway passes through the Franchising Director with the exception of certain freight grants and any capital grants. The Franchising Director's function is to define rail passenger franchises and sell them to train operating companies using a competitive tendering procedure. He defined

FIGURE 3.2 **The structure of the rail industry**

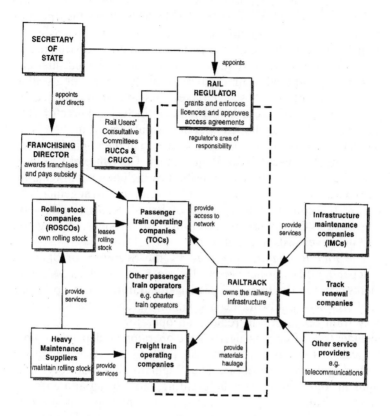

Source: Office of the Rail Regulator, *Annual Report 1996/97.*

passenger service groups that would be offered as 25 franchise agreements. Arrangements for through-ticketing and concessionary fares are enforced through these agreements. On the basis of the charges set for track and station access, costs were expected to exceed passenger revenues for most of the franchises; prospective train operators thus bid for the lowest subsidy for which they would be willing to operate the defined services. The Franchising Director funds the subsidies from a budget fixed by the Secretary of State. Chapter 9 shows the outcome from the first round of bidding.

The Passenger Service Requirement lies at the core of the

franchising agreement. It comprises two components: a minimum guaranteed level of services to be provided by the operator, and a degree of flexibility above this level which allows the operator room to develop and improve services. The Office of Passenger Rail Franchising has specified certain mandatory service characteristics, such as train frequency, stations to be served, first and last trains, and peak train capacity. Franchise agreements allow for adjustments of these characteristics over time, subject to consultation and a veto held by the Franchising Director. The Franchising Director hoped operators would find it in their commercial interests to offer a better service than the minimum specified in the Passenger Service Requirement. The Office of Passenger Rail Franchising's other responsibilities include encouraging investment, improving services, and developing arrangements to ensure the continuation of some of British Rail's former services, such as concessionary travel for staff, through-ticketing and certain travelcards and railcards.

The *Rail Regulator*, appointed by the Secretary of State, is independent. His or her approval is required for all access agreements between Railtrack and passenger and freight train operators. Railtrack has a network licence administered by the Regulator. Any train operator will require an operator licence. Operators include: franchised passenger service operators; independent, non-franchised (that is, 'open access') passenger service operators; and freight train operators. The Regulator has statutory functions in four main areas: the granting, monitoring and enforcement of licences to operate railway assets; the approval of access agreements between facility owners and users of railway facilities; the enforcement of domestic competition law; and approval of railway line closures.

The Regulator's duties are to protect the interests of both providers and users of rail services, to promote competition together with efficiency and economy, to promote the development and use of the network, to safeguard through-ticketing for the benefit of the public, and to ensure that Railtrack does not find it unduly difficult to finance its activities. In fulfilling those duties, the Regulator must take into account the financial position of the Franchising Director, whose budget is decided separately. The Regulator can vary licences by agreement: if the licence-holder does not agree, the matter can be referred to the Monopolies and Mergers Commission. The Regulator will ensure that arrangements for allocating train paths and settling timetable disputes are fair and reasonable. In relation to the monopoly supply of railway services the Regulator has concurrent jurisdiction with the Director General of Fair Trading.

A significant difference between privatized rail and other British regulated utilities is the role Parliament has given the Regulator over the commercial contracts which give infrastructure users permission to operate. In other industries, the regulator's role is based primarily on the licences the industry players hold. In the case of the railway industry, however, much of the important economic regulation – particularly the control of prices charged for the use of railway assets – is based on access agreements not licences, and the Regulator's approval of every access agreement is required. If it is not approved, it is void.

The Regulator has considerable powers. However, there are many things over which he or she has no power. Some may come as a surprise to those familiar with other regulated utilities: most stem from the railway's more complicated regulatory structure. That structure, in turn, ultimately derives from the fact that the railway receives, and will continue to receive, substantial subsidy from central government. Many contracts are not regulated, such as the terms of leases for rolling stock and for stations, and the contracts between Railtrack and providers of engineering services (the greater part of Railtrack expenditure). Most important, and most surprising to the general public, the Regulator has no power to regulate passenger fares. This power belongs to the Franchising Director through the contracts offered for passenger franchises, presumably on the grounds that fares regulation has direct implications for subsidy and therefore for government expenditure.

Local transport responsibilities

At local level, counties in England and unitary, all-purpose authorities in Wales, Scotland and some parts of England, are both highway and passenger transport authorities, with the ability to integrate traffic and transport policies for their areas within limits set by central government. In the six major conurbations outside

FIGURE 3.3   The organizational structure of transport in London

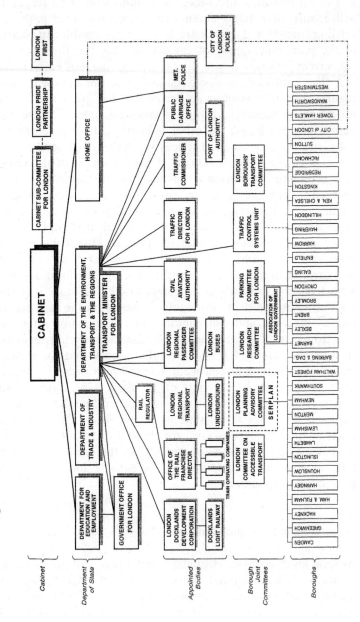

London the metropolitan district councils are grouped into Passenger Transport Authorities (PTAs), joint boards of councillors which represent each council. Their role is less than that of the metropolitan counties abolished in 1986, but they continue to sponsor (that is, subsidize) local rail and bus services, levying a charge on their constituent councils. The policy they decide is implemented by officials in Passenger Transport Executives.

London Regional Transport, which runs the Underground and oversees the provision of bus services in the capital, has been a nationalized industry since 1984, subject to the strategic guidance of transport ministers. But LRT has no responsibility for mainline suburban rail services, for taxis and for roads. Figure 3.3 illustrates the complexity of the current arrangements for the governance of London and its transport networks since the abolition of the Greater London Council in 1986. The Labour government elected in 1997 is committed to creating a new Greater London Authority to take control of most aspects of London's transport and roads.

The metropolitan and London boroughs are now land-use planning authorities, their plans subject to the Secretary of State's approval, and strongly influenced by the government's regional offices, whose position in the planning system is pivotal, since they are in a position both to advise the planning authorities at the preparation stage and to advise the Secretary of State when resources are required for implementation. It can be argued that one effect of abolishing the metropolitan county councils (and the GLC) was to give Whitehall departments more control over the transport policies of the conurbations (Truelove, 1992: 29). It is certainly true that both before and after the change DoT exercised considerable influence through its deployment of resources.

Outside the conurbations, roads are of more direct concern than railways, reflecting not only the greater emphasis on roads in statutory duties but their direct relevance to local people. In West Sussex, for example, 90 per cent of all major journeys made within the county are on roads (West Sussex, 1993a: B35). Together with responsibility for much of the road network come provision and maintenance of pavements, bridges, drainage, lighting, verges, trees, traffic signs and signals, and pedestrian crossings. Under the Transport Act 1985, councils can support the cost of bus services through their support for concessionary fares, and they subsidize non-commercial services by asking operators to tender for running specified routes or services.

Central government oversees local government's executive responsibilities on road and rail. It lays down advisory standards which apply to all roads, for instance on highway markings, traffic signs and signals, traffic calming works. Since the mid-1980s local government has been increasingly hampered in coordinating services and deciding levels of provision by progressive reductions in standard spending assessments and capping of local authority expenditure, including (since the abolition of the metropolitan county councils) the Secretary of State's power to set the maximum precept which boards including PTAs may levy on constituent district councils. More particularly the 1985 Transport Act which deregulated bus services led to the withdrawal of central government support for non-commercial bus services, which had previously qualified for Transport Supplementary Grant, now restricted to capital investments. All PTAs and councils are limited in their spending by tight controls on levels of income from local taxation, government grants and credit approvals. Since grants and credit approvals are mostly awarded for particular projects, councils are inclined to follow central government's transport priorities.

The division of responsibility for roads between central government and local government owes more to history than to technical criteria. National roads comprise trunk roads and nearly all motorways. The Trunk Roads Act 1936 led to the designation of a national network of trunk roads for which central government assumed full financial responsibility, and the Secretary of State has wide powers under the Highways Act 1980 to add roads or remove them. Until 1974 there was a policy of not trunking roads inside county boroughs, which left many gaps in the national network. Since then many of the gaps have been filled as motorways, bypasses and road improvements within the old borough boundaries have been constructed, though a number of gaps remain, for example in the Bradford and Bristol areas. Trunk roads account for only about 4 per cent of total road length in Great Britain. But their national importance is confirmed by the fact that they carry traffic out of all proportion to their length – 32 per cent of traffic in England in 1991. Moreover they carried

56 per cent of the heavy goods traffic which causes most of the structural damage to roads (DoT, 1993a: 42).

Roads not designated as trunk roads are 'local' roads and the responsibility of councils as local highway authorities. The local highway authorities may also act as agents for national government, maintaining national roads under contract to the DoT, but in recent years these contracts have been put out to competitive tender, and many have been won by road construction companies. Under the Highways Act 1980 the lower-tier shire districts may undertake maintenance for local roads subject to 30 mph speed limits. The county council reimburses them for 'any work necessary to their duty', though the district council can work to higher standards at their own expense if they wish. This arrangement allows borough councils to continue a responsibility they had before the 1974 reorganization of local government. Districts increasingly have little financial leeway to do more than maintain roads to county-determined standards. Under the Transport Act 1985 districts contribute to subsidies on county-tendered (non-commercial) bus services, but here too if the county council does not have enough resources to support all the services which the district council might judge to be desirable, the district can come under heavy pressure (as has occurred in Hertfordshire) to contribute financially if they wish to ensure that certain bus routes will in fact be put out to tender. District councils also implement local traffic-management schemes and have a few other specific functions, such as in parking regulation.

A National Audit Office report in 1985 recommended there should be some transfer of responsibilities for roads to local governments because local authorities were better-placed to judge priorities; the Commons Public Accounts Committee thought local authorities should have more control of bypasses and saw local government as being discriminated against (Mackie, 1987: 117). The DoT refused to consider any transfer of responsibilities before 1990 on the grounds that councils might not spend enough on major roads. At the time many counties wanted that responsibility, as did London boroughs when the GLC was abolished, though subsequent financial constraint caused them to have second thoughts about taking it on. The creation in many areas of unitary authorities smaller than counties has strengthened the case for retaining central government control over national roads, since maintenance is now very sophisticated.

There is a political advantage for DoT in retaining trunk road bypasses and smaller projects within its national remit, even though local authorities could administer them, because they counterbalance the equivocal image of larger schemes. Stephen Potter (1993: 37) thought the government made good public-relations use of bypasses. 'Although the bypassing of towns and villages is frequently cited as a justification for [the road-building programme], in practice bypasses amount to only 15 percent of the schemes; 85 percent of expenditure is to increase motorway and trunk road capacity.'

Local government–central government relationships

Arguments such as Stephen Potter's lend support to models of local government–central government relationships that see local government as the agent of central government, and inevitably in conflict with it. The dual-state thesis, as developed by Cawson and Saunders (1983), asserts that central government and its bureaucrats, relatively insulated from a wide range of interest groups and public debate, keeps for itself control over investment decisions in infrastructure important to private-sector producers. It allows local authorities and local pluralist competition the less critical social consumption goods or social welfare services. DoT's payment of Transport Supplementary Grant and the efforts by some local authorities to build their own light rail systems would not negate the validity of the theory since their spending and borrowing is very much determined by central government.

More significant, however, is the 'public choice' theory of Niskanen, not because it is necessarily valid, but because it was promoted by New Right think-tanks and believed by Mrs Thatcher as prime minister and Nicholas Ridley as Secretary of State for the Environment. By defining public bureaucracies as intrinsically wasteful and self-serving, Niskanen's work reinforced the determination of Conservative leaders to reduce public spending, particularly by those not closely under their control. Nevertheless, it would be a mistake to suppose that central government 'rolled back the (local) state' only under Mrs Thatcher. Jerry White (1993: 20) has shown there was a continuous transfer of power and functions from local government throughout the twentieth century, the period of greatest centralization being under a Labour government between 1946 and 1948. In the British unwritten constitution local government is always at the mercy of central government.

After John Major became prime minister, there was some repairing of the relationships between central and local governments, particularly in relation to transport policy. Moreover, local authorities and their regional associations have much to teach central government departments on how to cooperate in the strategic planning of land-use and transport (see Chapters 6 and 7). Central government for its part has begun to recognize the importance of cooperation among local authorities in neighbouring areas which form a coherent unit for transport purposes, and has encouraged this through the emphasis placed on the 'package approach' since 1993 as the preferred basis on which to bid for resources in the annual round of transport policies and programme submissions (TPPs).

The coordination of public responsibilities in transport

An account that sets out public responsibilities for transport department-by-department and tier-by-tier inevitably emphasizes its fragmentation; it would be unbalanced if it failed to acknowledge forces for integration. Several mechanisms exist for coordinating the work of departments, bringing them together at central and local levels or, more often, bringing together officials, local authorities and other interests to debate a particular issue. They are not easy to describe; some of the structures and responsibilities of ministerial committees have been made public, but much remains confidential and the work of informal gatherings is extensive, ever-changing and difficult to pin down.

Since April 1992 the existence of *Cabinet committees*, together with their names, membership and general area of concern, have been made public. The actual topics of discussion are made known only through leaks of information from participants. The general working principle is for them to handle any interdepartmental issue which cannot be settled by correspondence or meetings at official or ministerial level among the parties most directly concerned. The committees refer on upwards for discussion by full Cabinet items of high political significance only, or those unable to be unresolved at committee level. Otherwise Cabinet is merely informed. There is a supporting structure of committees at official level which may resolve some issues and clarify others for discussion among ministers.

Some Cabinet committees have particular relevance for transport policy. The Cabinet committee on the environment handles major cross-departmental issues on the environment, which would include controversial transport infrastructure projects. It is a large committee of more than a dozen ministers including senior ministers responsible for Environment, Transport, Trade and Industry, Agriculture, Scotland, Wales and Northern Ireland, together with the Chancellor of the Exchequer and the Chief Secretary. The Minister for Transport is also a member of the Cabinet committee on local government, which discusses local government financial issues, including transport finance. The Cabinet sub-committee on London, created after the April 1992 election, coordinates government policy on London and includes the Minister for Transport in London. Among other things, it discusses future transport projects.

The multiplicity of committees in central government discussing transport issues for London is a consequence both of the capital's special transport problems and its lack of a coordinating local authority. Other committees chaired by the Minister for Transport in London have included the Transport Working Group, the Docklands Steering Group, and the River Thames Working Group, whose membership includes the Port of London Authority, London First, London Docklands Development Corporation, the London Planning Advisory Committee and London Regional Transport. But such groups come and go as ministers and priorities change, and the position in London is certain to change as arrangements are developed to give Greater London a mayor and a new Greater London Authority.

The Cabinet committee on public expenditure, set up in 1992 so that Cabinet ministers could consider collectively the government's annual expenditure programme, is probably more important than all these committees combined, just as the Treasury is more important to transport than any other department. This committee has the last word in the annual review of transport spending (see Chapter 8), subject only to final endorsement by the full Cabinet.

At *official level*, coordination between departments takes place not only in committees preparing the ground for ministers to take decisions in Cabinet committees, but in dozens of other interdepartmental groups, formal and informal, for which no public list exists. To these should be added many advisory committees bringing together officials, experts, members of interest groups and professional organizations. In 1993 the Minister for Transport in London listed the bodies with transportation responsibilities in London with which DoT had formal liaison arrangements: his list covered most of the organizations identified in Figure 3.3 (*HC Debs*, 18 January 1993: 68). Though not typical of all regions, these organizations are a guide to the complexity of arrangements across the country. A full list would indeed add many other organizations with nationwide remits on highways and transport, such as the Standing Advisory Committee on Trunk Road Assessment (SACTRA) and the Royal Commission on Environmental Pollution mentioned earlier.

At local level, and particularly within the major conurbations, the Department has used *the package approach* since 1993 to encourage coordination between transport and planning authorities. Within an agreed package of transport works and measures designed to achieve locally agreed objectives, which may well include safety, enhanced modal interchange, cycling and walking as well as traditional road and public transport schemes, the cooperating local authorities get the benefit of flexibility in the allocation of the approved expenditure. By giving priority to such packages in the annual allocation of grants to local authorities, the department has encouraged integrated transport planning at local level.

Informal contacts between officials on transport issues are impossible to chart. Some of them are mentioned here and there in this book. The working methods and personnel management of the civil service are designed to overcome some of the deficiencies of Whitehall's departmental structure. Examples include: the Cabinet Office's use of departmental officials on two-year secondments to staff the Cabinet Secretariat; the telephone networks of civil servants in ministers' private offices and at all levels in departments; the secondment of officials from their 'home' department to other service departments or the Treasury, and from the Treasury to other departments (nearly all top civil servants have served in the Treasury or the Cabinet Office or both), absorbing a common culture. The advantage is that every senior official has a personal acquaintance of other departments and a set of easy contacts around the Whitehall community. The disadvantage of such regular movement is sometimes thought to be a lack of continuity and depth of knowledge, which risks being altogether absent from policy-making within government if it is not supplied by officials, since ministers seldom spend more than two or three years in the same department.

Conclusion

This chapter has described a very fragmented system for conceiving and delivering a national transport policy. For historic, and probably inevitable reasons, transport policy-making and implementation was already split between central government, public corporations and local government, between departments and divisions of departments, even before the New Right governments of the 1980s came into office. Those governments, searching for efficiency and a more effective public service, deliberately fragmented the system further, dividing the administration into separate agencies and the service-deliverers between a multitude of public- and private-sector bodies.

The ideological drive towards a greater use of market mechanisms and privatization in air, rail and bus services in the 1980s and 1990s removed some large enterprises and large numbers of employees from the public sector. But the changes did not imply government had lost all power to direct and control the transport industries. Contracts are finite, and the powers of the Secretary of State to set objectives for regulators and public corporations could be used almost as easily to facilitate government intervention as to reinforce market disciplines.

The positive features of the current, fragmented system are first, an increased 'transparency', a clarity of objectives, budgets and relationships which, because they had to be set out in documents, made ministers, officials and advisers think more carefully than before what they required the system and its separate parts to deliver. Second, those documents often provide a means for ministers to exercise a far closer control over the system than the market rhetoric makes it appear. They can change the orientation of the system by changing the directions and objectives given to their appointees, directors and agency chief executives. Third, there has been a growing recognition of the value of cooperation among government authorities in tackling transport-related issues at the local level. The actions of central government are being more effectively coordinated through the enhanced regional offices set up to manage urban regeneration budgets. Neighbouring local authorities, especially in urban areas, are being encouraged to cooperate more closely in dealing with transport issues through the preference given since 1993 to bids based on the package approach in the annual transport policies and programme submissions. The need for more effective cooperation between central and local government was also acknowledged when such a possibility was postulated in *Transport: The Way Forward* (DoT, 1996b: appendix 1), which proposed that the preparation of regional planning guidance should in future include formal consultation on the trunk road programme within the region. Previously local authorities had been asked to treat the trunk road programme as a given.

These are some of the foundations on which an integrated transport policy was already beginning to be constructed at local levels and potentially at a regional level under the Major government. At the level of national policy, however, new structures and organizations were still being created, notably under railway privatization, or proposed (as, for example, the privatization of the London Underground) to facilitate and entrench competition and individual choice. A new Labour government committed to the development of an integrated transport policy is more likely to emphasize structures which facilitate cooperation and collective choice. The bringing together of the Transport and Environment departments in 1997 was a clear signal of their intention to reconcile and integrate the policies of the two departments. How much further the structures of government will need to be changed is perhaps debatable, though new structures can sometimes signal a new direction as well as providing a useful catalyst for new thinking. What has been lacking in recent

years has been not so much the administrative structures which
a more integrated approach to transport policy would require,
as the political will to use for that purpose, at national level,
the extensive powers and the substantial resources which the British
government with its strong executive has the capacity to deploy
when it chooses to do so.

4 Making Transport Policy in the European Union

Transport in the Treaty of Rome

The founding members of the European Economic Community (EEC), the precursor of the European Community (EC) and today's European Union (EU), had high expectations for a common transport policy when they signed the Treaty of Rome on 12 March 1957. In a common market based on the freedom of movement of people, goods, services and capital, what could be more natural than a common transport policy?

The Spaak Report of 21 April 1956, which provided an agreed framework for the negotiations leading to the Treaty of Rome, had drawn attention to three aspects of transport policy which would need to be covered in the Treaty:

(1) the charging of all passengers or freight at the same price for the same journey within the common market;

(2) the development and financing of infrastructure investment;

(3) the formulation of a common transport policy.

Agreement was quickly reached on the principle of non-discriminatory pricing (Article 79). For infrastructure investment it was decided to rely on the general provisions of the Treaty, an omission that was to be rectified only in 1994 by Articles 129b–d of the (Maastricht) Treaty on European Union. But as the main negotiations for the creation of the EEC approached a successful conclusion in the winter of 1956–7, the working parties of transport experts were still far from agreement on the principles which should underlie a common transport policy (Abbati, 1987: 29–33).

Of the six original EC members, the Dutch, with some support from their Benelux partners, Belgium and Luxembourg, favoured an approach based on the liberal market-driven policies which best suited their compact trading economy. France, Germany and Italy on the other hand, with large territories and dispersed populations, were much more accustomed to extensive state intervention in the provision of both road and rail networks, and wanted a common transport policy which would allow such policies to continue (ibid. 33).

At that time almost all transport of goods and passengers within the six member states was protected from international competition. Lorries carrying goods across frontiers were subject to parsimonious quotas. International trains carried both passengers and freight, but there was no competition between the various national operators, each of which enjoyed a monopoly on its own tracks. Cross-frontier trains were operated under the Bern Convention of 1890 (originally relating only to goods) with the revenues shared out among the railway companies in proportion to usage. A parallel Convention for passenger travel was signed in 1924. Air transport was relatively insignificant and conducted on the basis of duopolies regulated by bilateral treaties which allowed the business to be shared equally between the national airlines at either end of each international route.

The only significant transport market open to international competition was on the Rhine where a regime dating back to the Congress of Vienna (1815) provided for freedom of navigation under the authority of a Commission which included Britain as a member along with all the riparian states. The liberal regime governing Rhine shipping was to remain for many years an isolated exception to the managed transport markets of the EU member states, but it was important enough to warrant the determined efforts made by the Dutch to defend it; in 1962 the Rhine and its tributaries carried about 25 per cent of the freight transported on all the rail systems of the six original member states (Despicht, 1964: 54–6). It remains a major transport artery for the industrial heartland of northern Europe.

The negotiators could not reconcile the conflicting positions which the member states derived from their history and geography and their perception of national interest (Abbati, 1987: 29–33). This posed a dilemma for the intergovernmental conference negotiating the treaty. They attached too much importance to transport to leave it out altogether, but not enough to risk delaying the negotiations while transport experts struggled towards a more detailed agreement. So they settled for a few short articles, hurriedly drafted to specify the procedures under which the new institutions would establish a common transport policy, leaving the content to be filled in later.

As a result the transport articles of the Treaty are a compromise. The germ of a liberal policy is buried deep in the apparently innocuous wording of Article 74, which requires the member states to pursue the objectives of the Treaty within the framework of a common transport policy. (The objectives of the Treaty, as set out in the preamble and principles, are essentially liberal.) But when it comes to implementing that commitment, there is plenty of room for debate about how to proceed. Article 75(1) requires the Council to take account of the 'distinctive features of transport', which Nigel Despicht (1964: 35) described as 'a permanent pretext for treating the transport sector differently from the rest of the economy'. He continued:

In our view, the 'special aspects' are the words used to indicate the fundamental reluctance of many EEC states to accept the full effects of competition in the transport market – either for users because transport is held to be a public service, or for carriers because unrestrained competition is regarded as leading inevitably to an uneconomic use of resources.

The first relatively uncontroversial steps were laid down clearly enough in Article 79 which required the Council to adopt provisions within two years to make it illegal to protect domestic industries by charging less for the transport of their goods than for the transport of similar goods produced elsewhere in the community. But the uneasy balance between liberal and interventionist policies is reflected in the terms of the remaining Articles. For example, Article 80 seeks to control subsidies through the fare-box to particular transport undertakings by requiring Commission authorization for any state-imposed rates and conditions, but wide-ranging exceptions are envisaged on account of regional economic policy, areas seriously affected by political circumstances (see also Article 82), and even for the effects of competition between the different modes of transport. The interventionist stance is even more positively endorsed in Article 77, which justifies the provision of state aids to 'meet the needs of coordination of transport' as well as to cover public-service obligations, and in Article 78 which requires any measures affecting fares to 'take account of the economic circumstances of carriers'.

If the negotiators really envisaged a common transport policy consistent with the objectives of the Treaty (Article 74), the qualifications with which such an intention was hedged about in the following articles were so extensive as to give the Commission little help in devising acceptable proposals. Moreover most of the member states saw the transport articles as a defence against the general provisions of the Treaty governing such matters as competition, state aids and the freedom to provide services, which in their view could be applied to transport only within the framework of a common transport policy. In their support they pointed in particular to Article 61(1) which states that 'freedom to provide services in the field of transport shall be governed by the provisions of the Title relating to transport'. Within the transport Title, most decisions were to be taken by qualified majority vote after the end of the second stage of the transitional period (end of 1965), and this should have made it easier to reach agreement, but Article 75(3) provides for the Council to take decisions by unanimity (even today, after the increasing membership has made the achievement of a unanimous view more demanding) 'where the application of provisions concerning the principles of the regulatory system for transport would be liable to have a serious effect on the standard of living and on employment in certain areas and on the operation of transport facilities'. The application of the Treaty to sea and air transport was even more uncertain, since Article 84(2) merely provided that 'the Council may, acting unanimously, decide whether, to what extent and by what procedure appropriate provisions may be laid down for sea and air transport'. For many years the Council regarded this text as justifying the complete exclusion of sea and air transport from the ambit of the Treaty in the absence of any decision to establish a framework of common policies.

The conflicting views of transport policy barely concealed within the terms of the transport chapter of the Treaty would not have mattered if there had been some way of resolving them later.

There was, but it took nearly thirty years to find it. The basic principle of the division of powers within the European Communities is that the Commission has the sole right to make formal proposals, but the Council of Ministers, in which all the member states are represented, decides – after hearing the views of advisory bodies including the European Parliament – whether to accept or reject the Commission's proposals. The Commission, as guardian of the Treaty, was to make many proposals which the Council rejected or ignored, as discussed below. In the end, after some 25 years of inconclusive debate, the log-jam was broken by the European Court of Justice (ECJ) which ruled, in a case brought by the European Parliament (Case 13/83, *European Parliament* v. *Council of the European Communities*, 22 May 1985), that in the absence of a common transport policy duly laid down by the Council, the general provisions of the Treaty, which include the freedom to provide services, should be held to apply to transport. Spurred on by the implied threat of more or less unrestricted competition, the Council finally put in place a set of measures which could credibly be described as a common transport policy.

1958–72: gridlock in the Council

In the years before British accession, 1958–72, the Commission did its best to devise a common transport policy consistent with the objectives of the Treaty and with the distinctive features reflected in the transport articles. On 10 April 1961 it sent to the Council a memorandum outlining the main features of a common transport policy, followed on 23 May 1962 by an action programme. In 1964, despite the meagre progress which had been made so far, it was still possible for an optimistic British observer to refer, perhaps more in hope than in expectation, to 'this historic period of transformation when six national policies begin to merge into a single common policy' (Despicht, 1964: 293).

Such optimism was misplaced. Unable to win support in the Council for a liberal policy, the Commission tried a less radical approach in 1965. It entailed allowing carriers freedom to set fares within a limited range (so-called 'forked' tariffs), but this approach was vetoed by the Dutch, since any liberalizing effect on road transport was outweighed by the introduction of price controls on inland waterway transport. Any hope there might have been that agreement could be reached in the Transport Council was overtaken by the wider institutional crisis precipitated by the French over the common agricultural policy. The crisis was resolved in 1966 by the Luxembourg compromise, which allowed member states to insist on unanimity where they felt that important national interests were at stake. This reinforcement of the unanimity rule made it even more difficult, if that were possible, to reach agreement in the Transport Council. With timid proposals blocked by the Dutch and radical proposals blocked by the majority, the Council decided in October 1966 to concentrate on a range of less contentious issues on which proposals had been made by the Commission, such as the abolition of import duty on fuel in the tanks of commercial vehicles, and did in fact manage to implement between 1968 and 1972 a number of modestly useful measures in accordance with a programme adopted at the Council on 14 December 1967. But such measures were at best peripheral to the evolution of a common transport policy. In his study of the formative years of the European Community (1958–66), Hans von der Groeben, a German Commissioner from 1958 to 1970, could point only to the benefit of the Council of Transport Ministers being able to discuss difficult problems with complete frankness, and in some cases to find joint solutions or at least to coordinate attitudes. Noting that the Council had turned down or deferred most of the Commission's proposals for a common transport policy in 1965–6, he adds that 'expectations that this could some day be the basis for progress towards a common transport policy have not been fulfilled in the 15 years that have elapsed' since then (von der Groeben, 1982: 219–21).

1973–82: the Court breaks the ice

The decade following British accession was even more unproductive for the common transport policy. The Paris Summit of October 1972 looked forward to the establishment of an economic and monetary union buttressed by closer links between a common transport policy and regional, social, industrial, environmental and economic policies. Seduced by these new horizons, and convinced that only government intervention could overcome the diseconomies inherent in transport operations and the growing social costs incurred by the use of land and energy, the Commission came forward with grandiose new proposals for a common transport policy in which governments would bring everything together in an intermodal network in which the different modes of transport would play complementary roles (COM (73)1725; Abbati, 1987: 29–33). The Council took no action to implement the Commission's proposals.

However, if the Commission and the Council were still deadlocked, developments elsewhere were beginning to break the ice. In 1974 two cases before the ECJ gave rise to judgments which at last made it essential for the Council and the Commission to act, and tipped the balance of the debate decisively in favour of liberal policies consistent with the general rules of the Treaty. First, in Case 2/74, *Reyners* v. *Belgian State*, the Court established the principle that the right to freedom of establishment under Article 52 of the Treaty is directly applicable in the member states. In the absence of Council regulations laying down rules for the application to transport workers of the right to freedom of establishment, the terms of the Treaty applied as they stood. This same reasoning was to be applied by the Court in subsequent cases to the rules on freedom to provide services and to the competition rules of the Treaty.

Then in Case 167/73, *Commission of the European Communities* v. *French Republic*, generally known as the French Seamen case, the Court rejected the French government's contention that it was entitled to continue to apply discriminatory rules concerning the free movement of seafarers until such time as the Council had adopted a common policy for sea transport. In practice this meant that free movement of seafarers could be put off indefinitely, since agreement on a common policy for sea transport required unanimity under Article 84(2) of the Treaty. The Court held that the general rules of the Treaty applied to all economic activity in the European Community, and that 'far from involving a departure from these fundamental rules, therefore, the object of . . . the common transport policy is to implement and complement them by means of common action' (ECJ, Case 167/73, point 25).

Other factors were also driving the Community towards the development of common policies. In 1974, two days after the judgment in the French Seamen case, agreement was reached in the United Nations Conference on Trade and Development on a code of practice, known as the UNCTAD Liner Code, which would regulate access to seaborne freight among the signatories. EU member states wanted to sign up, but without a common transport policy under which they could apply for exemption from the competition rules of the Treaty, their rights to a protected share of the trade covered by the Liner Code would be open to challenge at the ECJ on the same grounds as had succeeded in the French Seamen case. Another stimulus to the development of common policies was provided by the grounding of the *Amoco Cadiz* off the Brittany coast in 1978, which led the Council to take several steps towards improving ship safety and guarding against pollution (Aspinwall, 1995: 90–5).

Air transport is governed by the same Treaty provisions as sea transport, but progress towards the development of a common air policy was even slower. From about 1981 Lord Bethell's 'Freedom of the Skies' campaign in the European Parliament, and the case he brought in the ECJ, began to focus attention on the high level of European air fares and the failure of the EU to apply the competition rules of the Treaty to the arrangements between airlines and their governments which kept them high (Case 246/81, *Nicholas William Bethell* v. *Commission of the European Communities*. The Court ruled (ECR 2277) that the plaintiff did not have *locus standi*). But up to 1983 there was little progress towards the adoption of a common policy for air transport.

In 1983 the European Parliament, frustrated with the continuing lack of progress towards a common transport policy, brought an action against the Council in the ECJ seeking a declaration that the Council had infringed the Treaty by failing to introduce a common policy. The parliament was only partially successful in its submission, because the obligation to establish a common transport policy was not expressed in the Treaty of Rome in sufficiently specific terms for an action for infringement of the Treaty to succeed. However, the underlying complaint – the failure of the Council to establish a common transport policy more than 25 years after the Treaty was signed – could not seriously be contested, and the Court did find, in its judgment of 22 May 1985, that the Council was in breach of the Treaty on a narrower point, the obligation set out in Articles 75(1)(a) and (b) to ensure freedom to provide international transport services within the Community, and to lay down the conditions under which non-resident transport carriers may operate transport services in a member state (Case 13/83, *European Parliament* v. *Council of the European Communities*, ECR 1513–1603).

One further landmark judgment of the Court, known as the *Nouvelles Frontières* case after the travel agency involved, confirmed that the fundamental principles of EU competition law, set out in Articles 85 and 86 of the Treaty of Rome, applied directly to transport even if the Council had laid down no regulations or directives to guide their application (Cases 209–213/84, *Ministère Public* v. *Asjes*, 30 April 1986). Since these Treaty articles ban anti-competitive agreements among companies and any abuse of a dominant position, the Nouvelles Frontières company was free to sell air tickets at bucket-shop prices not approved by the International Air Transport Association (IATA) or the French government which endorsed them. This judgment, with its implied threat that the terms of competition among the airlines would be determined by judgments of the Court if the Council failed to act, was wonderfully effective in compelling the member states to agree the first package of air transport liberalization measures in 1987 (see below) including a regulation which applied the competition rules of the treaty to air transport in an acceptable manner.

1983–93: the common transport policy takes shape

After 1983 major developments affecting road, air and sea transport proceeded in parallel, with a common thread of liberalization. Provision had been made since 1972 for motor insurance policies issued in one member state to cover all risks compulsorily insurable in others (the green card), and the harmonization of driving licences, begun in 1980, was completed in 1991. Although a reference to measures to improve transport safety was added to Article 75 of the Treaty only at Maastricht, the technical standards member states require vehicles to meet, mainly for safety reasons, have been the subject of a steady flow of harmonization directives since the early 1970s. Without such provisions the European market for the construction and sale of motor vehicles would be fragmented and uneconomic.

However, there were still many impediments to the free movement of goods and passengers by road. It was 1985 before the Community could reach agreement on a directive setting maximum weights and dimensions for heavy lorries to have access to all member states, and then only on the basis that the directive would not apply to Britain and Ireland until almost the end of the century, to allow time to strengthen roads and bridges. On the key right to provide road haulage services, agreement was reached in 1988 to abolish quotas on the transport of goods between member states by the end of 1992. A further agreement, negotiated in June 1993, governing cabotage – the right to carry goods between two points within another member state – is being phased in gradually between 1993 and 1998, but countries which do not charge motorway tolls, notably Germany, are to be allowed instead to require all lorries, including those licensed in other member states, to purchase an additional tax disc to help pay for a road network which has to carry much international traffic. On the railways a start has been made with Directive 91/440/EEC, which provides for railways to be commercially managed, with separate accounting for infrastructure and transport operations, and which governs the provision of access and transit rights for certain international services. The provision of bus and coach services remains severely restricted. The main directives and regulations governing the provision of transport services by road and rail are set out in Figure 4.1.

In the air the minimal liberalization of inter-regional air services that broke the ice in 1983 was followed by three further packages of regulations in 1987, 1990 and 1992, which progressively liberalized the rights of airlines to carry passengers on any route within the EU subject to certain time-limited exemptions for the Greek islands and for the Azores, ended restrictions on capacity and frequency, and on fares, and even provided for the gradual phasing in of cabotage rights between 1993 and 1997. The main regulations and directives governing the provision of aviation and shipping services are set out in Figure 4.2 on page 94.

FIGURE 4.1   **Road and rail transport regulations and directives**

ROAD HAULAGE

03.01.1985	Directive 85/3	maximum weight and dimensions
03.08.1989	Directive 89/460	derogations for UK and Ireland until 1999
30.06.1988	Regulation 1841/88	abolishes quotas from 1993
30.12.1989	Regulation 4058/89	freedom to set tariffs
14.05.1992	Regulation 881/92	licensing of road hauliers
12.11.1993	Regulation 3118/93	phases out cabotage by 1998

BUS AND COACH SERVICES

20.03.1992	Regulation 684/92	each member state to authorize bus services on its own territory
29.08.1992	Regulation 2454/92	permits cabotage operation of coach tours from 1996; cabotage on regular services severely restricted

RAIL SERVICES

24.08.1991	Directive 91/440	requires commercial management, separate accounts for infrastructure and operations, some access rights

The freedom to provide services, which signatories to the Rhine Convention already enjoyed, was extended to all EU member states in 1985, and cabotage rights were approved in 1991. At sea a package of regulations agreed in December 1986 freed up the provision of maritime services between member states, applied the Treaty competition rules to maritime transport, and made provision for levies to be imposed against the unfair pricing practices of subsidized foreign carriers. In 1989 the Commission sent the Council a second package of shipping measures. State aids were covered in a document, not requiring Council approval, setting out the conditions under which they would be allowed. The package included a further attempt to establish a

FIGURE 4.2   Aviation and shipping regulations and directives

AIR SERVICES

24.08.1992	Regulation 2407/92	licensing of airlines
24.08.1992	Regulation 2408/92	freedom to provide services – routes, frequency, capacity; cabotage from April 1997, with some exemptions to 2003
24.08.1992	Regulation 2409/92	freedom to set fares
24.08.1992	Regulation 2410/92	apply the Treaty competition rules
24.08.1992	Regulation 2411/92	apply the Treaty competition rules

INLAND WATERWAYS

22.10.1985	Regulation 2919/85	freedom to provide services extended to all member states
31.12.1991	Regulation 3921/91	cabotage rights
31.12.1991	Directive 91/672	mutual recognition of boatmasters' certificates

SEA TRANSPORT

31.12.1986	Regulation 4055/86	freedom to provide services
31.12.1986	Regulation 4056/86	apply competition rules
31.12.1988	Regulation 4260/88	apply competition rules
12.12.1992	Regulation 3577/92	cabotage, some derogations up to 2004

European Register of Shipping (Euros) with restrictions on employment conditions and on foreign crews, but this has not been agreed, because the conditions proposed would result in further and probably irresistible pressure for shipowners to register their ships elsewhere in order to avoid the penalty of uncompetitive conditions in an internationally competitive business. The Commission's 1989 proposal to open up cabotage was finally adopted at the end of 1992, but there was an exemption extending to 2004 for all Mediterranean cabotage and the Atlantic coasts of Portugal, Spain and France.

Developments since 1993

By 1993 the regulations and directives summarized in Figures 4.1 and 4.2 had gone a long way towards creating a single market in transport services. Subject to licensing for safety and financial fitness, which is generally undertaken by the state of registration within guidelines laid down in EU directives, road freight, air and shipping companies were generally free to provide services throughout the EU (or will be when transitional derogations expire), free of quotas and other economic restrictions on their activities. However, further work has been needed to complete the single market where the framework of Community legislation left gaps or loopholes. For example, the provisions of Directive 91/440/EEC granted only limited scope for competition in the provision of rail services, but the Commission is trying to prise the market open with further Directives on licensing (95/18/EEC), and enhanced access starting with freight (95/19/EEC), within the overall framework of its White Paper, *A Strategy for Revitalising the Community's Railways* (COM (96)421). The Commission has also pursued an active policy of safeguarding competition within the single market by monitoring state aids (particularly in aviation) and it has pressed its right, though with only limited success, to conduct external relations in those areas where an internal policy has been developed, notably in relation to air service negotiations between the European Union and the United States, which have hitherto been conducted by each member state on a bilateral basis.

Beyond these practical moves to complete and consolidate the single market in transport services, the Commission has tried to give a more coherent shape to its transport policies by presenting them within the context of a White Paper (COM (92)494) and an action programme for 1995 to 2000 (COM (95)302). Thoughtful papers have also been produced on urban transport (COM (95)601), and on the principles of fair and efficient pricing (COM (95)691), as well as sectoral White Papers on railways (see above), civil aviation policy (COM (94)218), air traffic management (COM (96)57) and maritime strategy (COM (96)81). These activities have the potential to affect policy within the UK, but with only a few exceptions they are unlikely to do so because for the most part the Commission's policies are consistent with those already adopted within the UK. Besides, their impact on policies for purely domestic transport is limited, provided that the market for providing such services is open to any EU citizen or company.

Probably the most prominent focus of EU activity in transport policy since 1993 has been the development of Trans European Networks (TENs) within the framework of the new provisions of the (Maastricht) Treaty on European Union and the Delors White Paper on Growth, Competitiveness and Employment (COM (93)700) The development of TENs responds to the Commission's longstanding ambition to become a major player in the development of transnational infrastructures, and several of the 14 priority projects identified by the European Council are partly or wholly located within the UK, including notably the Channel Tunnel Rail Link. But once again the impact of the EU is limited, this time because the financing regulation (adopted by the Council of Finance Ministers) sets a firm ceiling for EU intervention of 10 per cent of the total investment cost of any project, regardless of the form of intervention chosen, including loans from the European Investment Bank.

EU policy in the Department of Environment, Transport and the Regions

Within the DETR, EU policy is not a separate branch of activity but rather one means among others of achieving the government's policy objectives. DoT had a small European division which provided advice on dealing with the EU, and coordinated activities where necessary, for example in assembling briefing for meetings of the Transport Council. But the functional directorates carried the primary responsibility for all policy development and implementation within their respective fields. Thus EU measures affecting road safety were handled by the Road and Vehicle Safety Directorate, those affecting shipping were handled by the Shipping Directorate and so on. Similar arrangements apply within the united DETR, with the Environment policy group in particular continuing to deal with issues handled in the Environment Council.

The gestation period for EU policies is often long. The department aims to influence policy development by maintaining contact with the Commission's Directorate-General for Transport (DGVII) at every appropriate level from the Commissioner and the Commissioner's cabinet downwards. The presence of British staff at all levels helps to ensure that channels of communication are easy and that British concerns are at least well understood within the Commission. Neil Kinnock was not the first British Commissioner to hold the transport portfolio; Stanley (now Lord) Clinton-Davis was the Commissioner for Transport between 1985 and 1989. There have also been three British Directors-General for Transport – Ray Le Goy (1973–81), John Steele (1981–6) and Robert Coleman (since 1992). The department also attaches importance to placing good staff on secondment to DGVII as detached national experts, and has taken the initiative in consulting the Commission about appropriate opportunities. Good communications are also fostered by the staff of the UK Permanent Representation in Brussels, many of whom are drawn from Whitehall departments on secondment. The first secretary dealing with transport issues has always been a principal (grade 7) on secondment from the DoT.

If the British government wishes to secure some change in EU policy, one of the department's ministers may well arrange to meet the Commissioner either in London or in Brussels to press the case for proposals in the sense desired. Such lobbying, even at ministerial level, would not necessarily have much effect in isolation, but ministers, officials and British embassies in the EU member states all have their own networks which can be used in a carefully orchestrated campaign, or as opportunities arise, to generate sufficient support for the British position to influence EU policy as it takes shape. If the Commission itself is taking an initiative, or is persuaded to take up an initiative suggested by others, it will generally explore its ideas with politicians, officials and expert opinion in the member states, and may well convene a working group in which to take soundings collectively. Once the Commission has decided what to do, it prepares a report with formal proposals to the Council.

The Transport Working Group

The Committee of Permanent Representatives (COREPER), which has the responsibility of preparing all Council business, sends the Commission's proposal to the Transport Working Group

(TWG) for discussion and the preparation of a report. All the member states are represented within the TWG, which is chaired by the country holding the Presidency of the Council for the time being, which rotates every six months. The Presidency, supported by the Council Secretariat, sits at one end of a long table, with the member states ranged down the two long sides, and the Commission at the far end. The regular members of the TWG come from the Permanent Representations in Brussels, but they are often assisted by representatives from their capitals who may be more expert in the particular business on the agenda. With 15 member states to take part, a single exchange of views on just one important point can easily occupy a full morning or afternoon session, particularly if the Presidency does not keep the meeting on a tight rein. Progress may also be frustrated if the representatives of some member states have not yet received instructions from their capitals, or if they set out to delay matters by expounding their point of view at considerable length.

Once the different delegations have been given an opportunity to state their positions in general terms, the Presidency has to judge whether there is any chance of carrying the debate forward to a constructive conclusion with such amendments to its proposal as the Commission may be prepared to accept. In most cases a sufficient basis of agreement can be identified eventually, but where the proposals are complex, sensitive or controversial it may take several meetings spread over more than one six-month Presidency before a way forward can be found. Sometimes it may be necessary to prepare an interim report referring the papers to the Council for an 'orientation debate' before attempting to reach agreement.

When the time comes for the papers to be sent to the Council for decision, the Secretariat, guided by the Presidency, prepares a draft report to COREPER which begins by outlining briefly any fundamental differences of opinion which may remain, expressed in terms of general reservations ascribed to one or more delegations. The report then turns to the text of the Commission's draft proposal, taking each Article in turn, stating which delegations are in favour and which have reservations (meaning not merely concerns but stated objections to the text proposed), with alternative proposals where these have been put forward. This draft report will be discussed at a further meeting or meetings of the TWG, at which the Presidency will try to reduce to a manageable number the points of difference between the delegations, who will themselves be keen to ensure that those points of difference which go forward to COREPER and ultimately to the Council are clearly articulated and of sufficient importance to merit debate at ministerial level.

There is no voting at the level of the working group, or even in COREPER, the function of officials being to reserve the position of their ministers until they are authorized to indicate agreement, but qualified majority voting now applies to almost all decisions based on the transport articles of the Treaty, and each delegation will be well aware of the number of votes ultimately required to carry particular proposals or to block them in the Council. As the negotiation proceeds, the British officials in the TWG will review their position, consulting their own ministers and others where necessary. In the light of the voting arithmetic, they may decide to concede some points of lesser importance, or to join with other delegations in building a potential majority in favour of changes which may help to make the proposal more acceptable; or they may decide to stand firm on some points, with or without the support of other delegations.

Ministers will be particularly concerned about any point on which they are likely to be isolated in the Council. Depending on the political importance of the point at issue, they may decide to withdraw their reservations at COREPER or at the Council, perhaps in exchange for concessions elsewhere, or they may prefer to go down fighting at the Council itself, with or without a formal vote, in order to make it clear to Parliament and the public that the point has only been conceded in the face of an overwhelming majority.

The role of the Presidency

The Transport Working Group usually meets two or three times a week (except in August), but it may have a dozen or more Commission proposals under consideration at any one time, so that any one proposal may be discussed much less frequently. The agenda is determined by the member state holding the Presidency of the Council (and all its working groups) for the time being, so that progress is very much dependent on the priority which the Presidency is prepared to give to any particular proposal, and the skill and effort which the Presidency is prepared to devote, with the cooperation of the Commission, to finding ways to reconcile the different positions adopted by the member states.

The opportunities open to the Presidency to pursue its own priorities are limited but should not be under-estimated. It is the duty of every Presidency to carry forward all the business of the Council in the interests of the Community as a whole, and this responsibility precludes any bare-faced pursuit of national interest, but priorities have to be decided, and within the limited range of available business (the proposals sent by the Commission to the Council), there is a natural and legitimate tendency for each Presidency to give the highest priority to those topics which it considers to be of most importance. For example the British Presidency in the second half of 1986 gave high priority to the Commission's proposals on aviation and shipping. The room for progress was explored at an informal meeting of the Council in September, and intensive negotiations and lobbying took place throughout the autumn. At the December Council meeting, the shipping day produced agreement on a major package of shipping measures (see above). The aviation day also resolved most of the major issues in the first aviation package, though its final adoption was delayed for a year because of a last-minute dispute with Spain over the use of Gibraltar airport.

The Transport Council

All this activity reaches a frenetic climax in the month or so leading up to the Council meeting. Although the Council meets almost every working day in one configuration or another, and proposals which have been agreed in COREPER can be endorsed as 'A' points (without discussion) at any Council, the Transport Council usually has only two meetings in each Presidency, with each meeting lasting at most two days. (There is a separate Council of Shipping Ministers, but many of the ministers are the same, so it often meets on the day before or after a Transport Council, reducing the latter to a single day.) If agreement cannot be reached, the next opportunity may be several months later under a different chair who may prefer to use the limited time and resources at his or her disposal to resolve some other issues. So preparations for any Transport Council meeting are intensive whenever issues of importance to British interests are at stake, and never more so than for the final Transport Council of the British Presidency. The report from the TWG will have been discussed in COREPER, perhaps more than once, and the areas of disagreement among the delegations reduced to the minimum, but there may still be several points outstanding, each one clearly set out in the final report from COREPER to the Council.

On the morning of the Council meeting, the chair may well begin by calling on one or more of the other ministers to confirm support from an important ally or to assess the degree of resistance to be expected from an opponent. He or she will also meet with the Council Secretariat to review the agenda, the handling of the meeting and any points of procedure which need to be dealt with. At the start of the meeting the chair will run through the agenda and outline provisional plans for the day. If there is a major dossier requiring discussion, he or she will usually allow a *tour de table*. This allows everyone to make the points they have been instructed to make by their own governments, and to declare either their enthusiasm for what is proposed or the serious difficulty which certain aspects of the proposal may cause them. It is unusual for any new points to be made which are not mentioned in the COREPER report to the meeting, but the Presidency team will listen carefully to gauge the strength of support and opposition around the table. The chair will be particularly sensitive to any political difficulties which ministerial colleagues may have.

After the first round of discussion the chair may well appeal to certain delegations to lift the reservations which they have maintained up to that point on particular aspects of the Commission's proposal. Some delegations, having made their point, may be content not to press their concerns any further. But others may have more serious reservations which cannot be so easily set aside. This will probably have been anticipated, and a compromise proposal prepared and canvassed with the Commission and some other delegations. This proposal may then be circulated by one of the delegations or by the Presidency, whilst the formal meeting is suspended to allow the President to broker a final compromise in a series of bilateral meetings with those principally concerned. Sometimes a restricted session of the

Council (ministers only) can be helpful. If the basis for an agreement can be found, officials may need to broker a precise text with other delegations and with the Commission, whose proposal cannot be changed without its consent. All this may take several hours if the issue is complex, and there is always a risk that some ministers may have to leave the meeting before the business is finished. However, if there is a real chance of reaching agreement on a measure which is generally regarded as important to the EU, the Council can usually be kept in session, if necessary until very late at night or the early hours of the morning, while the final compromise is hammered out.

Often there is a certain amount of tidying up to be done afterwards, including review of any new texts by the panel of jurists-linguists, and the lifting of any final reserves which may have been maintained pending the completion of national parliamentary procedures, but provided agreement has been reached on all essential points, the members of the Council disperse to brief the press at the end of a long and difficult negotiation with a considerable sense of achievement and even euphoria.

Parliamentary procedures

Although the negotiation of EU legislation takes place mainly between the ministers of member states, or between officials acting within the framework of ministerial authority, all legislation proposed for adoption by the Council is subject to parliamentary scrutiny both within the member states and by the European Parliament. The purpose of such scrutiny procedures differs between Strasbourg and Westminster. The European Parliament seeks to be an active partner in the legislative process, with its own views of how it wishes to influence the terms of the legislation which comes before it. The British Parliament has a narrower focus on the implications of proposed European legislation for UK law and policy, bringing its views to the attention of ministers by means of reports and debates, so that they in turn can take the views of parliament into account in their negotiations within the Council.

Scrutiny procedures at Westminster

As soon as the Commission sends to the Council any formal document, and particularly any proposal for Community legislation, the Cabinet Office arranges for the document to be deposited with both Houses of Parliament. This triggers the scrutiny process in both Houses of Parliament. The first step is the preparation of an explanatory memorandum (see Figure 4.3 for its structure and content). The Department of Transport prepared more than thirty memoranda in 1994. This short document, which must be sent to Parliament within ten working days, describes what is proposed and how it might affect British interests. All explanatory memoranda of any substance must be approved and signed by a minister, though an unsigned memorandum (the DoT submitted seven in 1994) is considered sufficient where a document sets out amendments of little or no consequence, or where a factual report has no legal or policy implications. EU documents, together with their explanatory memoranda, are considered by both the Commons and Lords scrutiny committees who decide what parliamentary action to take on them. The Commons committee meets each Wednesday when the House is sitting, to decide whether the documents before it raise questions of legal and/or political importance, and whether they should be debated. Another option is to ask for further information, which the department provides in the form of a Supplementary Memorandum – six of the memoranda submitted in 1994 were prepared in response to requests of this kind.

If the scrutiny committee recommends a debate, the private secretary of the relevant transport minister must write within four weeks to the private secretary to the Chief Whip (whose task it is to manage the government's business in parliament), with copies to other interested ministers, setting out the scrutiny committee's recommendation, giving a preferred date for the debate to take place having regard to tactical considerations including the progress of negotiations in Brussels, naming the minister who will take the lead in the debate, recommending whether the debate should be in committee or on the floor of the House, and setting out the exact wording of the motion. Debates usually take place on an extended 'take note' motion; that is to say, the committee is invited to take note of the

---

FIGURE 4.3   Structure of an explanatory memorandum

TITLE – of document and responsible department

SUBJECT MATTER

MINISTERIAL RESPONSIBILITY – normally in the case of transport documents the Secretary of State for Transport, or Secretary of State for the Environment, Transport and the Regions, but other ministers will be mentioned if they have an interest as well.

LEGAL AND PROCEDURAL ISSUES – including the legal basis in the Treaties, the relevant procedure in the European Parliament, the voting procedure within the Council (unanimity or qualified majority vote) and the impact of the proposal on UK law.

APPLICATION TO THE EUROPEAN ECONOMIC AREA – much, though not all, EU legislation applies to EEA countries such as Norway, Iceland and Liechtenstein which are not EU members.

SUBSIDIARITY – comments on whether the proposal requires Community action, or whether it could more appropriately be carried out by member states.

POLICY IMPLICATIONS – some indication of how the proposal affects British policy, including a compliance cost assessment, where appropriate, evaluating the possible impact on business costs and employment.

FINANCIAL IMPLICATIONS

TIMETABLE

OTHER OBSERVATIONS

ANNEXES – frequently used to summarize the history of past scrutiny of related documents. In four cases in 1994, the compliance cost assessment was added as an annex.

Commission's proposal, but the motion will go on to give some general indication of the government's position, perhaps inviting the committee to support the government's view that the proposal will need amendment if it is to be acceptable, or that further measures will be needed. The department will consult the scrutiny committee clerk before writing to the Chief Whip's Office, and the terms of the draft motion will be agreed, where necessary, with other interested departments.

The arrangements for debates are negotiated by the Chief Whip's Office through the usual channels, and announced in the business statement on the Thursday of the preceding week. Debates are usually held in one of the two European standing committees (Committee A for Transport), but they may take place on the floor of the House if they are of major importance. If the debate is in committee, the chair will first allow the minister to make a brief introduction, followed by questions. Officials are present and can pass notes to the minister if points are raised which are not covered in the ministerial briefing. After a maximum of one hour, the chair brings questions to a close and invites the minister to open the debate itself by moving the motion, usually with a short speech. Any amendments to the motion will normally have been tabled on the preceding day. At the end of the debate the chair puts the question on any amendments which have been debated, and then on the main question or the main question as amended. The minister has the right to intervene in the course of the debate, and to wind it up, but only members of the committee are entitled to vote. There were four debates arising from the explanatory memoranda which DoT sent to Parliament in 1994, all of them in committee.

The final stage of the Commons scrutiny procedure takes place a few days later on the Floor of the House when a motion is tabled which is usually the same as the resolution reached by the standing committee. Such motions are taken, and if necessary voted on, without debate. If the government is not able to accept the terms of the committee's resolution, it may put its original motion to the Floor of the House, or another motion which differs from that reached by the committee, but in those circumstances the minister, after consulting his colleagues and particularly the Chief Whip, would need to write to the chair and members of the committee explaining in some detail how the government intends to proceed.

Whereas consideration by the Commons Scrutiny Committee is focused on the need for and terms of motions for debate, scrutiny in the House of Lords, under the aegis of the Select Committee on European Legislation, is more inclined to the investigation of issues in some depth through the work of five sub-committees which call expert witnesses and prepare reports with recommendations that may go well beyond the terms of the immediate proposal under consideration. Transport proposals are referred to the sub-committee on energy, industry and transport. The government has undertaken to respond to the reports of the Lords Scrutiny Committee normally within two months of publication, and no later than a week before a debate. Debates in the Lords are usually on a straightforward 'take note' motion. In principle ministers should refrain from accepting a proposal in the Council until the scrutiny process is complete. This stage is reached only when the scrutiny committees in both Lords and Commons have decided that no further consideration is required, or when appropriate motions have been passed in either or both Houses following any debates that may have been arranged.

Every effort is made to complete the scrutiny procedures before decisions have to be taken in the Council, and there are arrangements for speeding matters up when necessary, but there may occasionally be cases where national parliamentary procedures are not complete in time. If ministers are unable to delay a decision in the Council, it is possible to enter a parliamentary reserve pending completion of the scrutiny process, but such reserves are of a formal nature and it is not clear what would happen if parliament were to pass a motion which precluded the lifting of such a reserve. Ministers can also decide to agree Community legislation without scrutiny clearance, but they must have good reason for doing so, and they need to explain themselves afterwards.

Most important transport legislation, and certainly anything controversial, is discussed and agreed at a meeting of the Transport (or Shipping) Council, even if it may be adopted in final form as an 'A' point at another Council when any final drafting points have been resolved. The Secretary of State normally reports the outcome of each formal meeting of the Council to Parliament by means of an arranged Parliamentary Question, or if the business is sufficiently weighty, an oral statement. This action brings the parliamentary procedure to a conclusion.

European Parliamentary procedures

Under the terms of the Treaty of Rome the Commission has always been obliged to seek the opinion of the European Parliament (EP) on a Commission proposal. Opinions normally take the form of a report prepared by a rapporteur for the Transport Committee of the EP, to which is attached any amendment of the Commission's proposal which may be judged necessary. Once debated and approved by the Transport Committee, the opinion goes forward to be endorsed by a plenary meeting of the EP before being transmitted to the Council.

In the past such opinions had little influence on deliberations within the Council. The position began to change in 1987 with the Single European Act which established the 'cooperation procedure'. This procedure, applied to most transport legislation by the 1992 Maastricht Treaty on European Union (TEU), strengthened the position of the EP in the legislative process by requiring unanimity in the Council to overturn a change proposed by the EP if it was endorsed by the Commission, but in practice the Commission has proved reluctant to side with the EP if by doing so it would risk destabilizing the consensus secured in earlier negotiations within the Council. The effect of the cooperation procedure has therefore been marginal.

However, the co-decision procedure, introduced in the TEU (Article 189b) and extended to all transport legislation by the 1997 Treaty of Amsterdam, gives the EP a much more significant role in the legislative process. The procedural details are complex (see Nugent, 1994: 314–23) but the key point is that if the EP is not satisfied with the Council's response to its proposed amendments, it can insist on the establishment of a conciliation committee which has to hammer out a compromise acceptable to an absolute majority in the EP and a qualified majority in the Council. If no text can be found which is acceptable to both parties, the proposal falls. These new procedures will take effect only after ratification of the Treaty of Amsterdam, but their impact can already be gauged because they were applied under the earlier TEU to the guidelines for Trans European Networks. The conciliation procedure enabled the EP to add a large number of additional projects to the lists annexed to the guidelines, and to insert fiercer environmental conditions than the Council and the Commission had proposed.

It is too early to assess the practical consequences of extending co-decision to all EU transport legislation. The pivotal role of the Commission is diminished in the final negotiation between Parliament and Council, though it will continue to exercise a significant influence as facilitator. But those in the Commission or the member states who are concerned to shape EU policy will clearly have to expend much more effort than in the past to secure the support of the EP for at least the key aspects of policies which cannot now be enacted without their assent.

The European Union and British transport policy

The EU is unlike any other international organization to which Britain belongs in the extent to which its legislation impacts on policies which might otherwise be regarded as matters of domestic concern. The concept of a single market within which firms compete for business on equal terms across national frontiers requires common rules governing the standards to which vehicles are designed, the hours which coach and lorry drivers can work, or the environmental standards which must be met by road schemes or vehicle emissions. Sometimes these rules, set in negotiation with others, may be uncomfortable for Britain, for example in increasing the scope for objections to new roads on environmental grounds (Chapter 7), or in limiting ministers' freedom to insist on the fitting of seatbelts in coaches and minibuses (Chapter 5). But it may also be convenient to blame 'Brussels' for imposing a change which, although desirable, is unpopular or even unattainable in a purely domestic political context (Smith, 1997). For example, the Labour government of the 1970s may not really have minded being forced to accept the tachograph or 'spy in the cab', despite the bitter opposition of some of its supporters among the unions whose members would not be able to fiddle the tachograph as easily as the manual records. Similarly, in 1985, the Conservative government may not have minded conceding access to British roads for heavier lorries, despite a strong show of resistance. Ministers will have been well aware of the economic case for well-designed heavier lorries, which do not have to be any bigger or more damaging to roads than less heavy older models, but the public were not persuaded, so it may well have been politically convenient to allow the EU regulation to go through under protest, with a long derogation for Britain.

Another source of difficulty relates to the structures of the EU institutions which are characterized by a rather rigid separation of policies and much less effective arrangements for coordination than exist across Whitehall. Thus transport business comes to the Transport Council, environment business to the Environment Council, and proposals affecting taxation are taken in the Finance Council. The different Councils have their own special preoccupations and the difficulty inherent in getting agreement among 15 ministers, not to mention the Commission and the European Parliament, means that the implications for transport of, for example, a directive on environmental appraisal, may not be uppermost in the minds of those assembled around the Council table.

Conclusion

For all these reasons it would be wrong to suggest that British transport policy has never encountered problems as a result of EU membership. British politicians and civil servants have learned to accept that their decisions on controversial road schemes may be subject to appeal to the European Court if they have tried to ride roughshod over interests protected by the EU's environmental directives. They have come to recognize that standards for seat-belts in coaches cannot be imposed unilaterally as an instant reaction to the latest motorway crash. They may in time have to concede that the Commission must negotiate air service agreements for Europe as a whole in place of the complex network of bilateral agreements which exist today. But the policy adjustments faced by Britain are much less fundamental than those faced by many European countries, for whom the concept of a competitive transport market, substantially exposed to private-sector disciplines, represents a very considerable policy shift. In the construction of a common transport policy acceptable to British interests, the Department of Transport has shown that, when there is political commitment to playing a full part in European policy-making, Britain has the official and diplomatic skills and procedures required to make a major impact on EU policies.

5 Interest Groups and Transport Policy

Central and local governments, Parliament and European Union institutions are formal actors in the British policy-making process, given express authority to make decisions. Trying to influence these structures of elected representative democracy are the informal actors called interest groups, pressure groups or lobbying groups. They are often divided into two categories: 'sectional' groups – that is, groups defending or expressing the 'self-interest' of their section of society, such as the Freight Transport Association (FTA), rail workers' unions, and the Cement and Concrete Association; and 'promotional' or 'cause' groups, which promote changes in attitudes or in policies that affect the general public, such as Transport 2000, which campaigns for increased public transport provision, and Friends of the Earth, or the Royal Society for the Prevention of Accidents. However, to make rigid distinctions in interest-group politics is to miss much of the action. First, many 'self-interested' groups would argue they also promote the wider public interest, not only when they take up outside causes (as the RAC did over coach seat-belts), but even in promoting their own interests, if they contribute to national economic growth. Second, 'cause' groups may be supported primarily by sections of society whose interests they promote. Transport 2000 was initiated in 1972 by a rail workers' union, part-funded from 1977 by British Rail, and incorporates a wide range of user groups – for example, cyclists and pedestrians – which would benefit from less road traffic. Transport 2000 is, of course, supported too by environmentalists and others with no personal benefit from the promotion of public transport. Yet even environmental groups are, according to some critics, promoting their own sectional view of the world, seeking to impose costs

110

on a less enthusiastic general public. Third, the use of the convenient word 'groups' rather than 'interests' distracts attention
from the influential part played by professional bodies, firms and
some individuals, and by others who appear to be neutral or
'holding the ring' (public bodies, the media or ministry officials).
Andrew Marr noted that the debate over road-building was not
taking place in Parliament (where parties were split on this issue), and lined up two groups either side of the argument: on
the one hand, the Department of the Environment, Transport
2000, the Council for the Protection of Rural England, Friends
of the Earth, and the National Trust: on the other, the Department of Transport, the big road construction companies, the retail
motor trade, oil companies, gravel firms, the AA and the RAC
(*Independent*, 27 September 1994). Any analysis of how interests
are promoted or defended in transport policy needs to draw in
all these participants.

The principles of interest-group action

It is hard to evaluate with certainty the impact of particular groups
or individuals on any particular decision. The decision-makers
themselves may be unaware how much their 'own' ideas were
stimulated by organized pressure. Policies may be so long debated and involve so many interests that it is difficult to ascribe
the crucial influence to any group within society or government.
Nevertheless, some general principles have been put forward about
how special interests are, or should be, represented.

According to the pluralist theory of democracy, as expressed
for example by Dahl, policy is made through individuals and
groups competing freely for influence at many levels and places
in society (Dahl, 1956). Thus a national transport policy would
be debated openly by the broadest possible spectrum of groups
and the outcome would reflect the balance of views, giving greater
weight to groups with larger memberships and stronger feelings.
Pluralists see the representation of interests as legitimate participation in the decision-making process. However weak the theory
turns out to be in British practice, it still has a normative value
– that is, it sets a standard for government behaviour. Transport
ministers and officials are keen to show they have consulted

relevant groups. Nevertheless, the participation of interested parties in British policy-making is not guaranteed – in comparison, say, with the 'remiss' system of Sweden, which deliberately and systematically incorporates the opinion of any interested group into parliamentary discussion. Nor do British interest groups have the wide access to government documents guaranteed to Swedish citizens.

The pluralist theory was criticized by 'elite theorists', who argued that power over decision-making is not diffused widely but dominated by certain social elites, for instance business leaders, top professionals or senior civil servants. Pluralists had taken a 'one-dimensional view', basing their argument on evidence from observable public decisions, which constituted only 'one face' of power. A 'two-dimensional view' would recognize that an elite could also exercise power more subtly by promoting social values or governmental procedures which keep issues from being raised that would harm the elite's interest – the 'restrictive face of power' or 'veto power' (Bachrach and Baratz, 1962; Lukes, 1974). Environmentalists say the 'cost–benefit' calculations for guiding decisions on road projects have operated in this way by regarding as inadmissible other arguments based on landscapes, habitats, communities and history.

Steven Lukes added a 'third dimension of power', remarking that power is applied most insidiously when it persuades people to accept the existing state of affairs as natural or beneficial (1974: 24). Again, environmentalists would argue that we have been persuaded into regarding economic growth as evidence of good governance, and the free use of road space as a natural right. However, it is difficult to prove that power has in fact been exerted, whether insidiously or not, and that decision-makers have been persuaded to make a decision (or non-decision) they might otherwise not have made, or that people are mistaken in judging their real interests. Elite theorists rely on indirect or circumstantial evidence, for instance by showing the supposed elite groups have a reputation for influence, or that they share common goals with decision-makers. MPs are working on this 'elitist' assumption when they quiz transport ministers about departmental meetings with sections of society reputed to be influential (for example, with various consultants in the run-up to rail privatization).

Lindblom's important variant of elite theory, in *Politics and*

Markets, emphasized the crucial power of one elite group, business. This group had special power – Lukes' third dimension of power – because, Lindblom argued, its main interest (economic growth) was regarded as the public interest, and governments automatically took its views into account – a policy often summed up as 'what is good for General Motors is good for the country'. Although Marxist theory scarcely recognizes interest groups (the only interest is class interest), *Politics and Markets* shared the Marxist hypothesis that the needs of capitalism determine public policy decisions (1977: 172). Lindblom's theory seemed somewhat questionable in Britain in the 1970s when organized labour was able to obtain large pay increases, led notably by Ford workers at Dagenham, and rail unions could disrupt commuter services over long periods. But the workers were called to order with legislation in the 1980s restricting unions' freedom to strike, and privatizations of the transport manufacturing and service industries. The evidence for and against the influence of 'big business', including the Society of Motor Manufacturers and Traders (SMMT), the Railway Industry Association (RIA) and the Confederation of British Industry (CBI), is equivocal. For example, Geoffrey Alderman notes on the one hand that the DoT deferred to the motor manufacturers on the compulsory wearing of seat-belts – the pro-campaign in 1980–1 was welcomed by some MPs as a way out of the impasse. But, on the other hand, he shows that, the following year, the DoT refused to support British car manufacturers and importers by acting against the Consumers' Association when it showed buyers how to buy the same car more cheaply abroad (1984: 102, 145). Christopher Foster, as a transport economist who had worked in the DoT, thought that senior officials were made more vulnerable to outside interests by their lack of self-confidence on specialized, technical, managerial issues (Foster, 1971).

From the 1980s, political leaders were less likely to listen to the CBI and more likely to seek views on public policy from a newer financial elite, such as members of the Institute of Directors, management consultants and accountancy firms, who represented economic growth and efficient management. On rail privatization, ministers took advice from management consultants and marketing firms rather than the RIA and the heads of the old transport industries, with the added irony that the consultants were paid substantial fees to express their opinions.

A different type of criticism of pluralism has come from writers on corporatism, who thought that interest group activity is, or should be, more organized than the pluralist 'free-for-all'. They envisaged public policy being made by continuous negotiation between the relevant part of the state and a limited number of groups that both promoted the interests of their members and enforced the decisions (Cawson, 1986: 38). Policy-making in Britain is far less deliberately corporatist than in some other European countries (Austria, Germany, Scandinavia), though in policy sectors where the number of professional groups is small – the classic case is agriculture – policy-making can be 'corporatist' in nature. The symbiotic relationship between the National Farmers Union and the agriculture ministry has a parallel in the strong links between the roads industry and the highways engineers of the transport ministry (now in the Highways Agency). Enid Wistrich notes how the roads engineers were able to sustain their separate identity as an interest group within the ministry even when it was subsumed within the environment department in the 1960s and 1970s. 'It was not so much a question of excessive influence as of total identification of the department with its clients or pressure groups' (1983: 102). However, outside roads infrastructure, transport policy-making cannot be organized so tidily because transport interests are diverse, some looking more towards ministers and officials dealing with trade and industry, planning or local government. In short, all the existing theories offer insights but none seem to explain the whole spectrum of interest-group participation in transport policy-making.

Explaining group influence

Current methods of examining how interests wield their influence over particular policies fall into two broad categories. The first examines individual participants for characteristics which seem to aid influence, and which elites often possess: key information or technical expertise, valid claims to represent all members of their section of society, financial resources, economic weight, political weight, and access to decision-makers (itself a product of the others). The SMMT provided the stereotypical example.

The government sought its opinion in the 1960s on the question of making car seat-belts compulsory because its members had the technical information about providing safe anchor points, and also because it represented all car manufacturers in the UK – a source of valuable exports and employment which no government would damage lightly.

The second method examines the networks of groups acting in each policy area (see Marsh and Rhodes, 1992). The links between the groups are as significant as their characteristics as individual members. The term 'policy community', at one end of the policy network spectrum, refers to the close, stable working relationships which develop when a small number of participants deliberate over a topic. They are based on some shared professional understanding or economic interest, and the road-building lobby and road engineers duo is a typical example. A policy community often forms between a division of a government department and the public bodies or private groups it subsidizes or regulates. At the other end of the policy network spectrum is the 'issue network', a more volatile arrangement connecting a larger number of groups of varying resources and limited mutual agreement. The 'seat-belt' issue described below brought together such a network.

Neither of the two approaches enables definite conclusions to be drawn of who influenced whom (see Dowding, 1995). Rather they are ways to examine interest representation systematically. The four case studies below – one from each 'mode' of transport: road, sea, air, rail – illustrate these approaches. But their main function is to show the wide range of participants in transport policy-making and the variety of campaigning methods used at different scales and in different locations (the media, a public inquiry, a Commons committee room).

Some readers may be surprised not to see here an account of the transport events which regularly supply British news headlines; that is, 'direct action' protests against the construction of motorways and airport runways. Barbara Bryant's account of the efforts to save Twyford Down from a motorway cutting offers a detailed and thoughtful study of an important case throughout the cycle of planning and construction, reasoned argument and direct action. Her study shows that 'the time to alter decisions is before they are made' (1996: viii). Once construction starts, the activity of protest groups has no effect, beyond adding to the cost and influencing the climate of opinion for the next project. A further study of a similar case would have had little value; it seemed to us more useful to show the influence of interests on a wider range of decisions which were still in the process of being made.

Fitting seat-belts to coaches

Until the mid-1990s the Department of Transport (DoT), the Confederation of Passenger Transport (CPT, representing coach operators), the European Commission, and perhaps the Department of Trade (DTI), had a consensus that coach seat-belts would not be made compulsory, though in 1989 and 1990 DoT ministers had said they would like to see seat-belts fitted. The policy community accepted the technical-financial view that the expense and difficulty of fitting belts outweighed the financial value of the accidents they would save, even including police and ambulance time, loss of production, and an element for 'grief and suffering'. Furthermore, the accepted legal-economic view was that the UK could not prohibit coaches from other EU countries, so national legislation would impose unfair competition on British manufacturers and operators. The prevailing political view was strongly against regulations in general.

In November 1993 two serious coach accidents stimulated demands for action from a wide range of bodies outside the policy community and added the resources of sustained media attention to groups already campaigning for seat-belts (*Independent*, 11 November 1993). The Consumers' Association, the RAC and the British Safety Council (an official body for improving safety in the workplace) called for seat-belts to be installed. The National Consumer Council – a Department of Trade-appointed body – put pressure on ministers; the chair of the Northern Ireland Consumer Council was particularly active on this issue. But DoT said that European competition rules posed difficulties. A pressure group, BUSK (Belt Up School Kids), started by parents in Gwent in February 1993, had 43 branches by spring 1994. A loose issue network was forming with a variety of organizations trying to influence members of the policy community (see Figure 5.1).

FIGURE 5.1 Seat-belt networks

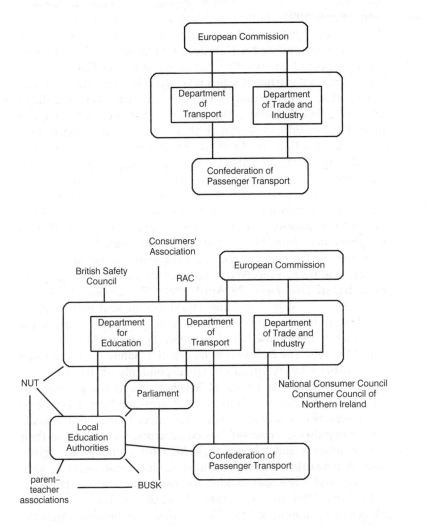

The Transport Minister asked his officials to conduct a review of technical and costs considerations, which took over six months to complete, despite conducting no new research (*HC Debs*, 26 May 1994: 285). The European Commission set up a working group of national experts and officials to examine bus and coach safety. The CPT started to shift ground; belts could be installed but operators first needed 'government-led research' on 'the optimum system' (in letter to *Independent*, 21 February 1994).

In March 1994 another accident renewed media interest in the parents' campaign. The Consumers' Association asked DoT to act without waiting for Europe. The Labour Shadow Minister for Transport, Joan Whalley, asked questions in Parliament to the education department which revealed it had recently reminded schools that pupils should be transported 'in reasonable safety', and had given financial authorization to Strathclyde Council to fit seat-belts. Education rather than transport decision-makers were taking action. In April, BUSK presented a petition with 156 000 signatures to Parliament. The Roads Minister, Robert Key, made a cautious response, saying there were no technical obstacles to fitting seat-belts in *new* vehicles; however, DoT would await the Commission's detailed proposals. But he volunteered that he had received 'over 700 letters plus a large number of telephone calls from MPs and others', – this could be interpreted as a sign of his support for the campaign (or he would have merely said he had received 'a number' of letters.) He agreed to meet BUSK (*HC Debs*, 29 April 1994: 377; 23 May 1994: 54). The CPT now said companies could not fit seat-belts without regulations because they might have to pay compensation for any injuries they caused (*Independent*, 26 May 1994).

In May 1994 *The Independent* launched a 'Safety First' campaign for seat-belts by its education correspondents on its education pages. The National Union of Teachers asked for government grants for minibus seat-belts. Under pressure from BUSK and parent–teacher associations, some local education authorities made belts compulsory for school bus contractors, fitted them in their own minibuses and lobbied their MPs for a change in legislation. A network focused on education decision-makers at local and national levels was making its own policy on seat-belts.

In June 1994 the Secretary of State for Transport, John MacGregor, announced the DoT review had demonstrated the case for compulsory fitment; the UK would take it up with the Commission, and meanwhile the government would encourage manufacturers and operators to fit belts. The CPT now agreed *new* coaches should have belts; but it still wanted standards for fitting them to *old* coaches. In July, at an inquest into a minibus accident, the coroner and the county chief constable urged the government to require seat-belts in all minibuses, old and new. Key said that many schools were fitting belts voluntarily so there was no need for a new law. The parents replied that a law was needed or 'it is left for money to decide' (*Independent*, 1 July 1994). MacGregor then said the UK would seek agreement from the Commission to act 'ahead of the EU' on vehicles used by children (*HC Debs*, 19 July 1994: 81–2). Nevertheless, the draft rules for consultation were not issued until March 1995, the day before the minister was required to appear before a Commons committee on European Legislation examining transport safety. The CPT said it welcomed any action improving safety. The Commission said it planned to issue legislation in 1996 making belts mandatory in all new coaches by 1998 (*Independent*, 16 March 1995; 11 July 1995). British regulations for British school buses were eventually made in February 1996 to come into force in February 1997 for new vehicles, February 1998 for older vehicles.

According to *The Independent*: 'Under pressure from a very effective parents' lobby, ministers agreed to ensure all coaches and minibuses carrying schoolchildren must be fitted with belts' (leader, 6 July 1995). On the surface, the policy networks imagery would suggest that an education policy community, backed by consumer bodies and parliamentarians, took over the agenda, forcing DoT reluctantly to take action against its policy-community partner. An examination of the changing balance of resources between the partners of the transport community offers a more subtle interpretation. Some transport ministers had expressed a genuine wish to see seat-belts in coaches. But the cost–benefit case for fitting belts in all coaches was finely-balanced (it required a calculated saving of five lives annually; there were 50 deaths in coach accidents 1985–95). The decision must have been a point of contention within DoT and the government, especially given the political emphasis on international competitiveness and deregulation. The strong pressure from a variety of outsiders, and the intervention of another department, would have helped the case of the more safety-minded DoT ministers and officials. They might have helped tip the balance against other ministers and officials, less keen to regulate the transport industry – or to be seen to regulate the industry. Decision-makers are unlikely to reveal whether they lost an argument with new groups, or got what they wanted against the wishes of older groups with whom they must continue to negotiate.

Fitting bulkheads to ro-ro ferries

In March 1987 the British roll-on roll-off ferry the *Herald of Free Enterprise* sank off Zeebrugge. The ship had left for Dover with its bow doors open. Water entered the vehicle deck and the ship capsized within four minutes. The report of the Sheen Inquiry into the accident recommended serious attention should be given to changes to Ro-Ro design, 'restricting the spread of water on the bulkhead deck' – the final words of the report (DoT, 1987b: 72). Nearly all Ro-Ro ferries lack bulkheads on the bulkhead deck (just above the water-line), because they slow down unloading. The Royal Institution of Naval Architects (RINA), the professional body, insisted that only bulkheads provide adequate safety on Ro-Ros. The families of the *Herald*'s victims campaigned for action. Yet the government introduced different regulations, less costly for ferry operators. If water entered, because of negligence or a collision, catastrophe was still likely to occur.

These regulations were in line with new standards, SOLAS 90, adopted in 1987 by the International Maritime Organization (IMO), an inter-governmental organization. Companies were given till 2007 to modify existing ships. The Sheen Report said although DoT had wanted IMO to bring in higher standards, it did not want them as high as the US, USSR, Poland and Norway had proposed, because they 'would gravely impair commercial viability of the ferries' (ibid. para. 53). DoT was using the same 'business competition' rationale as for coach seat-belts.

Seven years later, another accident to a Ro-Ro produced a very different reaction from the government, even though the vessel was not UK-registered. In September 1994 the ferry *Estonia* sank in the Baltic after its bow door came off. IMO set up a panel of experts to look at Ro-Ro design. DoT panel members were advised by a shadow panel including representatives from the British Chamber of Shipping (the industry's trade association), major UK ferry operators, the Consumers' Association and trades unions. The day before the formal report on the *Estonia* (the equivalent of Sheen), the Secretary of State for Transport,

Brian Mawhinney, made a statement to Parliament. He said it was 'incumbent on government . . . to introduce bulkheads to Ro-Ros . . .'. He added various caveats, including that of the cost–benefit ratio as noted above for coach seat-belts, but insisted he would go ahead. He had asked the DoT's Marine Safety Agency to do research on bulkheads (after the *Herald* sinking, DoT had left it to ferry operators to fund relevant research). He said if IMO could not agree, the UK would consider an agreement with other countries in the region (*HC Debs*, 5 April 1995: 1753–61). In November 1995, when the IMO panel recommended bulkheads but IMO itself did not agree, the government confirmed it would negotiate a regional agreement on bulkheads applying to all Ro-Ros serving UK ports. A Labour opposition spokesperson on transport, Paul Flynn, later paid tribute to the government's unusually speedy action (*HC Debs*, 21 February 1996: 286). (See Figure 5.2.)

Why were government reactions to the *Estonia* and the *Herald* so different? A second disaster was obviously an important factor. It stimulated a wide variety of bodies to put pressure on the government. The Parliamentary Transport Committee, chaired by Paul Channon, who had been Secretary of State for Transport at the time of the *Herald*, decided to examine ferry safety (Transport Committee, 1995a). The Consumers' Association, RINA and the Institute of Marine Engineers told the committee that SOLAS 90 had been a 'bare minimum' compromise. Eurotunnel complained it was subject to more stringent safety requirements than those of the rival ferry companies, including ironically an expensive change to truck design as a consequence of the *Herald* disaster. Opposition committee members put embarrassing questions to ministers. P&O, which operated about half the UK's ferries, said it had never been against bulkheads but it was not convinced they added safety. However, if bulkheads were shown to make their ferries safer it would gladly fit them (*Independent*, 6 April 1995).

Mawhinney put more pressure on the operators when he published in April 1995 a list of UK ferries showing which met SOLAS 90 standards (most did not). The sole UK survivor of the *Estonia* pleaded for the names of ferries with bulkheads to be published (Paul Barney in *Independent*, 27 July 1995). The transport committee report in July 1995 recommended ferries be awarded a star rating for survivability (the government refused). It said

FIGURE 5.2   Ro-Ro ferry networks

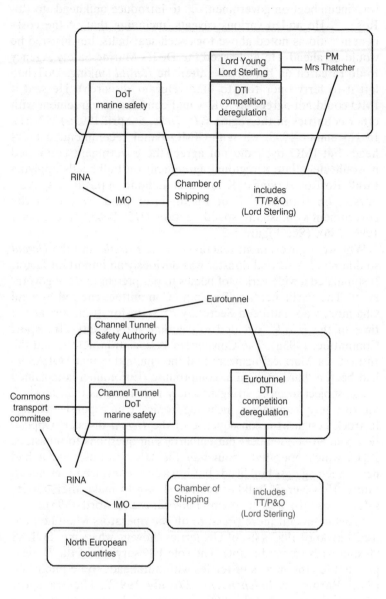

the government should impose design changes on all ferries using UK ports, if international agreement was not reached soon. Three committee members said they were not willing to travel on Ro-Ro ferries. The Chamber of Shipping said it agreed with the objectives of the report, and hoped to have solved the problems by autumn 1995 (*Independent*, 29 July 1995). In Stockholm in February 1996 the UK concluded an agreement with other North European countries that stricter survivability standards would be imposed on all ferries operating from their ports. They would be implemented in stages between 1997 and 2002, the more vulnerable first.

The activity after the *Estonia* would seem to confirm the pluralist theory that groups can make themselves heard; but what is the explanation for the government's limited response to Sheen, RINA and the *Herald* families? Gary Slapper, law lecturer at Staffordshire University, accused the government of having been 'over-acquiescent in catering to the interests of ferry operators . . during a time of intense commercial competition' (letter to *Independent*, 27 July 1995). Townsend Thoresen, which operated the *Herald*, and P&O had been engaged in takeover battles in the mid-1980s, won finally in October 1987 by P&O. The Labour MP, Dennis Skinner, asserted that 'Jeffrey Sterling[of P&O] . . . could have been required to insert bulkheads in all ferries if this minister [Mawhinney] had the guts to do that. The reason why he does not is that Jeffrey Sterling puts money into the Tory Party' (*HC Debs*, 5 April 1995: 1759). These allegations are not a sufficient explanation, because in 1995 there was still 'intense commercial competition', and P&O remained one of the Tory Party's biggest donors. Yet Mawhinney took action.

However, in the period after Sheen reported, the ferry operators had greater support from senior ministers for ideological, political and personal reasons. The Secretary of State for Trade, Lord Young, was a personal friend of Mrs Thatcher. He was appointed to bring business ideas to the Cabinet, and had a similar passion to deregulate – he called it 'lifting the burden from business'. Sterling was not only a political friend of Mrs Thatcher, but also a special adviser to Lord Young and other Trade and Industry ministers from 1982 to 1990. The two rival ferry companies embodied the New Right ideology (Townsend Thoresen's fleet was called *Herald of Free Enterprise*, *Spirit of Free Enter-*

prise, *Pride of Free Enterprise*). Furthermore, P&O was battling against strikes by the National Union of Seamen from January to May 1988, and by dock workers in January 1989. It was determined to beat the unions, another strategy in tune with the Conservative government's policy.

Mrs Thatcher's immediate reaction to the news of the *Herald* disaster had been that she 'understood it was a fundamental design fault ... that was the problem', yet two days later the Secretary of State for Transport was saying 'it was entirely due to operational error' (*HC Debs*, 21 February 1996: 283). The Sheen Inquiry found the immediate cause was operator negligence, but that the unobstructed car decks made even a well-managed Ro-Ro intrinsically vulnerable. The greater attention in media reports to human failings distracted attention from the design fault. But the ferry companies' greatest strength was that the government saw their interest as the national interest (the 'third dimension of power'). The DoT official giving technical evidence to the Sheen Inquiry assumed that 'commercial operation' had to be given high priority in the design of ferries (DoT, 1987b: 50).

Analysing the events using network theory (see Figure 5.2 above), the classic policy community network (DoT Marine Safety Agency–RINA–Chamber of Shipping–DTI) had an understanding on the balance to be struck between safety advances and 'commercial viability'. When the costly Sheen recommendations were unacceptable to one section of the network, it was able to minimize and postpone change by using its membership of another, more politically powerful network. That political network had disappeared by the time the *Estonia* again highlighted the dangers. Non-economic interests can therefore get issues placed on the agenda and settled to their advantage when an event with public impact is followed by sustained pressure by a wide variety of bodies. But the absence of policy change in the late 1980s confirms the veto power which important groups have when their interests are in tune with those of the prevailing ideology.

Heathrow Terminal Five

In May 1995 the inquiry opened into BAA's application to build a fifth terminal (T5) at Heathrow. About 70 organizations and

2000 people were expected to give evidence in the three years it was likely to take. On one side was BAA plc (the former British Airports Authority). It was supported by business groups, trades unions and one local authority (Brent). On the other side were 29 local authorities, a dozen residents associations and Friends of the Earth. The Secretary of State for Transport, Brian Mawhinney, had declined to give his opinion on T5 – a position in keeping with his quasi-judicial role as final judge of the planning application – but he firmly ruled out alternative ways of increasing airport capacity. So his statement, 'The Government wish to ensure capacity available for future demand but take reasonable account of environmental impact', was interpreted as meaning the Conservative government was on BAA's side but unwilling to upset local voters (*HC Debs*, 2 February 1995: 859–62).

BAA's most authoritative support came from the Civil Aviation Authority (CAA), a public body responsible to the Transport Minister, which (among other things) regulates airlines and airports. The CAA's official status gives it an aura of neutral expertise. But its function and outlook meant it saw BAA's case more clearly than it did that of BAA's opponents. The CAA was market-oriented even before New Right governments took office. After 1982 its terms of reference had required it 'to impose the minimum regulatory burden' and 'to further the interests of users'.

The CAA gave evidence in October 1995 to the Parliamentary Transport Committee examining UK airport capacity. Its statements all pointed in favour of providing extra capacity at Heathrow: the lack of surplus capacity was a 'major impediment to competition'; users greatly preferred Heathrow; traffic could not be shifted to other British airports because the government (on the CAA's advice) had abolished the relevant regulations; high charges for using Heathrow would penalize private airlines more than state-subsidized airlines; and constraining capacity at Heathrow risked airlines transferring business to Paris or Schiphol-Amsterdam (Transport Committee, 1995b). The CAA's arguments, though often speculative or ideological in nature, would provide good support in favour of BAA's application.

BAA organized an intelligent campaign. It engaged Des Wilson as director of corporate affairs, a figure whose record as a crusader for liberal, humanitarian and environmental causes added credibility to BAA's case. BAA targeted different audiences with different products: 'A letter to our HEATHROW neighbours' from BAA's chief executive, delivered the day the inquiry opened; a credit-card-sized compendium: *T5: why it is vital*; a non-glossy booklet on *The case for terminal 5*. Each gave favourable 'facts' and countered opposition 'myths'. BAA commissioned Gallup to poll local people and emphasized the increase in those saying 'yes to T5' (there was still a majority against it). It made sure the special report in *The Times* the day the inquiry opened (16 May 1995) was well-informed on its case.

BAA started 'good corporate citizen' projects, to provide material for the campaign leaflets and help win people over. It stimulated direct backing from a Heathrow Airport Support Group, bringing together the CBI and over 120 businesses, trade associations and trades unions which would give evidence to the inquiry. Support Group newsletters told members how to help: by writing to policy-makers and the media; by issuing company press releases; and by introducing the case for T5 into normal business presentations. BAA kept up-to-date on the groups opposing T5.

Ranged against BAA were local authorities, residents associations and environmental groups. The local authorities' campaign was conducted by the Airports Policy Consortium (APC), a group of 20 councils affected by Heathrow and Gatwick, professionally-run from Surrey County Council. APC called for a national strategic aviation policy, rather than the voicing of exclusively NIMBY ('not in my backyard') claims. It produced a booklet equivalent to BAA's *The case for terminal 5*, but did not have the statistical information to challenge BAA's figures convincingly. Ten councils around Heathrow formed a second group, Local Authorities Against Heathrow Terminal 5, LAAHT5. Their newsletter, *No to Terminal 5* (Winter 1995), gave poll data contradicting BAA's poll. LAAHT5, even more than APC, is handicapped by limited funds and political divisions, but it attracts wide support. Dozens of village associations were fighting individual campaigns, particularly against noise. FHANG (Federation of Heathrow Anti-Noise Groups), had an office and noise complaints line; HACAN (Heathrow Association for the Control of Aircraft Noise) was chaired by a leading PR professional, and worked closely with senior councillors on Richmond Council and the *Richmond & Twickenham Times*. Its campaign focused on reducing the number of night flights, an achievable target.

The opposition groups BAA seemed most to respect were those which were technically well-informed and running professional campaigns. It had a working relationship with FHANG, which it knew from when both were members of RUCATSE – the working group on Runway Capacity in the South-East. In internal documents BAA described some other groups as 'unpleasantly aggressive', 'forming a pack', and 'spreading rumours', largely it seems because they worked in an unconventional manner (for instance, phoning Heathrow in the middle of the night to complain about engine noise). The distinction drawn by BAA confirms Wyn Grant's observation (1995) that policy-makers categorize groups into respectable 'insiders' and illegitimate 'outsiders'. Yet, as Geoffrey Alderman points out, an effective campaign can make use of two types of action, the public and the discreet (1984: 12–22). The anti-T5 campaign may need both the smooth professionals with their pre-paid postcards supporters are asked to send to MPs (which do not much impress ministers or civil servants), and the vociferous individualists whose personal lives are so affected by the nuisance they are prepared to be a nuisance themselves.

The protesters could not match BAA and the Heathrow Airport Support Group in financial resources or expertise, or with technical backing such as that provided by CAA. But the government veto on new runways, and BAA's substitute of the less environmentally-contentious T5, show this opposition is feared. BAA's position was undermined by cutbacks to the roads programme after the inquiry started, which threatened its ability to assure the inspector that road access was adequate. Its offer in January 1997 to consider funding a second rail link between Heathrow and central London, with local stops, in addition to the Heathrow Express it was already funding, was a measure of its need to placate local and environmental opposition. Despite BAA's highly professional presentation of its case, the outcome of the inquiry could not be a foregone conclusion.

Rail privatization

There was little opportunity for informed debate on the government's scheme for rail privatization. The government published the White Paper, *New Opportunities for the Railways*, in July 1992, said Parliament would examine the legislation in 1993, and the first franchises would be awarded in 1994 (DoT, 1992a). Interest groups did not have much time to put their points of view. On the other hand, the options were debated in a more public way than usual, in Parliament. In addition, groups were able to put their own cases to the Commons Select Committee on Transport, chaired by Robert Adley, a rail enthusiast, author of railway books and Conservative opponent of rail privatization.

Between November 1992 and February 1993 an extensive range of witnesses gave evidence to the committee. Those listed by the committee's report comprised the Department of Transport, British Rail, consumers' groups, individual companies, freight operators, potential passenger franchisees, leasing specialists, local authorities, railway line users groups, trades unions, the Confederation of British Industry, retired railway workers, leading industrialists, and 'pressure groups' (sic), including Transport 2000 – as though the CBI, user groups, retired rail workers . . . were not considered to be 'pressure groups'. The committee also received the written views of about 40 individuals, 15 individual councils, 12 rail traveller or action groups, the AA, the Consumers' Association, Royal National Institute for the Blind (RNIB), Institute of Mechanical Engineers, British Transport Police Federation and the Centre for Policy Studies (Transport Committee, 1993).

Operating an open access railway

The White Paper proposed a system of 'open access'; no operator would have exclusive rights to any track. Ministers were following the advice of the free-market Adam Smith Institute (*Economist*, 30 March 1991). If one company operated all the passenger trains on a line, they argued, there would be no incentive to improve services. Open access was strongly supported by freight customers or operators, such as the Railfreight Users Group and Power Gen, which could be flexible about timetabling. In contrast, nearly all potential passenger-train operators were opposed to open access: it would disrupt their timetables, hinder planning and allow peak-time demand to be creamed off. Only smaller companies, such as British Bus plc, welcomed open access as a chance to run a few passenger trains.

The Adley Committee recommended the government should introduce open access for freight operators, but counselled against open access for passenger trains. The most important interest groups for the government on this topic were the few companies who had expressed interest in franchises; they might have been deterred if other operators had access to their lines. By February 1993 the government had recognized the problems, ministers saying they 'did not rule out open access', but that 'in respect of the first franchises, there may have to be a degree of exclusivity' (*HC Debs*, 2 February 1993: 242).

Franchising

Potential franchise holders were worried too by the proposed division of responsibilities between Railtrack and train operators. Their long-term management would be dependent on Railtrack's investment; their day-to-day service would rely on Railtrack's signalling. British Bus, which did not want responsibility for maintaining infrastructure, was happy to have Railtrack. But other groups, including Sea Containers and Stagecoach, rail unions and BR management, recommended vertical integration, that is, the franchisee controlling both trains and track (Transport Committee, 1993: paras 95–107). Sea Containers and Stagecoach still held this view as the bid deadline for the first franchises approached (*Independent*, 29 July 1995).

The government rejected the arguments by Adley and others for a return to 'regional railways', even though it had been John Major's preference, and promoted by the Centre for Policy Studies, a New Right think-tank (*Economist*, 30 March 1991). Ministers argued that such a division would split up the profitable Intercity business, and would militate against open access. In the event, each of the major Intercity route networks was offered as a separate franchise. But franchisees were not given control over the track.

Railtrack

Prospective franchisees were critical of the proposal for Railtrack. They would not be able to make efficiency savings on maintenance, and Railtrack would be a monopoly like BR. Stagecoach suggested Railtrack should be decentralized to units based on the franchise areas. Railtrack was not defined in the privatization bill, but in the Commons ministers said Railtrack would be a 'government-owned company', 'independent' but 'commercially driven' (*HC Debs*, 2 February 1993: 161). In November 1994 the government announced Railtrack would be sold. There seems to have been no interest group pressure for the sale, and commentators believed the government was anxious to put more of BR into the private sector before the next election; Railtrack, with its substantial property portfolio, would find a buyer.

British Rail bids

The government bill included a clause forbidding BR to apply for franchises; private bids might be deterred since BR had expertise and could borrow more cheaply. In the Lords, a former Conservative Transport minister, Lord Peyton, supported by a former Labour Transport Minister and BR Chairman, Lord Marsh, said BR should be able to bid. It was illogical to allow foreign nationalized railway companies but not BR to bid. The Consumers' Association feared BR would otherwise become a demoralized bidder of last resort, providing services no-one wanted to run. The Peyton amendment, giving the Franchising Director authority to decide whether BR could bid for any particular franchise, was agreed in the Lords by a majority of 38 votes. The clause shuttled to and fro between the Commons and the Lords. The eventual compromise clause (which let Conservative MPs openly against privatization off the hook), allowed BR to bid unless the Franchising Director, having consulted BR, decided not to invite it to bid (BR would have to go to the courts if it disagreed). On this issue interest groups provided support but the most important defenders of BR were within the Lords.

Railway supply industry

In evidence to the Adley Committee, the Railway Industry Association (RIA) said railway manufacturers 'were staring annihilation in the face' during the uncertain transition to franchised operation (Transport Committee, 1993: para. 183). In response, the government introduced an amendment enabling the franchising director to assure rolling-stock companies (which lease trains to franchisees) that new stock would be used beyond the seven-year franchise period; it might give them more confidence to place orders. After the bill was passed, MPs continued to raise RIA problems. The government repeatedly referred to the same few orders. In 1994, in what observers regarded as 'a face-saver exercise', ministers invited manufacturers to put forward proposals to build Networkers (commuter trains) as a 'private finance initiative', that is, the industry would make much of the investment itself. The companies refused to bid, considering the project too risky because of the short leasing period *(Independent,* 25 May 1995).

Rail closures

The White Paper said the government would continue to subsidize socially-necessary services. But the National Consumer Council (NCC) was worried that rail closure procedures in the bill might allow socially-necessary lines to be abandoned. The Central Transport Consultative Committee (CTCC) criticized the loose definition of 'minor closure', and the short warning period given for consultation. The Adley Committee said it was 'partly in response to representations from the CTCC' that the government amended the bill, extending the warning period, and transferring responsibility for deciding what was a minor closure from the Franchising Director to the Rail Regulator, who has a duty to protect users' interests (Transport Committee, 1993: para. 231).

Through-tickets and inter-availability

The government at first argued that operators would find it in their commercial interest to sell and accept each other's tickets; there was no need for regulations. Yet the CTCC, BR and other witnesses to the Adley Committee feared passengers would lose the right to board any train. Stagecoach said, from its practical experience, that agreements between operators after bus deregulation had been obstructed by 'short-term commercial considerations'. The committee recommended 'all passenger operators should be required to participate in revenue allocation schemes which enable cross-validity of tickets to be preserved'. The

Secretary of State then said that the government would require through-ticketing at major ticket offices (ibid: paras 243, 443). By the time the Bill arrived in the Lords the government had accepted that 'operators will be required to participate in common ticketing and revenue allocation arrangements' (*HL Debs*, 15 June 1993: 1428).

Facilities for disabled people

The government's document on franchising said the rail regulator would include a requirement in franchisees' licences that they 'have regard to the needs of passengers with mobility handicaps'. The NCC and Transport 2000 wanted stronger wording, for operators to be required to accommodate disabled passengers and have a duty to consult representative groups. The RNIB said service providers should consult users on standards and needs. Though DoT has a procedure for showing its Mobility Unit all legislative proposals this routine seems to have been forgotten in the case of the privatization bill. However, Mobility Unit officials were instrumental in introducing an amendment, improving disabled people's rights, at the Lords committee stage. The regulator was required to consult the Disabled Persons Transport Advisory Committee on a code of practice for protecting the interests of disabled people. The regulator has a duty to encourage compliance with the code of practice. But there is no obligation on train or station operators to adopt it.

British Rail pensions

Organizations representing BR staff and former staff were able to modify the pension scheme arrangements proposed in the White Paper. In 1992 the BR pension fund had a large surplus. In addition the government made contributions to the fund under obligations from a previous pension scheme. Railway employees and pensioners were concerned about future pension arrangements in a fragmented, privatized and changing industry. There was also suspicion about the use the government might make of the surplus in the pension fund. The two unions, RMT and ASLEF, said they wanted an industry-wide scheme. The RMT wanted the current pension funds ring-fenced, so they could not be dispersed by the government or BR's successors. Parliament received 60,000 letters from BR pensioners about the pension fund.

The government discussed pension arrangements with BR pension trustees and rail unions, and published revised proposals in January 1993. The new suggestions for a joint industry scheme for current BR staff were generally accepted. The government offered two options for existing BR pensioners. Jimmy Knapp, General Secretary of the RMT, said neither scheme offered the protection currently available or included the government contributions owed to the pension fund (Transport Committee, 1993: paras 326–31). Ministers then received 'extensive' representations from the trustees, trades unions, 'pensioners' bodies', and many other interested organizations. In May 1993 the government announced a scheme for existing pensioners that met the wishes of rail unions and pensioners; but clauses allowing the scheme to be changed in future raised their doubts about government intentions. In the Lords the government was forced to introduce an amendment guaranteeing the protection of the pensioners' fund, though it later emerged that the government's contributions would remain within the general government fund (the Treasury), the trustees being given an IOU, as MPs called it. The Lords passed a further amendment, moved by Lord Peyton and Lord Marsh, requiring the trustees' consent to any change to the government's contributions. The government criticized the Lords for giving 'an independent third party' (the trustees) a veto over a government financial decision (*HL Debs*, 27 October 1993: 918). Partly for that reason, the Peyton–Marsh amendment was not supported by the House of Commons, but the wholesale rewriting of the pensions section of the bill was testament to the delaying and revising powers of the House of Lords, and the ability of some groups to influence the policy-making process.

The privatization bill

At the end of the Lords debate on rail privatization, opposition peers thanked the interest groups – their 'expert advisers from the transport industry, local authority associations, trades unions, insolvency experts, pensioners' organizations and British Rail pension trustees', for the help they had given in dealing with so much legislative material in so short a time. Expertise offered by the various groups to peers and to the Transport Select Committee enabled the proposals for privatization to be examined more thoroughly, and allowed the interests to be heard by the legislators. But what impact did this advice have?

Potential passenger train operators were not able to persuade ministers to abandon the separation of track from services; nor did the rolling-stock industry overcome government reluctance to increase public expenditure. Some other parts of the programme were modified because of the strength of opponents' views. The government was forced to allow BR to become a potential franchisee; but in practice it would be only the 'bidder of last resort' as the original bill provided. The proposed pension scheme was changed; but not to the extent the Lords wanted, and not in the way Commons backbenchers were led to believe – moreover, the surplus the pension fund had accumulated from investments was later distributed to successful bidders in the privatization process. Interest-group views prevailed on through-ticketing and inter-availability, provision for disabled users of rail services, and rail closures; but two of these issues might well have been resolved at least as well without interest group pressure, and the third is unlikely to have much effect.

More important, the efforts of these interest groups and organizations had no impact on the overall aim of the bill, to privatize British Rail. Yet, apart from freight users, the witnesses to the Adley Committee thought increased investment in British Rail was more important than changing its ownership (Transport Committee, 1993: paras 53–6). Those groups which were not against privatization in principle were against 'the practicality of the Government's proposals' (*HC Debs*, 12 January 1993: 811). Just after the Bill was passed, *The Economist* reported: 'the government's plans to return [the railways] to private hands have been attacked by almost everyone in Britain except a few zealots and this newspaper' (25 December 1993). Thus, whether rail privatization is ultimately seen as successful or not (and even *The Economist* judged it could go either way), this case shows the limited impact not only of Parliament but also of interest groups when British government ministers and 'a few zealots' are determined to succeed.

Conclusion

These brief studies were chosen, one from each 'mode' of transport, for the diversity of the participants and their modes of action, not for their representative nature. However, the seatbelt and ferry studies indicate how 'outsider' groups can bring about policy change if there is a change in the 'environment' of an existing policy consensus. On both issues a series of tragedies brought a disparate set of interests – from citizens' groups to professional associations to public bodies – to put pressure on government. No really new technical or financial information had become available, but the political priorities changed. On seat-belts it seems a new network centred on local and national education authorities stimulated (or enabled) transport ministers to act. On ferries, the fading-away of an important network linked to Mrs Thatcher made it easier for transport ministers to take action. In either case, the first 'dimension of power' (multiple groups openly pressuring for change) had – perhaps only temporarily – overcome the 'second dimension of power' (the pressure from business groups keeping stronger regulation off the agenda) and the 'third dimension of power' (an assumption that business must be helped to thrive).

The arguments over T5 were like those over coach and ferry safety in providing some confirmation of the pluralist theory of democracy – that government policy decisions are the outcome of many groups and individuals promoting their views, and seem to reflect the balance of opinion among the affected parts of society. The opinions of some groups (in these cases, business groups) weigh more than others – an elitist bias – but they are not overwhelming. Rail privatization provides no support for a pluralist theory of democracy. Support for the policy was very limited. It was virtually restricted to ministers and New Right policy advisers who believed, almost as an article of faith, that the private sector provides a better service than does the public sector. The Treasury is generally regarded as the most influential of all government departments on public policy. It was especially so in the case of British Rail, seeing privatization as an essential part of achieving its wider aim of micro-efficiency, and a smaller public sector. Yet, though privatization had the advantage of attracting private-sector investment to the railways and reducing public expenditure, the policy was essentially driven by ideological dogma that was not vulnerable to interest-group pressure. The Bill was carried because in the British system of party democracy a government with a parliamentary majority can always win a vote – it is less a pluralist democracy than an 'elective dictatorship' as Lord Hailsham said (under a Labour government) (Hailsham, 1976).

During the period of Conservative government, Mrs Thatcher and the ministers brought to power by her proclaimed their intention not to listen to interest groups. They pushed to one side the vested interests, including transport officials and professionals, regarding them as part of the country's problems. They refrained from appointing Royal Commissions. Influenced by the theories of Niskanen, New Right politicians regarded the officials at the heart of the policy communities as just another pressure group, working in their own interest rather than that of the consumer (Niskanen, 1972). The advice of the Royal Institution of Naval Architects on ship design, and BR managers on rail privatization, was not advice that transport ministers would necessarily trust. Treasury officials seemed until the mid-1990s (when their own work was subjected to 'a fundamental review') to have been exempt from this loss of influence, above all because, as their critics would claim, their departmental interest in cutting back expenditure chimed with the goals of the ministers they served. Indeed, as Enid Wistrich noted, Treasury restrictions on spending provided more successful counter-pressure against the pro-roads lobby in the 1980s than the environmental groups had been able to achieve (1983: 104).

The large parliamentary majority possessed by Tony Blair leaves Labour MPs much freer to campaign on transport issues, because they know their government cannot fall, but by the same token his government does not need to placate small groups of supporters. Though the Labour government is less 'ideological' in conventional terms than that of Margaret Thatcher (which usually implies a government that can more easily be swayed by pressure-group arguments), it is equally as firm as hers on one goal – a determination to hold down spending, which armourplates it against certain types of demand. The Labour government of the 1990s is more likely to move with the general temper of public opinion, using focus groups and surveys to test the views of a broad band of voters across the middle of the political spectrum.

Despite the Conservative government's claims, it too was influenced by groups if they appeared to have wide support. However, some would argue that the seat-belt and ferry case studies describe atypical events in the lives of their respective policy communities. In general, policy networks are a source of policy inertia, not innovation (Marsh and Rhodes, 1992: 261). Because a broad consensus has to be maintained among members of the group if all are to remain within it, policy changes that have an adverse effect on one member can only be introduced cautiously and incrementally. Case studies such as these, focusing on issues that are part of open debate, may well be exceptional. The second dimension of power in many areas of transport policy-making (that is, the power of some groups in a policy community to veto change), is, paradoxically, often made clear only when it collapses and outsiders are successful in challenging the power of the insiders to resist reform.

Part III

The Planning Framework

The Planning Framework

6 Local Planning for Transport and the Environment

Central influences over local transport planning

The increasing focus on the needs of the environment within transport planning is shifting attention towards the part local government can play in changing patterns of travel. In the Conservative government's final years in office it called upon local authorities to implement new policies for transport and the environment in its planning guidance document, PPG13, and policy document, *Transport: The Way Forward* (DoE and DoT, 1994; DoT, 1996b). Since 1947, 'town and country planning' has been the responsibility of local councils. The making of land-use plans, which try to match the demands of developers and the environment with transport provision, is a task that falls to 'local planning authorities'. Councils make the first judgment on whether a planning application meets the transport criteria laid down in their plans. Most journeys are local, and therefore perhaps susceptible to being modified by the transport policies of local authorities. Thus councils seem to be in a prime position for using their transport and land-use planning strategies to minimize the need to travel, and to reduce the use of transport in its more environmentally damaging forms.

This outlook is marred by three factors. First, local journeys form only a small proportion of the total distance travelled by people and goods in Britain. While optimists look to councils to make a considerable impact on the way people choose to travel in urban areas, pessimists fear that grander strategies are needed, chiefly by central government, if there is to be a significant effect on the contribution of motorized transport to the damage of buildings and landscape, to poor air quality, and to climate change. Local authority public transport and traffic management policies could help to reduce the high concentrations of pollutants, especially particulates, which are thought to be damaging to health, but much more could be done by stricter national and international standards on vehicle emissions.

Second, since the Town and Country Planning Act of 1968, council plans have been required to be flexible documents. They have not specified closely zones for housing, industry and other activities, as had been demanded in the 1947 Act. After planners in the 1950s and 1960s failed to understand and predict what citizens and developers wanted, 'planning ideology' became less prescriptive and more open-ended. That emphasis on 'non-planning' sharpened during the Thatcher decade, when a series of Environment Secretaries (Michael Heseltine, Patrick Jenkin, Nicholas Ridley) believed the market was intrinsically better at making planning decisions than council bureaucrats were. So council plans and planners are not as well-prepared for a proactive role as fifty years of town and country planning would make it appear.

Third, throughout the postwar period, central government has dominated local government planning through legislation, circulars, criteria for awarding transport grants, and its position as final arbiter of planning applications. The weak position of local authorities was summed up in two clauses of the 1990 Town and Country Planning Act. One said all *'adverse development control decisions'* (councils saying no to developers) *were appealable* to the Secretary of State, by virtue of a 1971 Order. The other said the Secretary of State could *call in for decision any planning application*. The 'rolling back the State', and 'leave it to the market' rhetoric of governments of the 1980s and early 1990s distracted attention from the very real control central government still exercised over local councils, even if, paradoxically, it intervened mainly to ensure councils did not interfere with market preferences. So while council planners welcomed the more active role they are now expected to play in planning for transport and the environment, many must have been sceptical about how long it would last.

The chief means through which central government controls the overall planning objectives of local councils is Planning Guidance, circulated by the Secretary of State for the Environment but sometimes issued jointly with a relevant minister. Councils are required to submit their development plans to ministers for approval and show they fit ministers' national and regional strategic guidance together with a series of Policy Planning Guidance documents (PPGs), and a vast array of regulations and circulars. PPGs specify the type of policies ministers would like to see implemented on particular issues, such as PPG4 (Industrial and Commercial Development), PPG6 (Town Centres and Retail Development), and PPG17 (Sport and Recreation). The most important PPG in the context of this chapter and book is PPG13. Planners and environmentalists were encouraged by the title of the 1994 version of PPG13, *Transport*, which replaced the PPG13 of 1988: *Highways Considerations and Development Control*. The new document, though often unrealistic in its expectations of what councils could achieve, set a different tone, and the Labour government of 1997 said it did not expect to issue an early revision.

Central government 'guidance' is more constraining on councils than might be supposed from the everyday use of the word 'guidance'. Its practical effect is that of a regulation or law. If a council refuses planning permission on grounds inconsistent with its plan (which must comply with guidance), or on grounds inconsistent with guidance (for those councils that have not yet produced an approved plan), it is likely to be overruled by the Secretary of State. Since being overruled wastes councils' resources they feel obliged to comply with guidance. Central government has more direct ways of controlling council transport provision: for example, since 1973 councils have had to submit annual transport policies and programmes (TPPs), and central government decides which major local transport projects to support financially. But Planning Guidance can have greater significance, especially if it is very prescriptive on what councils either should or should not do. The 1994 version of PPG13 and *Transport: the Way Forward* marked an about-turn from guidance of the 1980s which emphasized that councils should not hamper private developers – for instance, Nicholas Ridley's strategic guidance for Greater London (DoE, 1989). For the sake of the environment central government was returning to land-use and transport planning that did not leave decision-making only to the market.

A second about-turn could be detected a few years later in central government's attitude to local councils. Guidance inevitably reduces councils' freedom to decide what they think best for their citizens, but they recognize its value in imposing regional and national coherence on what could otherwise be a set of local development plans at odds with each other. Indeed in the absence of strong guidance in the late 1980s, councils in some regions, such as East Anglia, came together voluntarily to plan a joint transport strategy. But guidance that reduces local choice is accepted more willingly if it reflects the considered views of local authorities in their joint planning fora, such as SERPLAN for South-East England and the London Planning Advisory Committee for Greater London. Whereas in the 1980s councils in general felt their views counted for very little with ministers, from 1996 their participation in policy-making was being more actively sought by transport ministers and officials. For the cynics, this new appreciation of local government was the result of environmental and budgetary pressures on national transport policy: the contribution of local councils was needed if travel patterns were to be altered at minimum cost, and they could try out on a small scale innovatory traffic management policies (for example, urban road pricing), which central government found it difficult politically and technically to introduce.

The British government had given commitments on the environment at the Earth Summit in Rio in June 1992 (Agenda 21), especially on the reduction of carbon dioxide (a greenhouse gas). In 1990 the DoE White Paper, *This Common Inheritance*, had already stated that all public policies affecting the environment should rest on the principle of sustainability. The DoE's White Paper, *Sustainable Development: The UK Strategy* (1994), identified transport as a priority for action. PPG13 was drafted in the knowledge of the forthcoming report of the Royal Commission on Environmental Pollution on Transport and the Environment (1994). The Royal Commission made 110 recommendations on actions to be taken. Its overall conclusion was that improvements to vehicles (cleaner engines and more effective exhausts) would be insufficient to meet the government's targets on air pollution, and that road traffic growth must therefore be restrained. The government responded with two papers: *Transport: The Way Ahead* (1995) and *Transport: The Way Forward* (1996).

In 1996 it appeared that the UK would meet its Rio greenhouse gas targets for 2000 because of a transfer from coal to gas-fired power stations and a reduction in economic activity. The government's opponents (for example Matthew Taylor, MP, in *Liberal Democrat News*, 26 July 1996) denounced this finding as a 'one-off' serendipity that did not relieve government of the need to encourage a modal switch from cars and lorries to buses, cycles and trains. However, following the election of a Labour government keen to emphasize its green credentials, the new prime minister, addressing the United Nations Earth Summit follow-up conference in New York on 23 June 1997, committed the government to reducing carbon dioxide emissions by 20 per cent by the year 2010 (*Guardian*, 24 June 1997). To reach this new target there will have to be a considerable improvement in fuel efficiency, or a change in the balance between private and public transport, or both. A Steer Davies Gleave report for Transport 2000 argued that improving public transport was part of 'a balanced approach' which offered a less environmentally damaging form of travel that fitted existing social and economic patterns. The alternative approach promoted by environmental groups, of returning to local production and consumption to reduce drastically the volume of travel and transport, was regarded as too radical (1995: paras 7.10–11).

But although concern for the environment made it easier for a central government that wanted to reduce public expenditure to announce cutbacks in the road programme in March 1995 and November 1995, there was, for that very reason, no equivalent addition to public transport investment. Nor did it seem likely that the position would change greatly during the lifetime of the Labour government elected in 1997, given its manifesto commitment to holding down public expenditure. PPG13's guidance of 1994 was still in place but without much expectation of financial support for encouraging a switch to public transport.

Minimizing motorized travel

PPG13 requires local authorities to set out land-use planning and transport policies that have three goals: (i) to 'reduce growth in the length and number of motorised journeys'; (ii) to encourage alternative means of travel which have less environmental impact; and thereby (iii) to reduce reliance on the private car

(Introduction to PPG13). The first objective implies slowing the increase in car, bus and lorry mileage below forecast growth – by bringing closer together the sites of different activities (homes, shops, work, leisure). The second objective implies favouring walking, cycling, buses and trains over cars, lorries and taxis. The third objective reinforces the message about cars (though it should also mention lorries).

Some councils had already taken a different view from central government in their willingness to draw up land-use and transport plans that were environmentally sensitive (for instance, Surrey County Council, West Sussex) or in encouraging the use of public transport (West Sussex, Devon County Council). Some councils have other priorities and problems, even in drawing up an approved plan. But in many councils, PPG13 will tip the balance, because its authority will be used by a planning or highways chief officer, or the leading councillors on the planning and transportation committee, to encourage the rest of the council to take decisions that minimize transport emissions. PPG13's prescriptions are thus highly important.

Minimizing motorized travel, whether in planning for new housing, employment, retail, leisure or education, can be implemented in two ways. The first is through *transport strategies* promoting other forms of travel, such as cycling, walking, and using public transport, and discouraging car use, for example through parking restrictions and urban road pricing. The second is through *land-use strategies* which reduce travel distances by concentrating new development in areas within walking or cycling distances of established centres of activity, or by locating it near public transport routes. How realistic are the possible tactics within each strategy?

Transport strategies

Walking and cycling

PPG13 suggests that 'better conditions for pedestrians and cyclists', linked to locational policies that promoted local activity, could 'lead to a significant change in travel choices' (para. 4.12). Walking, it says, can be encouraged by pedestrianization schemes and

TABLE 6.1 Percentage of journeys by foot or bicycle

	% on foot of all journeys	% on foot under 2 miles	% by cycle of all journeys	% by cycle under 2 miles
1975–76	35.3	67.3	3.3	4.5
1985–86	34.2	64.4	2.4	3.3
1989–91	30.1	61.1	1.9	2.7
1992–94	29.1	60.2	1.7	2.3

Source: *HC Debs*, 7 May 1996 cols 61–2.

establishing pedestrian routes along 'canal towpaths or disused railways' (4.13). Cyclepaths could use 'redundant railway lines or space along canals and rivers' (4.16). These recommendations are not only a sad reflection of lost opportunities for low-pollution transport, but their serious contribution to a reduction in pollution has to be questioned.

First, the proportion of journeys made in Britain by cycle is small and declining, though the proportion of journeys on foot is still large if the walk is not too long (see Table 6.1). Second, and more important, car journeys up to 5 miles (short enough for potential replacement by walking or cycling) represent only 13 per cent of all travel in person-miles (Steer Davies Gleave, 1995: 40). Since for a proportion of these journeys, the time factor, small children, infirmity or bulky shopping will still make cars the first choice, replacing some short journeys by walking or cycling would contribute only a modest reduction to pollution. Third, people seem to have been making fewer short journeys (under 2 miles) that are, or could be, by 'low tech' transport (ibid. 39).

Nevertheless, cycling and walking could contribute to a useful reduction of congestion and emissions in urban areas, where levels of pollution tend to be at their highest. About 20 per cent of car journeys in urban areas at peak periods are school journeys (1996: para. 14.48). Some could be replaced by walking or cycling, to the benefit of children's independent development. The work of Mayer Hillman on this topic is particularly important (Hillman, Adams, Whitelegg, 1991; and see *Guardian*, 25 June 1996).

Sir George Young ('the bicycling baronet') was regarded as mildly eccentric for cycling in London, but under his direction as Secretary of State for Transport a target for cycle use was the one national quantitative objective towards 'Sustainable Development' the government was prepared to contemplate in *Transport: The Way Forward* (1996: 87). In February 1996 the Department of Transport produced a guide to cycle facilities that reversed earlier advice that cars had to be given priority over slower vehicles (*Independent*, 9 February 1996). It also gave an unusually firm commitment to fund over a five-year period the London cycle network, including along the roads it controls (for example, the A10 in Enfield, and along Red Routes).

Councils have much studied the experience of some towns in other European countries (especially Denmark, Germany and the Netherlands) because they show that up to 20 to 25 per cent of local journeys can be made by cycle if management schemes are extensive. Numerous local authorities have encouraged cycling in recent years by building cycle routes (paradoxically by dividing under-used pavements into two lanes); many offer their staff cycle mileage rates and cycle rather than car purchase schemes, or provide bicycle pools as well as car pools for officials to use on council business (among others: Sutton, Southampton, Surrey, Cumbria, Allerdale, East Sussex, Somerset, Worcester, York, North Devon, Welwyn Hatfield, Gloucester, Stafford, Worcester, Nottingham City Council and Nottinghamshire County Council). The London boroughs and the London Planning Advisory Committee are implementing the London network of 1000 miles of cycletracks, with Kingston-upon-Thames acting as lead borough, coordinating the efforts of groups of boroughs.

Yet the outlook for lowering pollution levels through shifting travel to cycling and walking seems bleak. Only York, Cambridge and Oxford reach Scandinavian levels of cycle use. A warning can be seen in Stevenage New Town, designed in the 1950s with few garages (future car ownership was underestimated) but a comprehensive cycleway system. Hertfordshire Constabulary's traffic management officers are resigned to showing their overseas visitors the extensive network of tracks, virtually unused since the 1960s. Stevenage's inhabitants did not cycle to work because they liked it but because they were used to it and their levels of income were low. Bicycles were gradually supplanted by Minis which kept the traveller dry and ready for work. The Transport Research Laboratory recently monitored seven cycle projects and concluded that 'none of the programmes resulted in a significant increase in cycle use' (DoE, 1995a: para. 6.45). The evidence is that cycle schemes do not generally shift modal use significantly and, where they do, they tend to replace walking and urban public transport, not car journeys. They need to be accompanied by simultaneous action against car use (ibid. para. 6.61).

Public transport

Local authorities can encourage the use of public transport alternatives to car travel for longer journeys, though the results may be modest. Many councils promote the use of public transport by bringing fares nearer car costs with special season tickets for over-60s, or discounted travel passes for council staff (as Nottingham City Council does), or by subsidizing tendered bus or metropolitan rail routes or services. They may issue up-to-date information on changing bus routes and timetables (as Hertfordshire does) – an important tactic in a deregulated bus industry. Though it could be argued that some of these policies encourage people to make additional journeys that replace staying at home or walking, nevertheless they are giving motorists an incentive to discover how many of their car journeys could be replaced by public transport.

Councils can take more positive measures to increase the quality and effectiveness of public transport, for example, by building bus priority routes into their traffic management schemes, and improving facilities at interchange points, perhaps in conjunction with town centre redevelopment. Some authorities are making intensive, experimental efforts to attract new bus passengers. Leeds, Suffolk County Council in Ipswich, Hampshire County Council in Southampton, Cambridgeshire County Council in Cambridge (and London Regional Transport, with the financial support of the DoT and boroughs) have upgraded their 'bus infrastructure' at pilot sites, with permutations of guided busways, traffic signals and junctions that give buses priority, and matrix displays of waiting times. The object is to remove some of the uncertainties and delays traditionally associated with bus travel. Other characteristics of ideal bus use, such as through-ticketing and ticket transferability, are hindered outside London by anti-cartel regulation.

Authorities in most metropolitan areas have been keen to provide new rail or tram infrastructure like the Tyne and Wear Metro, Manchester Metrolink, South Yorkshire Supertram and Croydon Tramlink (planned with London Regional Transport). But they can do it less easily than in the past because of problems in obtaining permission from central government to borrow or to use their capital assets; under both Conservative and the new Labour governments keeping down public expenditure has been a higher priority for central government than allocating additional public borrowing for environment-friendly transport systems.

A bigger question is whether such investment is really worthwhile in proportion to its limited effect on reducing transport-produced emissions (as distinct from providing efficient and effective transport, or adding to civic pride). The evidence so far is limited and difficult to interpret. Sheffield Supertram, built and owned by four local authorities in South Yorkshire, attracted so few passengers in its first phase of operation that the councils expected to have to sell it at a price below its cost. On the other hand, the bus companies competing for its passengers have been carrying full loads (*Independent*, 10 June 1996). In Manchester, about 13 per cent of Metrolink passengers used to travel by car, a 'significant modal switch' according to Steer Davies Gleave (1995: 43) and the Department of the Environment (1995a: para. 6.91). But the number of cars entering the city centre in the morning peak has fallen by only 2 per cent (DoT, 1996: 90).

The more relevant context for assessing what could be achieved with light rail is not Manchester as a whole but the travel corridor. Within the Metrolink corridor (2 km either side of the line), between 14 per cent and 50 per cent of car trips to destinations served by Metrolink have switched to the tram (Steer Davies Gleave, 1995: 43). Traffic on one of the routes parallel to Metrolink has fallen by 10 per cent in the morning peak, and the average peak hour reduction is between 4 and 6 per cent (DoT, 1996: 90). But this effect still seems disappointing given the size of the £140m investment, and an inadequate response given the size of the problem. Both DoE and Steer Davies Gleave thought that a greater overall reduction in road traffic would require additional, more constraining, traffic or land-use measures, such as parking restrictions, or confining new development to the rail corridor.

Efforts by councils to shift travellers from car to public transport are hampered by the adverse trend between the relative
cost to users of public transport and cars. The 'green indicators'
for sustainable development produced by the DoE in March 1996
showed that, while the cost of rail and bus fares had grown faster
than disposable incomes from the mid-1970s to 1990, the price
of petrol and motoring had fallen (DoE and Government Statistical Services, 1996). Fuel now costs the motorist about the
same as it did in 1964 compared to retail prices, having been 20
per cent higher in the early 1980s. In contrast rail receipts per
passenger kilometre have increased continuously since the 1970s.
While Kenneth Clarke, as last Conservative Chancellor of the
Exchequer, promised to continue to raise fuel tax by 5 per cent
above inflation, and Gordon Brown, in the Labour budget of
1997, mentioned 6 per cent, the Royal Commission on Environmental Pollution said the annual increase should be about 9 per
cent. Changing the relative use of less-polluting and more-polluting
travel requires the consistent application of clear policies by both
central government and local governments; local councils' actions,
though useful, will have much less impact than they should if
the price signals given by central government are weak.

Cars

PPG13's main strategies on motorized traffic are land-use policies to reduce car journeys to out-of-town stores, and traffic policies
to restrict parking in towns. The first policy objective received
greater attention. But the second poses equally serious problems, though it is agreed that high parking charges and parking
space constraints are substantial incentives towards the use of
public transport (Banister, 1994: 135). Councils experience difficulties in controlling parking provision. They do not have the
legal powers to control privately-owned off-street car parking.
(The Department of Transport, in *Transport the Way Forward*
(1996: para. 14.67) suggested councils might be given powers to
control 'private non-residential parking'.) Welwyn Hatfield District Council found town car parking spaces increased and its
own parking charges undercut by a further education college
seeking to raise money for its budget (colleges were removed
from the control of local authorities in 1988). Councils fear local

traders will lose business to areas that have not introduced stricter parking controls. The districts that have reduced town-centre parking seem to be those that can more confidently predict advantages for visitors or residents, or that can survive a loss of 'custom' (for example, Cambridge City, Westminster, Richmond-on-Thames). PPG13 suggested regional planning guidance and structure plans should set a standard range of levels of parking provision to which all plans would adhere; local authorities should ensure parking at peripheral locations did not disadvantage more central areas; and local authorities should be flexible in varying parking requirements according to other travel provision and traffic management consequences (paras. 4.5 and 4.6). Unfortunately, the flexibility, however sensible, may be exploited to negate the effect of setting standards. As in so many transport strategies, the policies are more complicated to apply than to prescribe. *Transport: The Way Forward* suggested regional groups of local authorities should consult each other on parking provision, with the aim of finding mutually agreed standards for incorporating into regional guidance (para. 14.82).

Yet local authorities fear applying parking restrictions since it is difficult to predict the consequences. The absence of sufficient parking provision in urban areas was a major reason in the 1980s for enterprises to move to out-of-town sites to find parking space for company visitors and delivery vehicles. This practice was especially noticeable amongst businesses in expanding parts of the economy, such as computer software houses and business information firms, which have moved to old country houses outside villages (for example, Mass Consultants to Little Paxton, outside St. Neots, and Esmerk-Infomat, from central Newbury to the public transport-free Bensham Valence on its outskirts). Councils are afraid of losing employment opportunities. Except for fully urbanized areas where the use of public transport is well-ingrained (such as central London), the strategy seems very risky for town centres struggling to survive.

PPG13 itself noted that limiting car parking may bring traffic congestion (para. 4.6), and thus pollution. It is careful to note that limiting parking provision 'on- or off-street' should be imposed 'where there are effective alternatives' to vehicle journeys (para. 1.8). There are less negative ways to reduce car pollution, such as the park-and-ride schemes in Canterbury and Cambridge, and car-sharing registers put in place by and coordinated with other policies by Nottingham City Council in its 'Green Commuter' strategy. They are less likely to penalize authorities that misjudge the willingness of people to switch transport modes, but perhaps they have a more limited impact. Even free park-and-ride schemes are poor alternatives to parking at a peripheral store and are mainly popular when people have to go in to the centre (for transferring to rail, for Christmas shopping or tourist attractions) and know they cannot park. But they have a strong role to play in historic cities, where limited space and the evident good sense of preserving the built environment make it politically easier for councils to persuade local voters that parking must be restricted. In all towns they can reduce urban congestion and its associated hazards.

The package approach: integrating transport measures

The lesson on alternatives to 'motorized travel' seems to be that inducements to use 'low-tech' or public transport need to be combined with restrictions on car use if they are to succeed – often called the 'carrot and stick' approach. The effect of these various strategies is assumed to be maximized if they are applied together. Steven Norris, Minister for Transport in London, 1992–6, said 'the package approach . . . is hugely helpful in achieving better value for the money we have' (*HC Debs*, 8 May 1996: 198). It has a public relations element, too. Cars and lorries are the primary cause of pollution, yet politicians and the public can only envisage constraining their use if travellers are offered other attractive options. Unfortunately, low-pollution alternatives are relatively weak in their effect – a direct reflection of the enormous comparative attractiveness of cars and road freight. The DoT estimated 'that a 50 per cent increase in rail traffic would reduce road traffic by a mere 5 per cent' (*Economist*, 12 March 1994). A very large carrot would have little effect, and politicians shrink from applying the stick. For example, first Conservative ministers, then Labour ministers have flown the kite of road pricing, only to draw back, even delaying time after time a 'pretend' trial on the M3 near Basingstoke.

Local politicians are equally wary of upsetting voters. Nottingham City in the early 1970s abandoned much of its road-building plans in favour of a traffic-control scheme which used traffic lights to keep cars waiting in side roads when bus routes were congested, and made city-centre parking more difficult and more expensive for private cars. Councillors wanted citizens to switch to public transport and 'park-and-ride'. It was abandoned quickly because it aroused public anger, partly a result of increases in bus fares but also because only one city was applying this scheme – motorists could go to out-of-town stores in a different district. David Banister thought hindsight showed Nottingham should have used a pricing mechanism instead, but recognized it too would have met problems of political acceptability (Banister, 1994: 34; and see Truelove, 1992: 158). But with more widespread concern for the environment in the late 1990s other cities may be able to conduct similar trials with less hostility.

The DoT's 1993 guidelines to councils on drawing up their Transport Policies and Programmes promised they would have greater freedom to switch resources between different forms of transport if they developed an overall plan 'in the context of broader strategic land-use, economic and environmental objectives'. The department used as an experiment the package approach developed by the West Midlands Passenger Transport Authority – the board of borough councillors which replaced the Metropolitan County Council abolished in 1985. Other councils have been active too in integrating transport policies. For example, in 1992 West Sussex County Council approved a package of measures for Crawley town centre which had been developed by county and district councillors, the New Towns Commission and Crawley Borough Planning Department working together. It balanced a relief road and car park with schemes for pedestrianization, bus improvements, traffic management, park-and-ride, safety management, cyclepaths and environmental improvements for residents.

The DoT advised other urban areas to use the package concept by 1995–6, if they wanted to increase their chances of approval to spend. The 'package approach' illustrates the typical process of policy adoption in local government: a council introduces a new policy, the policy spreads to neighbouring councils and through professional associations, and finally central government picks up the reform and imposes it on all councils (Jones and Stewart, 1985). Critics of recent central governments' transport policy might wonder whether the package approach could be adopted with more force at national level. Central government could integrate 'sticks and carrots' to much greater effect in its own areas of responsibility, such as in rail funding, lorry weights, fuel duty and vehicle taxation.

Land-use and development strategies

In pursuit of its goal to minimize polluting forms of travel, PPG13 asks councils to devise land-use policies that promote development at places that do not need car access; and to encourage types of economic development that do not rely on 'motorised travel'. It thought their plans should 'revitalise traditional urban centres', improving their attractiveness as 'places to live, work and shop', and 'promote healthy rural communities where people can both live and work' (para. 2.8). If these policies worked, it would reduce personal distance travelled (though not freight supplies), without simultaneously reducing the quality of life. The realistic prospects for 'town' and 'country' are examined in turn.

Revitalizing urban centres

The section of guidance on urban centres was one of the most publicized parts of PPG13 because it ran contrary to previous ministerial decisions on applications for building hypermarkets, and was contrary to previous regional strategic guidance. The subsequent draft guidance PPG6 on town centres (DoE, 1995b) confirmed John Gummer's willingness in principle, as Secretary of State for the Environment, to rule against out-of-town shopping complexes that affected town centre viability, or were not easily accessible by public transport. Sceptics were awaiting individual rulings – in March 1996 Gummer had not decided 11 applications for retail/leisure complexes six to 15 months after the inspector's report (*HC Debs,* 28 March 1996: 711).

During the 1980s there was a great expansion in out-of-town stores and leisure centres – whose trade was enhanced by the relative ease of access they offered customers and suppliers, compared with town centre sites. The chair of Surrey County Council's Highways and Transport Committee said the county

structure plan had provided for 12 out-of-town shopping centres; 15 had been built and she hoped 'we will be able to resist'
future applications (*HL Debs*, 23 November 1994: 307). Revital-
izing urban centres, or retaining such vitality as they have, is an
important objective of local authorities, but it is one they have
to fulfil as best they can. DoE's 1995 guide to local authorities
on implementing PPG13, called, confusingly, *PPG13: Guide to
Better Practice*, cited as a good example the town of Horsham
(West Sussex) which has an edge-of-centre store that provides a
car park within walking distance the town centre. Shoppers can
do other business in the town without making an extra journey.
But Horsham's associated town centre improvement and traffic
management scheme was financed by selling council land out-
of-town to a food retailer (1995a: para. 5.62). Local authorities
fearful of effects on existing town centres nevertheless conceded
planning permission because they knew developers could appeal
successfully to the Secretary of State on 'market' grounds. South
Somerset District Council agreed in 1993 to Sainsbury's edge-
of-town application in Yeovil despite opposition from environmentalists, because Sainsbury's earlier out-of-town application,
rejected by the council, had found favour with the DoE planning inspector. If the council had turned down the new edge-of-
town application, Sainsbury's might have revived the out-of-town
development.

Reducing pollution through changing modern shopping and
retailing habits seems unlikely to be swift. Moreover, the rise of
the hypermarket was accompanied by the rise of the out-of-town
warehouse distributor, based on cheap road haulage which has
encouraged chain retailers to buy their supplies from further afield.
Some firms, most notably Boots, have policies to remain or set up
again in town centres, but planning guidance can affect only future
development, so any reversal that occurs will take place slowly.

One way to revitalize a congested urban centre is to build a
bypass. Rarely as contentious as the Newbury A34 bypass, this
project, although a national decision, exemplifies the conflicting
transport and environmental consequences. On the one hand,
its construction was fervently desired by the district council, former
county council and nearly all of Newbury's inhabitants. The town's
old buildings and present community life would be liberated from
heavy lorries rumbling between the South coast ports and the

Midlands. On the other hand, many environmentalists mourn the disturbance of areas as diverse as a battlesite, sites of scientific interest or the habitat of the Desmoulins snail. They fear 'housing infill' between the old and new trunk roads will lead to more traffic and yet another bypass (housing was built in the narrow area between the old town and the current trunk road bypass). The alternative solutions of a less destructive route, or putting freight on rail, were too expensive or radical to consider. The political difficulty of the case was evident in the many postponements by ministers 'to relook at the evidence', culminating in Brian Mawhinney's last-minute decision, announced the day he left office (*HC Debs*, 5 July 1995: 244–5).

Promoting rural communities

PPG13 says the policies it recommends will help local authorities achieve 'a healthy rural economy and viable rural communities'. Respondents to the DoE's white paper on *Rural England* (1995c) questioned this claim, and the DoE admits 'there is less scope for reducing reliance on the private car in rural areas' (DoE, 1995d: 44), and probably for this reason PPG13 makes little further reference to rural areas.

The requirement to minimize travel by promoting rural communities in which people live and work at home seems unrealistic. Homeworking, tele-cottages and video-conferencing have the potential to alter the relationship between employment, homes and transport but they apply to relatively few people at present. About 1 per cent of workers in the UK (including in urban areas) are full-time 'teleworkers'; though about 3 per cent of workers always work from home, and 10 per cent of employees work sometimes from home (Northamptonshire CCTE, 1995: 31–2). The effects of homeworking on transport are complex and difficult to predict. If full-time or most-time teleworking tempts more people to move away from towns (rather than keeping current country dwellers at home), the net impact may be successful in 'promoting rural communities', but increase the volume of motorized journeys. People who work from home only part of the week may be more tempted to use the car for the whole journey (not just to the station) on 'going-in-to-the-office' days. Homeworking makes season tickets a poor bargain; and daily commuters develop a routine of travelling by public transport even if this choice of travel mode is not a rational decision when personal costs and inconvenience are considered. The children of homeworkers and teleworkers will want car lifts, and eventually cars of their own, to schools, colleges and leisure opportunities in the nearest town.

The fallacy of 'living and working at home' to reduce motorized travel is that rural communities are no longer self-sufficient. They are part of a national and multinational economy geared towards motorized transport and bulk distribution. To stay in business, small factories, food-processing plants and village shops depend on lorries designed for trunk roads.

The Rural Development Commission report on rural services (1994) said that 40 per cent of parishes had no shop or post office, 50 per cent had no school and three-quarters had no bus service. Its special report on rural transport (1996) showed that innovative local authorities can provide an excellent service provided they make full use of vehicles (by turn school buses, day centre ambulances, and hired out to self-help community groups). But they must be able to devote a substantial budget to public transport (Devon spends £20m a year whereas West Sussex, a determined supporter of public transport but more typical of local transport authorities than Devon, spends about £1m).

Local authorities can develop policies on the most cost-effective ways of providing public transport (minibuses, dial-a-ride, or volunteer-driven buses as in Bedfordshire and Devon). None the less, the self-help devized by many rural communities based on the car (shared shopping trips, rotas for collecting prescriptions and for school runs) may well cause less pollution than a near-empty bus. It will always be more difficult to plan for less need to travel in rural areas, as MPs from rural constituencies recognized when they opposed increased fuel duty on petrol.

The priority of transport objectives over other land-use imperatives

PPG13, paragraph 6.1, says that 'just as transport policies should support the locational policies in development plans, so land-use policies should support the transport aims of the plan'. This equivocation may have a positive role in improving coordination between planners and transport specialists (in central or in local government) because each will feel their views have equal weight. Yet transport policies must take unambiguous precedence over land-use policies if a primary objective of government is sustainable development. Paragraph 4.23 proposed that local authorities should draw up 'accessibility profiles' that would show which sites could accommodate development without car access; that is, sites that have good public transport connections to housing, employment, shopping and other activities. This suggestion offers a more systematic and more effective approach than the usual process of considering transport provision at individual sites when a developer seeks planning permission. If public transport access is the priority, the 'accessibility profiles' should designate the locations where development would be permitted, as they do in the Netherlands. A local authority should not give planning consent unless adequate public transport is available, or will be made available as a consequence of the development.

The very last paragraph of PPG13 put that point in an unobtrusive way under 'developer contributions' and is worth quoting in full:

> Where additional public transport or road provision would be required for a development to proceed this fact should be included in the development plan. The willingness of a developer to provide infrastructure to overcome objections to a proposed development may be a material consideration, but it will not necessarily justify the grant of planning permission particularly if there are other material considerations, such as the aim of reducing the need to travel. Where transport improvements will be needed to enable the proposal to go ahead, these should normally be provided first (para. 6.14).

To rely on 'accessibility profiles' for giving planning permission, councils need central government's backing: first, on supporting local authority planning decisions made according to these principles; and second, in the evolution of central government's own methods of transport programming and budgeting, so that a local council's plans to improve its 'accessibility' profile can be made with reasonable assurance about what grants and approvals to borrow will be provided within the lifetime of the plan.

The national context of local transport planning

National road policies and 'national roads'

Local authorities were warned by PPG13 in 1994 that local public consultation on their land-use and transport plans could not include discussion of national road schemes that had been or were to be examined at a public inquiry. The DoT offered in PPG13 to 'comment' on potential conflict between its schemes and local authority plans, but it did not offer a debate on the consequences of national proposals for their structure and local plans, or to modify national proposals if local authorities, working on their development plans, came up with better suggestions. The explanation in PPG13 (para. 5.11) for its treatment of local authorities was that they have 'little need or scope to vary the road programme' to meet local priorities, because the trunk road network 'is primarily to serve long-distance through traffic'. By 1996, central government was showing a different attitude to local government consultation. But this particular debate lives on in the recurring suggestion that 'local traffic' should be diverted from 'national roads' (trunk roads or motorways) through tolling, restrictions on classes of traffic, or perhaps the closure of some junctions.

There are political, logical, safety and practical arguments against these proposals. Motorists will assert that they are nearer to paying their way for these roads than long-distance freight vehicles, for instance, and use arguments of citizenship rights and market forces to say they should be able to choose which roads they use. The non-motorway trunk roads in particular make up a fairly idiosyncratic collection of busy roads that central government has, at various times in the historical evolution of local government boundaries, chosen to adopt as national – there are no formal or informal systematic criteria. They pass through urbanized areas and thus inevitably serve local as well as long-distance traffic. The rationale for building new sections of trunk road outside towns and villages was to remove all non-essential traffic from local roads, to improve safety, and to reduce urban congestion and damage to the built environment. (The cost–benefit criteria for building them included local users' safety and time-savings).

It is difficult to justify diverting non-essential non-national traffic from relatively safe modern motorways and bypasses onto local roads serving residential areas, schools and neighbourhood centres.

Local authorities are asked in PPG13 to think of urban vitality and rural viability. In some cases they will meet these objectives with traffic-calming measures to try to divert all but neighbourhood traffic away from local roads; in other cases they will invite tourists or commercial drivers to divert from trunk roads to break their journey. Finally, there is a practical limit to councils' abilities to direct traffic. PPG13 adds that local authority plans should 'ensure' that the use of trunk roads and other through-routes for short local trips does not 'undermine' their national role (paras 6.1, 6.3). It does not suggest any practical means by which authorities can ensure the prohibition is carried out should they wish to do so.

National environmental policies

Paragraph 5.6 of PPG13 asked local authorities to minimize the impact of new projects on the natural and built environment. They should keep away, 'wherever possible', from Areas of Natural Beauty, Sites of Special Scientific Interest, historic parks and gardens, National Parks and battlefields. Schemes should 'do as little damage as practicable' and schemes 'must be demonstrated to be in the public interest . . .' (paras 5.15 to 5.20). Local authorities will hope that the inclusion of these exhortations in PPG13 is a sign that central government will look favourably on TPP proposals for funding and credit approvals that include the cost of minimizing environmental impact. Local authorities are likely to be sceptical that central government is serious about the advice in paragraphs 5.15 to 5.20 until they see transport ministers willing to pay higher levels of grant funding to local authorities who do not choose least-cost solutions. The refusal of central government to forego least-cost solutions on its own roads – at Newbury (A34), at Twyford Down (M3), at Newport, South Wales (M4), and elsewhere – will not encourage local authorities to believe that central government will be prepared to support its guidance with the additional resources which would be required.

Conclusion

The most valuable contribution of PPG13 was to assure authorities that central government is now more likely to accept planning policies and decisions that help preserve the economic and social bases of their town centres and rural communities. Many local authorities do not have as their first priority the reining back of transport-related pollution, but rather a mix of objectives (sustain town centres, ensure residents without cars have access to chain retailers, keep tendered bus services viable, prevent dispersed development which is costly to service, adopt environmentally friendly policies if they fit tight budgets). But the effect of their policies will run in the same direction as PPG13.

Public comment focused on one aspect of PPG13: the turning away from planning through the market. Local authorities experienced this 'planning' as unrestrained pressure from developers and retailers to be allowed to build on greenfield sites with easy access to wide roads, and to be provided, even in urban areas, with free, abundant, parking capacity. Local authorities can now use PPG13 to justify their opposition – especially if the reason cited for turning down planning applications for out-of-town hypermarkets is transport pollution rather than *social* difficulties for non-drivers. Unfortunately PPG13 may have been a decade too late to have stopped the building of out-of-town stores, though the general response has been to regard its advice as better late than never.

PPG13 supports the arguments of those who would like to see public transport provision improved, but PPG13 is not and perhaps cannot be helpful in saying how additional public transport to replace car travel will be provided. The departments could say that Planning Policy Guidance is not the place to discuss resources for tendered bus routes and local rail infrastructure or for noting central government plans for funding national rail infrastructure improvements. But local authorities need to know what the national financial, legislative, and political context will be for their endeavours as passenger transport authorities – particularly in light of the structural changes that have recently taken place to both publicly-funded transport and local government – or they will be wary of planning for a reduction in motorized travel. DoT made overtures to local authorities in *Transport: The*

Way Forward (Annex 1 – titled, daringly in the last days of Major's government , 'scope for greater integration', a reversal of 'laisser-faire' ideology). Its offer to consult them on trunk road programmes in drawing up regional guidance was an encouraging U-turn from the attitude in PPG13 that trunk road projects were not local authorities' concern. Local authorities have much experience in drawing up coordinated land-use and transport programmes that could be transferred at regional level to departments.

Nevertheless, the constraints to action at local level have to be recognized. First, local authorities are limited in their effect. They spend only a fraction of total domestic expenditure (about 10 per cent of GDP, about one-quarter of general government expenditure). They have fewer legal and financial resources than they had at the beginning of the 1980s. They are more restricted in the requirements they can place on companies and individuals. Bus services have been deregulated. Contract compliance (imposing conditions on firms tendering for local authority work, such as local sourcing of supplies or the employment of local residents) – which might have been used to impose PPG13's policies on suppliers – was outlawed as anti-competitive behaviour in 1988. The Conservative governments' educational policies and health service policies have worked against planning for less travel. Councils have lost control of colleges, and catchment areas for schools can no longer be imposed. The trend in the National Health Service is to group its facilities into larger hospitals further apart. The Department for the Environment, Transport and the Regions may need to coordinate its activities with other departments of central government as well as with local government.

Second, councils are limited in relation to the size of the problem they are being asked to tackle. Planning guidance seems to be trying to go back to the transport modes of the 1960s without recognizing that society and the economy have changed. For example, an increase in the number of working mothers means more parents drive between school and workplace in order to reach both on time. Transport patterns have adapted to social and economic changes and vice versa; to change them significantly would need large-scale, long-term commitment – the acceptance of seat-belts and breathalyzers took decades, how much longer to persuade people to travel less, let alone to buy and sell goods produced locally? The flurry of reports by environment and transport ministers could be seen as part of an education process. They are trying to associate users with the decisions to be made, because habits must change. However, local authorities, no longer used to being a partner of central government, have to be somewhat sceptical about why they are now being associated with policies that have reduced budgets, uncertain outcomes and are mostly unwelcome to voters. Central government is asking councils to do at local level with relatively small means what it has been unable or unwilling to do at national level. The most powerful instruments for changing travel demand lie with national government. But local government could help to tilt the present balance.

7 National Planning for Transport and the Environment

At national level it is not just individual planning decisions which may be controversial but planning itself. The Labour manifesto for the 1997 general election stated unequivocally that 'a sustainable environment requires above all an effective and integrated transport policy at national, regional and local level'. The Conservative governments of 1979 to 1997 would not have agreed with that judgment. Their objections were expressed most characteristically by Cecil Parkinson, Transport Minister, 1989–90. He thought an integrated transport policy was 'socialist' and a 'way of keeping well-paid bureaucrats occupied' (Truelove, 1992: 8). But this attitude was echoed more moderately by people from across the political spectrum interviewed for this book, who mostly wanted a Greater London authority that could coordinate transport provision, but 'did not want GLC-type planning'. They were rejecting the prescriptive planning of the GLC, especially under Labour majorities, bearing down on London boroughs and private enterprises alike, which imposed patterns of travel that planners believed would be effective at regional level, but which did not find favour at local level.

However, it would be a mistake to make a clear association of 'Labour' with transport planning, and 'Conservative' with leaving transport decisions to the market and to the private sector. The picture is more complex. First, some 'one nation' Conservative prime ministers – for example, Baldwin and Macmillan – were in favour of planning. Even the Conservative governments of the 1980s and 1990s, so distinctive in their insistence that markets should decide where transport investment would take place, included more interventionist ministers such as Michael Heseltine, who introduced the 'planning' devices of Urban Development Corporations with their consequences for travel and transport. Second, across the political spectrum doubts have accumulated about the value of trying to predict and prescribe patterns of land and transport use. It has been increasingly difficult since the early 1970s to propose credible long-term transport plans, and to impose them on an informed public. There was a serious loss of confidence in planning and among planners in the mid-1970s when urban motorways, inner-city redevelopment and the destruction of historic buildings came under challenge from a broad range of groups from community activists to conservation societies.

The 1947 Town and Country Planning Act, which laid the foundations of the current planning system, had represented for many who demand an 'integrated transport policy' the ideal basis at local level, since it asked local authorities to set out in some detail their expectations for land use over the following decade. But rapid and unforecast changes in population and road use in the 1950s made such plans out of date almost before they were formally approved. The Buchanan Report on *Traffic in Towns* in 1963, and reactions to it, showed not only the unrealistic nature of the planning system, but also called into question the assumption that plans could or should meet transport demand. A transport plan, it was now clear, was not a technical document but a political choice. That realization was reinforced when it became evident in the 1980s that road space could no longer be provided to accommodate all the traffic growth forecast. It was further substantiated by the conclusion of the Standing Advisory Committee on Trunk Road Assessment that new road infrastructure could generate additional journeys (SACTRA, 94). That finding was particularly crucial because of the environmental aims agreed by the government at the Rio Earth Summit in 1992. These environmental objectives would seem to give a new lease of life to planners. However, as Brindley, Rydin and Stoker point out, the risk element in environmental planning itself precludes any certainty in planning (1996: 195).

Since the Town and Country Planning Act 1971, local authorities have not been expected to be specific in prescribing land use. The details of planning legislation vary over time, but essentially authorities prepare land-use plans, which include their main transport strategies for coping with problems that might arise. The structure plan must take account of any national and regional strategic 'guidance' issued by the Secretary of State for the Environment (the Planning Policy Guidance and Regional Planning Guidance notes described in the previous chapter), and accommodate any transport projects proposed by the Transport Minister. Arrangements are slightly different in Scotland from those in England and Wales because the local government structure is different, the Scottish Office (eventually perhaps the Scottish Parliament) exercises central government's responsibilities, and the key legal documents are enacted separately. But the general principles are the same.

Highways authorities (counties and unitary authorities) prepare an annual Transport Policy and Programme (TPP) for the following one-year and five-year periods, which implement the transport strategies set out in the structure plans (though central approval for their spending implications is something of a gamble). By assuming the future is uncertain, structure plans and TPPs now avoid the trap of the land-use plans of the 1950s. But their objectives have, correspondingly, to be couched in terms of high generality to accommodate a wide range of possible outcomes. Unless the council is very determined indeed to implement particular land-use and transport policies, it is more likely to follow development than to plan for it.

Under recent Conservative governments, ministers' guidance was either minimal or more about what councils should not do than what they should do. Regional guidance was absent in South-East England for much of the 1980s, until it was reinstated following an initiative by the local authorities (Brindley, Rydin and Stoker, 1989: 53). DoE Circulars in 1983 and 1985 and regional guidance to London boroughs in 1989 told authorities not to hinder developers by asking for 'planning gains' as a condition of granting planning permission (for example, junction improvements or subsidized bus services). The fragmentation implied by a multitude of local plans and weak national guidance was accompanied by a 'fragmentation of planning styles', as Brindley, Rydin and Stoker termed it, because authorities responded to 'Thatcherism' with a variety of planning strategies, according to their own attitude to market processes (critical or supportive) and the level of attractiveness of their locality to private investors (ibid. 7–13). But Secretaries of State can equally well use their powers of guidance and oversight to specify policies more closely, or to specify a different transport strategy – for example, one requiring high levels of public transport provision. Whatever the ultimate content of an integrated transport policy may turn out to be, the essential instruments of such a policy, which have been fashioned since the Second World War, remain on the statute book. But they were little used between 1979 and 1997 except to curb planning where it interfered with the initiatives of the private sector, or to facilitate major transport projects to which the government was committed – and especially those like the London Underground's Jubilee Line Extension and the Channel Tunnel Rail Link which were required by or for the private sector.

The patchwork quilt of local plans, tied together by central strategic guidance and voluntary cooperation between councils, was the nearest approach to a national transport strategy that Conservative governments between 1979 and 1997 could accept. Yet even this low-key attempt at planning transport is undermined by extraction or omission from the local planning process of schemes with a big transport impact, without them simultaneously being integrated into a wider national strategy.

These omissions concern, first, the Enterprise Zones and Urban Development Corporations, provided for under the Local Government, Planning and Land Act 1980. They are areas where, almost by definition, traffic growth is expected to take place. Yet they were deliberately freed from local authorities' land-use and transport planning so their development could not be restricted by regulations and by local politicians and bureaucrats. Local authorities themselves request the creation of an Enterprise Zone, so they should have considered the effect on travel patterns; but the nature of the development that took place in the 1980s, especially the rapid growth of warehousing and hypermarkets, caught many councils by surprise. Urban Development Corporations, on the other hand, while seeking to attract the maximum private investment by the minimum of regulation, nevertheless relied heavily on government intervention for transport infrastructure investment, especially in the London Docklands. The irrationality in technical terms of some of this investment, such as the

Limehouse Link road, 'considered the most expensive road ever built in Britain', or the Jubilee Line Extension's 'high-level poker game' over the ratio of public to private contributions, place these projects within a context of political commitment to an idea rather than within a context of national transport planning (Brindley, Rydin and Stoker, 1996: 202; Newman and Thornley, 1996: 138).

The second set of omissions from local plans are the largest transport infrastructure projects, such as major road schemes, railway lines or extensions, new airport terminals, the Channel Tunnel and its rail and road links. They will have a far-reaching effect on land use and the environment both in space and in time and are therefore properly decided at regional or national level. However, there is serious criticism of the way these projects have been divorced from a national debate on the overall direction and content of a national transport strategy, whatever the party in power. Discussion is confined to the project alone, not its place in a national air, road and rail transport policy. Moreover the debate responds to individual projects that public and private investors have decided to bring into being, not what might have been. It could be argued it therefore responds to identified demand, through the private sector searching for profit, or from the public's complaints about congestion or environmental nuisance. But it means that public debate about transport policy is fragmented into a series of arguments around a number of large infrastructure investments. Public participation in strategic transport decisions that are not related to a specific site is very limited.

In the absence of more coherent arrangements for debating priorities for a national transport policy, the procedures for deciding large transport projects are therefore highly important, because the discussions they precipitate – at public inquiries, at protests and demonstrations, in Parliament and in the media – have become by default the nearest approach Britain has known to a public debate about the goals of transport planning on a national scale. Even if there is in the future an integrated transport policy, decisions about major transport projects will continue to be an important test of its practical application and acceptability.

Planning by public inquiry

Most large transport projects, or land development projects with a significant impact on transport patterns, are resolved by local public inquiry followed by ministerial decision. For transport projects an independent inspector is nominated by the Lord Chancellor (the government minister who appoints judges), and appointed jointly by the Secretaries of State for the Environment and Transport (or by the Secretary for the Environment, Transport and the Regions in the combined structure). Planning applications to local councils for development projects to which the council objects, such as out-of-town shopping centres, are also examined at an inquiry, but the inquiry is held by a department planning inspector and the decision made formally by the Environment Minister, even if the main local concern is about transport. A large development project will probably be 'called in' by the minister for decision at national level, even if the council would approve it. If the developer is a statutory transport undertaking, the environment and transport ministers will decide jointly – as, for example, on the application by BAA to construct a fifth terminal at Heathrow.

The inspector hears witnesses and reports to the appropriate minister(s) on the objections, other proposals, and technical assessments of traffic, economic and environmental impact offered by transport civil servants and other witnesses. The report recommends whether the road project or development application should be accepted, perhaps with modifications, and sometimes suggests a different solution. Ministers may take decades to make the difficult and controversial decisions, as for the A34 bypass around Newbury, deferring time after time to 'relook at the evidence'.

Public consultation

Public consultation before the line of a proposed road project is announced is not mandatory. DoT officials consult as they think fit with interested parties while they are drawing up various solutions to the perceived road problem. Consultation may be extensive; the design project for dualling the A2 between Lydden and Dover included an exhibition, leaflets, questionnaires and advertisements in the local press. In contrast, the fast-track procedure was used for the A5 Kilsby Diversion in Northampton-shire; that is, there was no public consultation period before the department's preferred route was published.

Although the fast-track procedure leaves less time for opposition to be organized, it can provoke more confrontation. The draft order stage comes too late for meaningful participation by residents, landowners, amenity and conservation groups in the decision, since the department will not find it easy to accept that the route it has already selected is not the best. Barbara Bryant summarizes this point clearly in *Twyford Down*, when she notes that 'the time to alter decisions is before they are made' (1996: viii). Opponents will already be critical of the department over the loss of local consultation on alternative routes. John MacGregor, Secretary of State for Transport 1992–4, suggested in 1993 that the 'fast-track procedure' should be used more often to cut delays in construction. But one reason local authorities build roads more quickly than central government is that they are more likely to take consultation seriously, to clear away objections so a project does not have to go through the public inquiry stage. The Horsham northern bypass built in the 1990s did not go to public inquiry, because the potential objections were resolved.

Council officers assert that local projects arouse less conflict because councillors, implicated in the scheme from the start and accountable to a local electorate, take care to build up support and show they are making progress. The chairs of county transport committees and county surveyors regard it as part of their job to enter into debate and ward off dissent at public meetings. In contrast ministers and MPs rarely attend meetings on national schemes in village halls, and civil servants with a knowledge of the scheme would be uncomfortable about commenting on a minister's political choice. Government departments respond that they have more problems because their projects are bigger than local governments' (though the £11m Horsham bypass was bigger than many national schemes; the government defines 'larger schemes' as over £3m). Yet central government could apply similar strategies. For example, there was much activity by road protesters in the early 1990s over the construction of the M11 to Hackney Wick link road in East London. The government could have emphasized the advantages of the new road for people in the estates alongside the project area, where life had been made intolerable by drivers trying to avoid the existing, congested trunk road. The government could have considered associated schemes to build up the community currently split by these rat-runs, improving conditions for 14 000 homes, thus putting the destruction of 400 homes and street trees into perspective.

Nevertheless, councils too have outstanding projects where objections cannot be resolved because the community is evenly split for and against the project, and the mutually-acceptable solutions are too expensive to contemplate – a classic DoT problem. But councils seem to be more conciliatory, flexible and imaginative than government departments in their efforts to resolve the problem, perhaps because they are more in contact with the neighbourhoods and the people they serve.

The public inquiry

A public inquiry is 'a participatory process which, depending on your viewpoint, allows all information to be considered before a rational planning decision is reached, *or* allows all interests to be heard and involved in debate before a mediated conclusion is reached. . . . But the constraints of structure are more apparent than the mediation' (Rydin, 1993: 236). As a result of organized disruption by objectors to urban roads inquiries in the mid-1970s, restrictions have been placed on who may participate in public inquiries and what matters can be challenged (Wistrich, 1983: 104–9; Truelove, 1992: 142–3).

Following a Review of Highways Inquiry Procedures in 1978, the right to give evidence as a 'statutory objector' has been confined to those with a direct property interest (DoT and DoE, 1978). A pre-inquiry meeting takes place between inspector and major players to discuss the inquiry's agenda, and help the inspector decide which non-statutory objectors, such as representatives of environmental groups, will be heard, a procedure that both facilitates and controls participation. The planning inspector examining the case for Terminal Five (T5), for instance, selected as witnesses 1000 individuals and 70 representatives of airlines, airport operators, local businesses, trades unions and local groups opposing the proposals such as HACAN and FHANG (see Chapter 5).

Witnesses may raise issues only about the project which is the subject of the inquiry, not national transport policy, nor roads policy, nor national traffic forecasts, nor even some scheme of which the project forms a part. Objectors have argued that the practice of holding inquiries on short sections of a large scheme means the whole scheme and its potential effect on traffic movement, the generation of new traffic, and the environment are not properly evaluated (for instance, the North Circular Road through London suburbs, or the proposed widening of the M25 orbital route round London). The Transport Research Laboratory's survey of the impact of the 1989 Okehampton bypass, which went through the Dartmoor National Park, said that the environmental assessment of the project should have formed part of an appraisal of the whole route corridor, rather than being limited to the road (TRL, 1997). Approval for a controversial scheme, such as the stretch of the M3 that cuts through Twyford Down, may be given because it is the last connecting link in a route whose general need is not in dispute, whereas an earlier consideration of the whole route might have produced a less destructive scheme.

The 1976 consultation document on *Transport Policy* by the combined Department of Environment and Transport recognized in its conclusion the viewpoint and strength of the roads objectors: 'Central and local government must therefore set themselves a clear environmental objective when taking transport decisions' (Wistrich, 1983: 116). It suggested that annual White Papers should set out road construction policies and programmes and explain the thinking behind them. This was intended to overcome the difficulty that national roads policy was seen by the public as a legitimate topic for every local inquiry because it was not debated in Parliament. But though *Policy for Roads* in 1980 contained a substantial discussion of policy issues, the subsequent papers on the roads programme produced every few years have been little more than a list of schemes, organized by regions or (in 1994) by order of priority. SACTRA (1986) recommended the public inquiry process be divided into a first stage, which would consider the broader need for the scheme, and a second stage to consider the detail; but the idea was dismissed by the government as impracticable.

The court-like atmosphere of the inquiry is another constraint on real participation of all those affected by a scheme. To present an effective case against the technical and legal expertise of departments or developers, environmental groups and other objectors have had to take on professional advisers and lawyers. The 'inquiry' has become an expensive adversarial argument between experts, for and against the department's road scheme, the new airport runway or terminal. Local community groups can feel sidelined and that their case has not been heard. On the other hand, local objectors have an advantage when the benefit from a project is spread thinly and widely, because they can be coordinated and represented at the inquiry better than the project's beneficiaries (NEDC, 1992: 3; 23). The advantages of road schemes and airport expansion accrue to members of the travelling public, who individually have much less interest in debating the project than those whose homes are affected. In the T5 case, BAA encouraged the formation of the Heathrow Airport Support Group of business travellers, and organizations in the travel and construction industries, to put the case for airport development, as a counterbalance to residents' groups and councils who can claim they represent a large number of objectors.

Proposals for changes to a more participatory and compensatory approach to infrastructure decisions (for example NEDC, 1992) have in recent years produced some positive response from central government on compensation. Not implemented was a proposal by the DoE and the DoT that feasible alternatives revealed at the public consultation stage should be worked up in more detail and presented to the inquiry (DoE and DoT, 1978). (A similar procedure to that permitted for planning applications for buildings.) The inquiry itself would then be more like an examining magistrate process in which the inspector considered the evidence for a small number of options, avoiding the impression that the Highways Agency imposes 'its' route. It would encourage objectors to consider the advantages and disadvantages of each option on an equal basis. Development costs would not necessarily be more expensive, because highways engineers (the Agency or its consultants) probably already consider multiple proposals internally before recommending a preferred route publicly, and the cost of appeals and further public inquiries into alternative routes would be saved. However, this approach has the disadvantage of spreading planning blight more widely;

for example, there were loud protestations when British Rail published a wide corridor for several possible routes for the Channel Tunnel Rail Link. It would need to be balanced by more generous compensation payments.

The Planning and Compensation Act 1991 allowed government to pay 10 per cent above market value to owner-occupiers, though not to landowners or those whose property lies near but not on the route. The extra expense could be justified as representing the market price of an individual's disturbance for the sake of the general good, and would be offset by savings in the inquiry process (NEDC, 1992: 55). Such payments would reduce local resistance in some cases. For instance, a substantial part of the protest about disturbing the ancient Oxleas Wood for the East Thames River Crossing came from a nearby estate. Before its incorporation into the DETR, the DoT demonstrated publicly its reluctance to extend the grounds for compensation, in case expensive precedents were formed. It ignored the Parliamentary Ombudsman's advice on settling claims by people particularly seriously disturbed by works connected with the Channel Tunnel. The department was obliged to revise its guidelines on discretionary purchase of houses affected by planning blight, after it lost a case in the Court of Appeal, and had to pay compensation in 24 cases previously refused (*HC Debs*, 20 March 1996: 207).

But increased levels of compensation would not resolve objections where the issues are about environment, history and landscape (such as the cutting through Twyford Down, or across National Trust land at the Devil's Punchbowl and Hindhead Common in Surrey), rather than personal concerns about the loss of tranquillity or property value.

After the inquiry the minister is entirely free to reject the inspector's recommendations. Inspectors at two public inquiries in the 1980s into the controversial East Thames River Crossing endorsed the general route but recommended there should be a cut-and-cover tunnel under Oxleas Wood on the south bank. Successive ministers rejected this modification on grounds of cost, though one inspector estimated it would be about £10m – a small sum compared with £300m for the total project (1989 prices). However, the view of department officials was the tunnel would cost more than £10m and would have only limited environmental value

– because the wood would have been structurally damaged even if it appeared on the surface to be intact. Moreover, half the planned junction would be lost.

Objectors can appeal through the legal system (including the European Court of Justice) against the Secretary of State's decision. Residents brought actions in the High Court claiming the government had not carried out a proper environmental assessment of the damage to Oxleas Wood, and that land offered in exchange was inadequate. Some statutory bodies have powers to take their objections to Parliament. The National Trust threatened to ask Parliament to scrutinize the compulsory purchase of its land on the Devil's Punchbowl and Hindhead Common; the government then decided to provide a tunnel. If a preferred road route is altered, as in these examples, the process of inquiry to hear objections begins again.

Environmental impact assessment

For the objectors to trunk road-building through sites of high environmental value, European Union requirements for environmental impact assessment may provide a more comprehensive defence against future projects than they have had before. To comply with the Directive 85/337/EEC agreed between governments in 1985, ministers have had since 1988 to issue an environmental statement for all projects 'likely to have a significant effect on the environment'. Similar provisions for environmental assessment apply to local government and private-sector projects (such as toll roads, light rail projects, ports and airports).

An environmental assessment should be produced at every stage of a project, its level of detail being appropriate to the stage. Moreover the Directive expects an environmental assessment to be made for the whole transport project, not just individual tranches, which will make it easier for environmental groups at a local inquiry to discuss the broader effect of a section of a project. The environmental statement on widening the M40 to Heathrow section of the M25 would address not only that section but the whole scheme (that is, the total impact of altering all sections of the M25 transport ministers had planned to widen). Section 105A of the amended Highways Act 1980 requires the statement to include all information that can 'reasonably' be gathered on environmental factors likely to be affected by the project, 'the measures envisaged in order to avoid, reduce and, if possible, remedy significant adverse effects', and the data required to assess the main effects on the environment. The information must be published in a non-technical summary appropriate for the general public.

DoT officials have said the 'work involved had been an integral part of the Department's procedures since the mid-1970s' (in submission to NEDC, 1992: 33). Other officials have noted that the DoT has carried out 'proper appraisal' in accordance with its Manual of Environmental Appraisal published in 1983 (before the Directive). It is surprising therefore that the British government was reluctant to adopt the Directive, and the department unwilling to apply it to schemes already in its roads programme, and to infrastructure proposals approved through the private bill process (Newman and Thornley, 1996: 119; Rydin, 1993: 67; 209). The DoT interpreted the Directive in a narrow way as meaning that a project whose draft road scheme had been published before July 1988 did not need an environmental statement, even if it had yet to be discussed at a public inquiry or to be decided by the minister after that date. This definition removed from the Directive's obligations some contentious projects of the 1990s such as Twyford Down, the East Thames River Crossing, and the Newbury bypass. For some years the European Commission argued with the British government over this interpretation, suggesting the Directive had not been correctly incorporated into national law. However, in October 1995 the Commission announced its decision to agree with the DoT's interpretation, in the light of a ruling of the European Court of Justice. In particular, the Newbury bypass and the M77 in Scotland were, it said, not subject to the Directive, as 'lengthy consent procedures' had started well before July 1988. The UK government and the DoT had clearly won the legal argument with the Commission but it said little for their 'green' credentials.

Yvonne Rydin thought the experience of the first years of the Directive was support for it having 'at least some marginal impact' (1993: 210). Its more recent effect on transport projects is hard to judge, partly because budget cutbacks have been a more significant factor, and partly because negotiations between the government and the EU Environment Commissioner are confidential, and sometimes political in character. The DoT has never lost a legal challenge in respect of environmental appraisal. But it abandoned in July 1993 the East Thames River Crossing and its route though Oxleas Wood rather than allow the politically damaging controversy over this hugely unpopular scheme to continue while it settled its debate with the Commission (the warning letter sent by the Commissioner in April 1993 was not published). The Commission relinquished its objections to the Twyford Down cutting, but Peter Kunzlik has shown clearly that political bargaining between the UK government and the Commission was as important on this issue as the legal and environmental arguments (see his contribution to Bryant, 1996: 225–94).

Greater impact could come from implementation of the intention many saw in the Directive, and recommended too by SACTRA in 1992, of bringing in environmental assessment 'at the transport policy stage, and certainly before the Roads Programme was formulated. In this way, transport provisions to meet the nation's economic, social and environmental needs could be debated to ensure that a better balance was achieved between these important elements' – the view of the Council for the Protection for Rural England (submission to NEDC, 1992: 31; see also SACTRA, 1992). The Commission has made proposals for a strategic environmental assessment directive (COM (96) 511, 4 December 1996) but it remains to be seen when, and in what terms, these will be enacted by the Council of Ministers.

Planning by parliamentary bill or order

Until the introduction of the Transport and Works Act 1992, the planning of new rail infrastructure was treated differently in law from roads, since corporations such as British Rail and London Underground obtained planning consent for new infrastructure, such as the Jubilee Line extension, through Parliament's Private Bill procedure. Public hearings before a Private Bill committee in the Commons in effect replaced the public inquiry. This system was reformed in 1992 in response to complaints by backbenchers about the amount of their time taken up by such bills, and the backlog building up because of the surge of interest in urban rail schemes.

In England and Wales the Transport and Works Act 1992 brought the procedures for authorizing public transport projects nearer to those for roads. (In Scotland the Private Bill procedure will still be used). The Act gave power to the Secretary of State for Transport to agree the building and operation of small-scale rail projects. A 'negative procedure' order is laid before Parliament, and one of the houses would have to pass a resolution against the order to annul it, a rare occurrence, but one which provides some safeguard. Projects of 'national significance' are, on the other hand, required to have Parliament's positive consent; the proposals in the developer's application must be approved by both houses. If approval is given, the constructor will normally be required to seek detailed planning permission from the local authority, though the Secretary of State can decide it is not required. In addition the Secretary of State must consider objections from the public in deciding whether to hold an inquiry, and if a local authority objects to the proposals the minister must hold an inquiry.

Under the parliamentary bill procedure statutory consultation is restricted to the petitioning of parliament. The power to appeal is not insignificant. About 290 objectors presented petitions to the House of Lords on the Channel Tunnel Rail Link Bill (*HL Debs*, 21 May 1996: 767). Public hearings are available to those directly affected. Yet however intimidated individual objectors might be by a local public inquiry, they would need to be even more determined and well-organized to take their views to a parliamentary committee (Truelove, 1992). Planning through legislative procedures also has the disadvantage that small concessions made to petitioners (for example, on noise reduction measures) run the risk of setting a legal precedent. The Treasury scrutinizes bills carefully for these problems. Flexibility is therefore reduced.

Under the pre-1992 Private Bill (or hybrid bill) procedure Parliament had to confine itself to discussing the route presented by the developer or minor modifications, not raise alternative proposals. Under the Transport and Works Act Parliament will be expected to discuss the 'general features' of a major project and endorse (or reject) it in principle; the details will be discussed at the public inquiry if one is held; the final decision will be made by the Secretary of State (see DoT, 1992c). The practice may turn out differently if parliamentarians interest themselves in the details, though they may be ruled out of order. But local objectors will find it more difficult to sustain their protest if Parliament has given overwhelming endorsement to a scheme of national significance.

Though road and rail planning have long shared some essential features, the effect of the Transport and Works Act will be to put major rail projects on the same planning terms as major roads projects. Indeed, some peers accused the government of having avoided using for the Channel Tunnel Rail Link bill the Transport and Works Act 'which provides for planning inquiries pretty much like normal planning and conservation law in the case of railway works'. Using the hybrid bill procedure for the CTRL removed the protection of conservation law and inquiries from the historic buildings and gasholders at St Pancras and King's Cross (Lord Kennet, *HL Debs*, 21 May 1996: 810). The first 'positive approval' order under the Transport and Works Act was on an application made by Central Railways plc on 22 May 1996. The Secretary of State announced on 24 May that he had decided to submit it to parliament for debate; it was rejected by the Commons on 24 July by 172 votes to 7 on a free vote. Given such disapproval in Parliament it would be difficult for Central Railways to find strong endorsement at a local inquiry, or indeed further financial backing. Several small schemes had been approved by the 'negative procedure' within the first three years of the Act coming into force, and four cases had been examined at a public inquiry: one, the Usk barrage, had been rejected by the Secretary of State for Wales, and three (two relating to Manchester Metrolink extensions, one to the East London line) had been decided by the Secretary of State for Transport by February 1997.

The New Roads and Streetworks Act 1991 is a 'corollary' of the order-making principle in the Transport and Works Act, extending it to new 'special roads' (roads such as motorways that can be restricted to certain classes of traffic), meeting the government's desire for speedier approval and completion of road schemes than through public inquiries. It permits the granting of concessions to private firms to design, build, and run new motorways in return for toll (or shadow toll) income. The first road project to be authorized under this Act was the private-sector Birmingham Northern Relief Road, submitted to public consultation after the Memorandum of Agreement between the government and the developers in April 1991 and before the concession agreement in March 1992, and given what appeared to be the definite go-ahead by the Labour Secretary of State, John Prescott, in July 1997.

Coordination of transport planning

Much of this discussion has emphasized the fragmentation of planning between central government and multiple local governments, quasi-autonomous Enterprise Zones and Urban Development Corporations, and the substitution of argument over individual transport projects for coherent, comprehensive public debate over national planning for transport and the environment. The account needs to be balanced by a recognition of the coordination, or potential for coordination, which exists at local, regional and national levels.

Local authorities

Coordination between local authority transport and development policies can be encouraged by central government-imposed rules, especially on structure plans and local plans, and on Transport Policies and Programmes (TPPs). Guidance from the centre on planning was weak in the 1980s though it strengthened during the early 1990s under different ministers, and under the impact of the environmental agenda. But firmer recent planning guidance and central rules on transport planning for the environment – such as 'the package approach' in devising schemes that would attract transport funding (see Chapter 6) – may have more to do with persuading authorities to adopt policies approved by central government than with the desirability of improved coordination for its own sake. However, a new spirit of cooperation between central and local government was starting to emerge at the end of the Major government, as expressed in *Transport: The Way Forward*, in response to pressure on departmental budgets and in recognition of local government's greater ability to deliver the Rio Summit's 'Agenda 21' programme. The political congruence in the late 1990s between the majority party in Westminster and the largest party in local government is likely to ease relationships still further.

But more significant is councils' collaboration with each other, for example in the standing regional planning conferences of local authorities which advise the Secretary of State on regional guidance. The 'Houghton Report' of the Royal Commission on Environmental Pollution recommended that these conferences should be the site for deciding major road proposals that crossed council boundaries. Some councils deliberately work on transport strategy in tandem with other neighbouring authorities, outside the statutory framework. For example, East Anglian counties have coordinated their roads strategy since the early 1980s. These initiatives by local authorities reflect the practical need for a long-term and larger-scale approach to transport planning for which the machinery central government provides has proved inadequate. By themselves they do not answer the problem of coordinating transport investment, or coordinating transport with other policy areas, such as hospitals or tertiary education, for which local government is not responsible.

Regional coordination

Metropolitan authorities were set up in 1974 specifically to coordinate at strategic level the planning and provision of services in conurbations at a scale appropriate for transport. Joint working arrangements have been developed among the Metropolitan Districts and London Boroughs to deal with transport and the environment, nevertheless the joint working arrangements are far from ideal (Travers, Biggs, Jones, 1995). The efforts of their Passenger Transport Authorities to plan for and coordinate transport services were further undermined and complicated by deregulation of bus services and privatization of rail.

Evidence on the quality of coordination within the long-established joint DoE–DoT regional offices was always hard to establish with certainty. In the early 1990s DoE and DoT London region offices said they worked better together than did their respective colleagues outside London (Burnham, Jones, Travers, 1992) but even so, DoE–DoT strategic guidance for Greater London did not truly integrate advice on land-use planning and transport, appending maps from one department to development planning advice from the other (DoE, 1989). In 1994 these offices were recast on a grander scale, on the initiative – at ministerial level – of Michael Heseltine (Newman and Thornley, 1996: 124) to bring together officials from four departments, including Transport (see Chapter 3). The Government Offices were to work together on regeneration schemes, at the same time continuing to administer their conventional regional programmes. In *Transport: The Way Forward*, the Government Offices were proposed as the focus for coordinating and channelling to ministers the opinion of local authorities on what Regional Planning Guidance should comprise, as a way of improving the integration of transport infrastructure and land-use planning (DoT, 1996b: Annex 1). Together with the impetus to regional cooperation given by the EC's structural funds, and proposals by Labour and Liberal Democrat parties for eventual regional governments, these offices and the regional planning conferences could form part of the core around which regional consideration of transport policy coalesces.

National level

Even before the bringing together of the Departments of Transport and the Environment in the DETR of 1997, the interdepartmental boundaries between the DoT and DoE seem to have been breaking down with the growth of environmental concern. The DoT was more likely than in the past to ask broader questions about the effect of transport policies on the community and to consider issues which crossed intra- and inter-departmental boundaries. In 1990 it created a London Coordination Unit to treat these themes (though it quickly disappeared in the next restructuring). Its traffic policy and transport policy divisions considered issues beyond the bounds of the stereotypical departmental remit; for example: whether local authorities would retain the income from urban road-pricing and what effect this might or should have on local government financing arrangements; and the effects of transport policies on the environment and vice versa. Signs of change could be seen in the joint submission by DoE and DoT (1992) to the Royal Commission on Environmental Pollution, the joint advice to local authorities in PPG13 on how the land-use planning system can be used to bring about development patterns that reduce the need to travel and thus the use of fuel (DoE and DoT, 1994; and see Chapter 6), and in the much greater recognition of environmental issues in *Transport: The Way Forward* (DoT, 1996b). It remains to be seen whether good intentions will be translated into well-balanced decisions in controversial planning cases. The lessons of the recent past suggest that too often when decisions have to be made, out-of-town shopping centres and new roads tend to go ahead despite all that is said about better coordination between transport and land-use planning, and the need to safeguard the environment. The first decisions on major roads schemes by the Secretary of State for Environment, Transport and the Regions, especially the 'green light' for the Birmingham Northern Relief Road were no less bitterly criticized by environmentalists because the political motive appeared to be budgetary rather than ideological support for private toll roads.

Parliament has seemed to many reformers the ideal democratic location for debating and deciding a national roads policy and programme. Indeed this solution was assumed by the government itself in its 1976 consultation document: *Transport Policy* (DoE, 1976). The NEDC Construction Industry Sector Group's 'new approach to road planning' assigned Parliament a central role in legislating for a national, rolling, ten-year Transport Plan, covering 'all aspects of transport provision and need' (NEDC, 1992: 43). Yet despite the serious interest taken in transport issues by a few MPs, the procedures and habits of Westminster do not encourage sustained attention from a large core of parliamentarians. The normal legislative procedures of Parliament could not be guaranteed to settle the debate on a transport plan to public satisfaction unless some other forum had first established that it was very widely accepted by the public. The Act implementing rail privatization was passed by Parliament only because some Conservative MPs who had spoken against rail privatization in public put aside their reasoned arguments to vote for rail privatization in the cause of maintaining their party in government. In similar circumstances the political objectives of a transport policy would be queried at every public inquiry as they are at present. People are not persuaded that central government has listened just because an issue has been debated in Parliament; those closely affected by a project do not find it acceptable just because it has democratic credentials of a superficial kind at national level.

The Transport Select Committee has been proposed as a suitable preparatory forum, for instance by the National Economic Development Council's Vaizey Committee (NEDC, 1984). Departmental select committees are seen as cross-party, since they do not automatically have a government majority or government chair. They do not have government ministers as members, and their activities are less dominated by party whips than are standing, legislative committees. But, apart from the older Public Accounts Committee, select committees do not have much prestige. They are poorly resourced in money and expertise, their reports are rarely debated by Parliament and have had little impact on ministerial thinking. Andrew Adonis (1993: 150–76) summarizes the evidence. The transport committee's handling of rail privatization shows it should not be underestimated as a serious investigative body, which can explore and improve subsidiary aspects of sensitive topics (see Chapter 5). But it did so by accepting the basic premiss of rail privatization. The committee is at its best when examining limited topics that can command wide political support, such as the safety of roll-on, roll-off ferries. In short the Transport Select Committee, like Parliament itself, is not a suitable, nor a powerful enough body.

The Cabinet is the only body within the British political system with the authority and power to decide and impose a transport strategy. National transport programmes and policies, like county TPPs, cannot be apolitical. They reflect the views of the political leaders of the day. Transport programmes, because of their highly technical content, are easily assumed to be objective and ideology-free. Yet there is no ideal transport policy, or even an ideal roads programme on which all will agree, but a variety of possibilities each of which would help bring about a different array of economic and social goals. To ask what the roads programme is for is to ask a political question. The collective judgment and responsibility of the Cabinet must be engaged in reconciling the political, economic and social goals of transport policy.

Though a final decision would be promoted by the Secretary of State with the primary responsibility for transport, the support of the Cabinet as a whole is crucial. For any minister's policy to succeed, Treasury ministers have to be as committed as others to allowing spending to be directed in line with policy. But there are particular problems facing a Transport Secretary who decides to implement a roads or transport plan, because of the long timescale needed to build infrastructure and to change travel patterns. The political decision would need governmental support at the highest level over an unusually long period. But the political system thinks of a four-or five-year maximum period between elections, and parliaments cannot constitutionally bind their successors. There can be no guarantee a subsequent parliament, even one dominated by the leaders of the same party, will not reverse the decisions of its predecessor, as in the 1992 budget for London Underground.

A baser reason for acknowledging that transport programmes must be decided at the highest political level is that, however independent and expert a forum is, and however widespread the public support for its recommendations, if the government does not like the political effect of the recommendations it will not implement them. Reports from Commissions and Committees will be followed up by political argument. The reality is shown in microcosm by ministers' decisions after a planning inquiry that do not reflect the inspector's report. Examinations of 'big transport projects' (for example, Banister (1994) on the Third London Airport, and Bryant (1996) on Twyford Down) reveal a transport policy-making system which does not in practice match up to the technical, economic and procedurally rational arguments that appear in public documents.

Conclusion

The Conservative governments of the 1980s and 1990s had other preoccupations which were not conducive to planning-led policy-making. In particular they were concerned to bring market pressures to bear on the provision of transport services through policies designed to give maximum scope to private enterprise which, when freed from the shackles of bureaucratic control, was expected to deliver better services at keener prices. The need for regulation in the interests of safety and the orderly management of a competitive market-place was accepted, but there was little room for planning, since it was assumed that this was more likely to inhibit than to assist the provision of the services which the market would deliver best with the minimum of interference.

The declarations of ministers about 'markets' and 'choice' gave a *laisser-faire* appearance to the transport planning system that faithfully reflected their ideological approach, but the absence of a national transport plan did not mean the absence of central government control over transport programmes. The DoT determined to a very large extent the distribution of public expenditure on transport not only by the department, but also by nationalized industries, privatized rail and local authorities (see Chapter 8). Much new legislation gave the Secretary of State powers to appoint individuals (such as the Traffic Director for London) and give them instructions. 'The Secretary of State shall issue to . . . the Traffic Director guidance with respect to the management of traffic in London . . . Any such guidance may (a) include provisions setting out the Secretary of State's objectives . . . (b) be varied at any time by the Secretary of State' (Road Traffic Act, 1991: S.51). The Secretary of State for Transport, usually with the Secretary of State for the Environment, made the decisions on most major transport projects. Whether under Conservative 'non-planning' or Labour 'integration' much coordination takes place at all levels; and decisions on big transport projects are always significant.

The combining of the two departments into DETR should improve coordination between transport officials and environment officials. Brindley, Rydin and Stoker (1996) found that local authorities too have come closer in their planning styles than they were in the 1980s, probably for pragmatic and temporary reasons, the remaining differences depending chiefly on the state of their economy and infrastructure. The current 'planning assumptions', such as the value of public–private partnerships, are very widely shared. Relationships between levels of government, mediated in some circumstances by regional offices, are becoming less one-sided. So the conditions for deciding and promoting a truly national transport policy have improved. There was evidence in *Transport: The Way Ahead* that central government had identified many of the issues that would be raised by the evaluation of transport policies at the strategic level. The chorus of disappointment that greeted the more formal sequel, *Transport: The Way Forward*, bore eloquent testimony to the widespread conviction that tinkering with the planning procedures whilst relying on the market to provide transport services would not procure the coherent transport policy – flexible, affordable, environmentally acceptable – the public looks to government to deliver. The concept of an integrated transport policy is attractive, though it will be hard to steer a course between a framework which is so loose as to be meaningless and one which so shackles the initiative and enterprise of the companies which now provide transport services that the benefits of privatization are lost.

Part IV

The Economic Framework

8 Sources of Finance

When Mrs Thatcher's Conservative government came to power in 1979 the road haulage industry and private vehicles were paid for by the private sector, as was shipping and much of the civil aviation industry; but large parts of the transport sector – buses and trains, roads and railways, ports and airports – were still wholly or largely owned and operated by agents of central or local government. In the case of roads construction and maintenance, finance also came from central or local government, and central or local government made substantial financial contributions to subsidize users of public transport. The Conservative administrations sought to disengage government from the transport sector: to privatize, to deregulate and to put residual administrative control in the hands of new, single-purpose bodies such as the Highways Agency and the Office of Passenger Rail Franchising. There has been a parallel policy of shifting responsibility for funding from the public to the private sector. Chapter 3 discussed the new administrative arrangements. This chapter outlines the responsibilities for funding that remain with central and local governments, and the new sources of private-sector finance.

Public finance

Department of the Environment, Transport and the Regions (DETR)

The DETR's annual budget, which now includes transport alongside housing, environment and support for local government, is determined within the context of the Cabinet committee on public expenditure, the baseline for negotiation being the figures agreed for Year Two in the previous annual exercise. Every year in the early summer the Treasury launches the expenditure round with an overall assessment of the government's financial position, which shows why the forthcoming expenditure round is going to be exceptionally difficult, requiring sacrifices from all departments. The Cabinet notes the position and endorses general guidelines for the bilateral negotiations between the Treasury and spending departments which follow. Two short papers are prepared during the summer recess, one by the department and one by the Treasury and neither more than a few pages in length. The department's paper is itself the outcome of hard-fought negotiations within the department among the proponents of the different blocks of expenditure, with the figures in the final paper being decided by the Secretary of State to reflect his or her judgment of priorities. The paper submitted to the expenditure committee makes the case for each major block of transport expenditure, such as new roads, road maintenance, support for transport expenditure by local authorities, and the requirements of London Regional Transport (LRT), concluding each section with an estimate of any change in the resources required by comparison with the baseline. Almost invariably the Treasury's companion paper makes a case for lower figures.

Ministers consider these papers in the committee during the early autumn and agree where to settle. Each spending minister attends the committee for discussion of his or her paper, even if not otherwise a member, but the presence of the Chancellor of the Exchequer in the chair and the Chief Secretary as hatchet man stack the odds pretty heavily against departmental spending ambitions, especially in circumstances where the government's reputation and perhaps its electoral fortunes depend on keeping spending in check so as to minimize the need to raise additional revenue from new or increased taxes. Moreover no individual spending minister has sufficient information about other departments to challenge the Treasury's overall assessment of the vital importance of securing savings on his or her departmental budget in order to meet the Cabinet's agreed target. A disappointed spending minister can insist on taking to full Cabinet a difference of opinion about the resources required, and in most years this gives rise to some intensive horse-trading in October and early November as the budget deadline approaches. Transport expenditure is seldom a high enough priority to figure in the endgame, and the Transport Minister rarely carries enough clout in Cabinet and ultimately with the Prime Minister to take the risk of a bruising encounter, almost certain humiliation and diminished career prospects. He or she is usually left trying to juggle the figures to meet the overall ceiling which the committee has set for transport by spreading the pain to minimize the damage to politically sensitive priorities.

The final outcome, announced to Parliament in the government's annual expenditure statement in November is divided into several votes (Highways Agency, transport industries, and so on). Each vote has sections (transport industries in 1996 included separate sums allocated to the LRT core business, the Jubilee Line extension, CrossRail and BR pensions). The sections change over the years; for an up-to-date list readers should look at DETR's annual report setting out the government's expenditure plans for transport (for example, DoT, 1997a, which is the source for figures here on the department's budget, unless otherwise stated). DETR cannot vire (that is, transfer) money between votes without going back to Parliament, but it can vire between sections of the same vote, such as between CrossRail and LRT, providing it informs the Treasury. DETR divides the National Roads budget between capital and current expenditure, and the capital budget between new roads and structural renewals.

The department and the vote-financed transport industries take great care to avoid overspending. Any overspend, however small, causes the permanent secretary (the top official) to face an uncomfortable hearing with the powerful Public Accounts Committee of the House of Commons. A substantial overspend will usually become apparent well before the end of the year and will require a transfer to the vote concerned from the departmental votes or from the reserve. When such a transfer is required, as it was for both BR and LRT in 1991–2 when the recession led to much lower levels of revenue than forecast a year earlier, the Treasury is put in a strong position to insist on unwelcome conditions not just for the current financial year in which the reserve contribution is needed, but also in the negotiations for the following year. In order to avoid these risks, the department and its industries err on the side of underspending, particularly in the early months of the financial year. Up to 3

per cent of any budget head can be carried forward from one
year to the next. But underspending is also risky since it invites
the Treasury to reduce the budget in subsequent expenditure
rounds. Modern on-line accounting has made budgetary management easier, but the department still tends to hold back spending in the early months of the financial year, and rush to spend
in the last quarter, in order to live within the tight constraints
of annual cash limits. This lack of flexibility in the current year,
allied to uncertainty about the availability of resources in subsequent years, means that many contracts have to be short, even
when longer ones would give better value for money. The potential savings cannot be quantified, but are among the benefits
which arise when finance can be moved into the private sector.

Central government support for roads

Spending on national roads increased sharply in real terms between 1989, when the Roads for Prosperity programme was announced, and 1991 (see Figure 8.1). It continued to rise until

**FIGURE 8.1   DoT spending on roads, in 1995–96 prices
(estimates from 1996–97)**

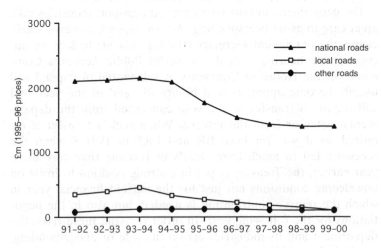

Source: DOT (1997a: 98).

1994. But the November 1995 budget forced the Secretary of State to announce a long postponement to a substantial number of priority schemes. The cutbacks were presented by the department as its recognition that building roads to meet demand was not environmentally or financially sound (DoT, 1996a: 38). DoT's spending on local roads was also cut. Comparing 1993–4 with the plans for 1998–99, there has been a cut of 40 per cent in the total roads budget.

However, these figures give a misleading impression of the quantity of physical roads investment which will be possible because of the rapid growth in privately-financed roads construction and maintenance. By August 1997 the go-ahead had been given for the tolled Birmingham Northern Relief Road and schemes which involve the construction or maintenance of 385 miles of trunk road. The capital value of these contracts is £750m (DoT, 1997b). If, as an approximation, this is averaged over a three-year period, the rate of spend of £250m a year goes a considerable way towards making good the decline, shown in Figure 8.1, between the 1995–96 spending on national roads and

FIGURE 8.2   DoT spending on public transport, in 1995–96 prices (estimates from 1996–97)

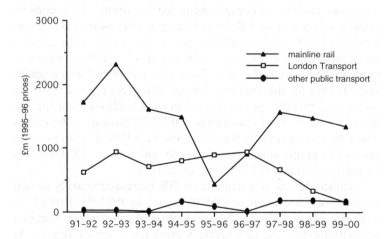

Source: DOT (1997a: 98).

TABLE 8.1   CAA's external financing limits in cash prices (estimates from 1996–97)

	1991–92	92–93	93–94	£ million 94–95	95–96	96–97	97–98	98–99	99–00
CAA's EFL	33	51	91	46	34	−13	−34	−39	−23
CAA investment	88	119	145	117	67	73	61	62	60

Source: DoT (1997a: 52).

1997–98 and later years. The full funding costs will not appear on the public accounts for several years. We return to private finance later in the chapter.

Central government support for transport industries

DETR's expenditure on public transport is mainly through LRT, still a conventional nationalized industry, and through the Rail Franchising Director (see Figure 8.2). The government funds nationalized industries, such as LRT, the Civil Aviation Authority (CAA) and British Rail before privatization, by setting 'external financing limits' (EFLs), the maximum level of government grants and loans they will allow them to spend above their income from trading. 'External financing requirements' (EFRs) are the outturn figures – the amount they actually used in grants and loans each year. London Regional Transport's EFL consists entirely of grant since LRT is not charged interest on loans. From 1997 the CAA will probably be able to pay back to the government more than it borrows to finance its air traffic control services; its EFL is thus shown in Table 8.1 from 1996–7 as a negative sum. Following the privatization of BR, passenger services by public and private operators have been subsidized from the Office of Passenger Rail Franchizing (OPRAF), funded on the money voted by parliament to the Department. OPRAF's support replaces the grants and loans previously given by the DoT directly to BR (see Glaister, 1995; and DoT, 1994).

Spending by the department on BR increased sharply in real terms from a low point in 1988 to a peak in 1992–93. Part of the peak was associated with the programme of construction required to accommodate the new services using the Channel Tunnel. As Figure 8.2 shows, public spending on mainline rail services then

TABLE 8.2 LRT external financing limits in cash prices (estimates from 1996–97)

	1991–92	92–93	93–94	94–95	95–96	96–97	97–98	98–99	99–00
				£ million					
Core business	489	800	572	370	442	386			
Jubilee Line Extension	55	57	70	383	447	425			
Core business plus JLE							679	310	151
Crossrail	11	26	50	30	14	7			
Croydon Tramlink						25	50	40	10
Total	554	883	692	783	903	943	729	340	161

Source: DoT (1997a: 30).

reduced sharply. The DoT explained the drop in spending as being the result of a reduced need for spending on rolling-stock after a few years of heavy investment by BR (DoT, 1996a: 21).

The most noteworthy aspect of LRT's funding, shown in Table 8.2 and Figure 8.2 is its irregular nature. In the run up to the 1992 general election, London rail transport organizations (LRT, BR's Network SouthEast) were promised generous funding. There had been widespread concern over London public transport, following the King's Cross fire, and the report by the Monopolies and Mergers Commission (1991) on London Underground, which endorsed the need for much higher levels of investment. But budgets were reduced again once the election was over, in the more stringent conditions which followed Britain's exit from the European Exchange Rate Mechanism. Further cuts were imposed on the core business in the 1996 budget partly to compensate for overspending on the Jubilee Line Extension, and partly, it may be surmised, to demonstrate that privatization was the only way to obtain an adequate stream of resources for investments. The unreliability of DETR's support, depending on political and macroeconomic considerations as much as transport-related criteria, makes the planning of service levels and investment very difficult for LRT managers, particularly as figures for the years ahead carry no guarantee.

Table 8.3 shows how the funding made available to LRT has affected investment in both the core business and the two major

TABLE 8.3   LRT investment in cash prices (estimates from 1995–96)

	1991–92	92–93	93–94	£ million 94–95	95–96	96–97	97–98	98–99	99–00
Core business	340	693	520	554	590	539			
Jubilee Line Extension	62	67	255	371	510	514			
Core business plus JLE							894	343	512
Crossrail	10	29	46	30	16	7			
Total	420	789	821	955	1116	1062	894	343	512

Figures may not sum because of rounding.
Source: DoT (1997a: 31).

projects, construction of the Jubilee Line Extension and preparatory work for CrossRail. Another important factor influencing the availability of resources for investment is the level of surplus or deficit arising from the operation of the core business; the deficit rose from around £50m in the late 1980s to about £200m in 1992–3, though it moved into surplus from 1994–5 following implementation of London Underground's Company Plan and in 1996–7 the gross operating margin was £169m. Some changes in rail spending are out of the immediate control of the DETR. Both LRT and mainline London commuter services were affected by the recession of the late 1980s. Both industries have had to increase investment on safety measures (BR spent about £225m on them in 1991–92), following the Fennell Report into the King's Cross fire and the Hidden Report on the Clapham train collision.

Central government support for local roads and public transport

As Table 8.4 shows, although about £1100 million was available for local road schemes in the best year (1993–94) less than half this sum (£431m) was actually given by the department in Transport Supplementary Grant (TSG). The rest of DETR's 'support for local authorities' is in credit approvals (DoT, 1997a: 64) which are the sums DETR has decided to allow local authorities to borrow for their transport schemes. Repayments have to be found from local authorities' own resources.

TABLE 8.4 DoT support for local authority transport spending (estimates from 1996–97)

	1991–92	92–93	93–94	94–95	95–96	96–97	97–98
				£ million			
Transport Supplementary Grant for:							
Major schemes	234	222	219	185	154	140	105
Minor schemes	38	45	58				
Bridge maintenance	45	55	68	68	57	52	44
Carriageway maintenance		48	86	76	67	44	46
Total TSG	318	370	431	329	278	236	195
Public transport facilities	28	21	13	14	13	24	15
Metropolitan Rail Grant				146	72	1	
MRPS Grant							173
Other grants, etc	4	3	5	6	3	25	28
Credit Approvals	570	630	653	658	625	504	452
Grants plus Credit Approvals:							
in cash prices	919	1024	1101	1154	990	790	863
in 1995–96 prices	1027	1099	1148	1182	990	771	825

Figures may not sum because of rounding.
Source: DoT (1997a: 64, 98).

The DETR may fund local authority public transport investment under S.56 of the Transport Act 1968 if it can be justified by benefits to non-users of the service (for example, in reducing urban congestion) – though there is no compulsion in the Act that it should do so. In the seven years from 1991–92 the DoT contributed an average of £18m per annum through this 'public transport facilities grant' to local authorities' light rail projects, including £48m towards a total cost of £142m for Phase I of the Manchester Metrolink and a similar sum towards the cost of the £200m Sheffield Supertram. During the transition to BR privatization the DoT assisted the Passenger Transport Authorities in the former metropolitan counties to adjust to the new financial regime. Instead of being charged as marginal users of BR's network (charged only the 'avoidable cost'), PTAs now have to pay the whole ('fully allocated') cost of rail services they support. During the two years 1994–6 DoT planned to pay £220m towards the extra costs through a 'Metropolitan Rail Grant'.

FIGURE 8.3   DoT support for local authority spending, in cash prices (estimates from 1996–97)

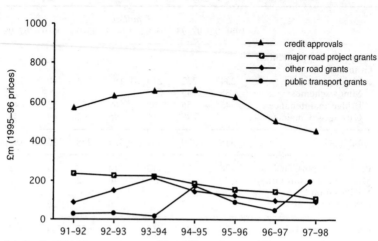

Source: Table 8.4.

The DETR (previously as the Department of Environment) provides general financial support to local highway authorities through Revenue Support Grant. RSG is based on central government's estimate of local needs and its assessment of the money each authority should spend to provide a standard level of service – the Standard Spending Assessment (SSA). There is a specific block within SSA for highways maintenance; other local transport services (subsidy for local rail and bus services, parking and concessionary fares) are grouped with a score of non-transport services in an 'all other services' element. The SSAs of metropolitan districts were increased from 1996–7 to reflect the additional costs of the new railway arrangements noted in the previous section. Associations of local authorities play a large role in the assessment of SSAs. The Department of Transport is represented on a working group on SSAs with representatives of local authorities' highways and transportation committees. The working group cannot increase the total highways SSA (though it can be increased as part of the Public Expenditure Survey negotiation), but there is negotiation about how it is shared.

Local authority spending on roads and transport

Local authorities are not obliged to spend their funds in accordance with the SSA decided by the DETR. Neither by law do they have to spend on transport the value of the Transport Supplementary Grant awarded to them by the DETR for projects specified in their grant application. They choose how much to spend on local roads maintenance and transport services according to local priorities, and these may change when councillors from different parties take control after local elections or for other reasons. Some county councils that changed control in 1994, such as Oxfordshire and Dorset, chose to spend less on road-building and more on repairing schools, for environmental or for educational reasons. But the DETR warns them that TSG may be withheld in a subsequent year if one year's grant is not used. On the other hand, the DETR sets strict limits to each council's total expenditure each year ('capping'). So councils are controlled closely by central government in the maximum they may spend in total, and they also have strong incentives not to diverge too much from the transport provision in what they actually spend on transport.

Since deregulation of bus services (outside London) and their privatization, the contribution to public transport of most local authorities outside the conurbations is in the form of subsidizing routes, perhaps at certain times of day, which they want for their community but which the private sector is unwilling to run on a commercial basis. They subsidize rail services in metropolitan areas. They subsidize public transport across-the-modes by offering concessionary fares to certain categories of residents. They invest in car parks and receive revenue from them in parking charges. Table 8.5 overleaf shows that local authorities planned in 1995–6 to spend about three times as much on roads as on public transport, including concessionary fares). The DETR responds to that division of spending priorities with its own pattern of grants and credit approvals.

The European Union as a source of finance

The European Union awards transport infrastructure grants for projects that improve Britain's links with the rest of the EU,

TABLE 8.5   Local authority transport spending

	£ million		
	1994–95 actual	1995–96 actual	1996–97 estimate
Current spending:			
roads	1690	1751	1717
car parks	−165	−181	−195
concessionary fares	420	420	436
support for buses	197	215	220
support for rail in metropolitan areas	253	218	–
Total current spending	2396	2422	2177
Capital spending:			
roads	1232	1166	1113
car parks	53	50	48
public transport	142	134	128
airports and ports	13	12	12
spending on DoT programmes	17	17	16
capital receipts	−126	−58	−42
Net capital spending	1331	1322	1276
Total local authority expenditure	3727	3744	3453

Source: DoT (1997a: 101).

varying between £2m and £10m a year in recent years (DoT, 1996a: 77). The European Regional Development Fund has provided capital grants for all British transport industries; that is, national roads, rail, harbour and airport authorities, the total sums varying from £64m in 1988–89 to £6m in 1990–91. In 1996–97 harbour authorities were expected to receive £6m from the ERDF, and the railway industry about £4m (ibid. 66). Local authorities have received larger grants for capital expenditure on transport, the sums varying from £12m to £58m between 1988 and 1993. The European Investment Bank agreed to loan £98m towards the cost of the Jubilee Line extension in cooperation with commercial banks to provide enough private-sector financing to allow the project to go ahead. Sums are small compared with total infrastructure spending, but they sometimes, as with the Jubilee Line example, encourage projects that might otherwise have failed to proceed.

Developers' contributions

Private builders sometimes pay for highways improvements associated with their housing or commercial development. They agree to commission work from the highway authority to persuade it to grant planning permission (under Section 106 of the Town and Country Planning Act 1991 or Section 278 of the New Roads and Street Works Act 1991). Although such 'planning gains' are usually small the total sum is not trivial. The DoT estimated that private developers contributed £126m (15 per cent) of the £806m provisional total figure for local authority capital expenditure on roads in 1991–92 (DoT, 1993a: 140). In the 1980s planning gain was frowned upon by central government, which did not want local planning officers to distort the free market, or left-wing politicians to drive away potential economic growth. Nicholas Ridley's strategic planning guidance to London boroughs when he was Secretary of State for the Environment told them not to seek planning gain (DoE, 1989). Only about 1 per cent of planning applications in the late 1980s included some planning gain but these few virtually always included money for roads. Very occasionally this 'positive obligation' included public transport (Healey, Purdue and Ennis, 1993).

A 1991 DoE circular, *Planning Obligations*, reaffirmed in Section 106 of the 1991 Act, implicitly recognized the value of developers' contributions to transport budgets. West Sussex County Council put the practical argument thus:

It is essential that development should bear the cost of changes to the infrastructure which it necessitates. Not only is this considered equitable but it is necessary because the Highway Authority has insufficient finance available to deal with all existing highway deficiencies and cannot therefore undertake to rectify additional problems arising from development . . . The requirements imposed upon developers are taken in context with the extent of their development and the feasibility of bearing the cost of the off-site works (1993b: 65).

Central government itself makes use of property developments to improve road infrastructure under Section 278. The Department of Transport improved three junctions on the A10 in Enfield in the 1990s, each in conjunction with the building of a new hypermarket. The improvement to the A23 Purley Way, Croydon, is another significant example.

Taxation

In setting taxes affecting transport the Chancellor of the Exchequer has to balance a great variety of policy considerations. DETR would like to use tax changes to influence the level of demand for both private and public transport and to reduce air pollution. The Department of Trade and Industry would like the tax regime to encourage sales of British-made vehicles, and assist the competitiveness of all British business by keeping down transport costs. The tax-gathering departments, which include Customs & Excise and the Department of Social Security as well as the Inland Revenue, prefer tax regimes that are easy to administer. The Treasury invites departments to contribute their views every year, but in contrast to expenditure which is subject to bilateral and collective discussion (see above), many decisions about taxation are so sensitive, because they may affect market values, that the Chancellor has to take them under conditions of the tightest security within the very small circle of advisers who prepare the budget. As noted in Chapter 3, this regime of budget secrecy makes it almost impossible to conduct an open interdepartmental debate about the impact of taxation policy on transport, but the main issues can be described here in relation to each of the principal taxes concerned.

Vehicle excise duty (VED) raised £4 billion in 1995–6. In nearly all other European countries the corresponding annual vehicle tax differentiates between cars depending on their engine size, which tends to favour the use of smaller cars burning less fuel and therefore creating less pollution (the range is from 18: 1 in Italy to 4: 1 in Germany). In Britain there has for many years been a flat rate for cars, which is simpler to administer. Heavy goods vehicles do pay variable rates, which until 1991 were related to 'track costs' by a formula which measured the wear and tear imposed on roads by different types of HGV. DoT attached importance to this link because it gave transport operators a soundly based incentive to invest in less damaging vehicles. However, the link with track costs was abandoned in the 1991 budget when the increases indicated by the track costs formula were presumably thought likely to damage industrial competitiveness, and in 1994 the Treasury suspended publication of the track costs calculation itself. Both decisions were taken by the Treasury without consultation.

Fuel tax is an even larger source of revenue, raising £15 billion in 1995–6, plus £3.7 billion in Value Added Tax. Between 1974 and 1994 the real cost of fuel fell by 8 per cent, while incomes rose by 31 per cent, bus fares by 55 per cent and rail fares by 71 per cent (DoE, 1996: 34). A quite small differential in favour of unleaded petrol, introduced in the 1987 budget, proved extremely effective in persuading motorists to use unleaded fuel, which now accounts for a substantial majority of the market. Since the 1992 Earth Summit in Rio de Janeiro, fuel duties have been raised every year by at least 5 per cent more than the rate of inflation (6 per cent in 1997) as a measure intended to reduce emissions of carbon dioxide, the main greenhouse gas. However, the Royal Commission on Environmental Pollution (1994: para. 7.58) thought the cost of fuel would have to be doubled over a period of ten years to bring about substantial reductions in fuel use, which would imply increases of about 8 per cent per annum above inflation (they actually recommended 9 per cent to include market-induced price rises). In the event, falling world oil prices between 1994 and 1996 reduced the increases in those years to as little as 1.5 per cent above inflation.

Until 1991 there was, in addition to VAT, a special car tax of 10 per cent on the purchase of new cars but this was removed in two stages in 1991 and 1992 in order to revive vehicle sales in the depressed market conditions of those years, though 'it was made clear that this income would have to be made up by raising other car taxes at a later date' (Potter, 1993: 43). The Chancellor's promise was made good when VED was increased in 1992 and 1993, and fuel tax was raised 10 per cent in that year. However, whereas abolition of the special car tax cost the Treasury £750 million a year, the increase in fuel duty was expected to bring in £100 million a year (ibid.: 43). The fiscal measure guiding people towards using more fuel-efficient cars was very weak compared with the fiscal measure encouraging people to buy cars.

The absolute levels of fuel tax and VED are not the only issue.

The current level of road taxes is arguably quite close to the cost of providing road services and the additional environmental costs for cars, though not for lorries (Newbery, 1995). As currently structured, VED and fuel taxes apply more or less equally to all motorists, but since it is congestion in urban areas and on some motorways which imposes heavy costs on the economy and causes most pollution, there is a case for reforming the tax system so as to impose the heaviest taxes on those who impose the heaviest costs on others, in other words the driver who uses congested roads at the busiest times of day. The ability to do this would be one of the major attractions of electronic road charging, and would avoid the inequity of imposing heavy additional taxes on people in rural areas where there is often no viable public transport alternative to using a car.

These examples of what has happened to VED, fuel tax and the special purchase tax suggest that although successive Chancellors have sheltered behind the government's concern for the environment as grounds for raising fuel taxes, the dominant factors in determining taxation policy have in fact been concern for taxation revenue and the state of the economy, including particularly the car manufacturing industry. The latter emphasis would seem to be particularly apparent in the regime of tax incentives, much more generous in Britain than elsewhere in Europe, which apply to the company car. A survey by DoT statisticians in 1989 showed 85 per cent of cars entering central London in peak hours had received some form of travel assistance from their company or employer for that journey (surveys by the GLC in 1982 produced similar figures). About half the drivers had a parking space provided, and a quarter had parking charges fully or partly paid. Fuel costs were fully or partly paid for 38 per cent of drivers (*HC Debs*, 15 January 1993: 861). The importance is recognized of the parking space for encouraging commuters to travel by car when they could otherwise use public transport, but this benefit is not taxed as provision of the car itself is taxed.

According to a 1997 study of company car taxation by the Ashden Trust, London First and the University of Westminster, company cars account for around 20 per cent of all car mileage, but this understates their importance to the new car sales market, of which cars registered in a company name have comprised more than 50 per cent since 1988. Employees provided with a company car are taxed on the benefit at 35 per cent of the list price of the car and its accessories, but the tax is reduced by one third for employees who drive at least 2500 business miles, or by two-thirds for those who drive at least 18 000 business miles. In addition, half of all company cars receive some free fuel, and since this benefit is assessed at a flat rate for tax purposes it may well constitute an incentive to do additional mileage, particularly when linked to the tax benefits associated with the business mileage thresholds. The study concluded that:

On average company cars do around 35 per cent more commuting miles than private cars owned by people of similar socioeconomic group who commute by car ... This differential doubles to 70 per cent, when comparing low business mileage drivers with and without company cars, and is higher among drivers receiving a free-fuel benefit. The availability and cost of parking is an important factor influencing the decision to commute by car, equally affecting those with company and private cars.

The study recommended that fuel economy should be encouraged by applying a fuel consumption factor to the list price used as a basis for assessing the benefit of a company car for tax purposes; that the business mileage bands should be replaced by tax bands related to the amount of private miles driven, which would encourage drivers to reduce their commuting and domestic mileage; and that free fuel should be taxed on a pence per personal mile driven basis. The study also recommended that an evaluation of workplace parking policy, for both company and non-company cars, should be commissioned.

Vehicle taxation is an important indicator of the balance of government policies as between the interests of the car manufacturing industry and the preoccupations of transport and environment policies. Changes to VED, fuel tax and company car taxation, together with the eventual development of road charging, will be important indicators of the depth of any commitment the government may announce to an integrated transport policy designed to achieve a sustainable environment.

Criticisms of the current public finance regime

The procedures for raising and allocating public funding for transport are not rational or effective. Central government's budgetary process is composed of annual negotiations between individual departments and the Treasury, each defending its corner (usually the previous year's budget), and 'playing games' with transport finance. The yearly spending round encourages the short-term, narrow outlook typical of British policy-making. Further, the convention that the Treasury takes annual decisions on levels of taxation under closet conditions precludes proper debate, even privately, within the departments of government responsible for policy in the affected sectors.

The value of departments' three-year financial plans is lost if, as in 1993–4, there are considerable changes to mainline rail and LRT's funding from the figures announced in previous years, or the Treasury imposes new figures on the DETR for the forthcoming year, or the Secretary of State decides to make significant transfers within the total budget. Some transport experts have argued for a ten-year rolling roads programme and for a greater certainty about rail infrastructure funding (see NEDC, 1992) but the facility for programming medium-term expenditure within the UK public expenditure process is inadequate. Once schemes are agreed and committed they are usually supported, but DETR's total budget is insufficient for it to guarantee the future funding of a major programme of works. There is no provision for forgoing current expenditure and 'saving up' for some desirable large item of expenditure (such as the extension or thorough overhaul of an Underground line); indeed the idea would have only to be floated by Transport officials for the Treasury to set the transport budget at a lower level, a new historical baseline.

Despite the constraints of annual budgeting it is apparent from the investment record that the DoT managed to secure funds for both upgrading the existing railway to cater for Eurostar services to the Channel Tunnel (DoT, 1993a: table 4.2.4.1) and for extending the Jubilee Line. But the cost of such projects in relation to the spending plans of the department as a whole puts pressure on more routine expenditure programmes, particularly when there is acute overall pressure to reduce public expenditure. Once embarked on a major project of this kind it is virtually impossible to pull out until it is completed without incurring severe political and economic penalties. This constraint is one reason the Treasury is cautious about big projects, and searches for reasons to prevent or postpone them, or nowadays to transfer them and their attendant risks to the private sector.

Private finance

The demand for more investment in transport infrastructure at a time when the government has been trying to reduce public expenditure has led to much debate about ways of involving the private sector more fully. Britain has a highly developed capital market, internationally-successful construction companies and experienced contract managers, but successive governments have found it difficult to draw on these skills and resources to instigate, develop, construct and maintain road and rail projects. However, a number of creative ideas have been put forward, and although Treasury rules about what would count as 'private' contributions have in the past been interpreted so restrictively that few projects could be approved, there are signs now of a more flexible approach. The changes have been made through concessions by the government to points put by potential investors and other interested parties. By 1995 Treasury ministers had evolved a firm and positive policy towards the replacement of conventional public sector funding by private finance, encapsulated in the 'Private Finance Initiative' (PFI), described by the Treasury and the Private Finance Panel in *Private Opportunity, Public Benefit* (HM Treasury, 1995). But Labour politicians including, significantly, John Prescott (later to become the Deputy Prime Minister), had already identified the scope which leasing and franchising arrangements might offer to raise investment in transport infrastructure without increasing the annual level of public expenditure. These concepts, given the new name of Public–Private Partnerships (PPP), may in due course change the nature as well as the name of the Conservative government's PFI (Corry, Le Grand and Radcliffe, 1997).

The genesis of Treasury policy on private finance

In 1981 the National Economic Development Council believed a higher level of investment might benefit the economy and was worried the system of External Financing Limits was hampering investment by nationalized industries. A working party was set up, chaired by William Ryrie (then a Treasury second permanent secretary). The following criteria under which private finance might be introduced were presented to the NEDC:

(1) decisions to provide funds for investment should be taken under conditions of fair competition with private-sector borrowers; any links with the rest of the public sector, government guarantees or commitments, or monopoly power should not result in the schemes offering investors a degree of security significantly greater than that available on private-sector projects;

(2) such projects should yield benefits in terms of improved efficiency and profit from the additional investment commensurate with the cost of raising risk capital from financial markets.

These criteria, known as 'the Ryrie rules', are mild, reasonable requirements, but over the years the actual rules were forgotten; many commentators appeared not to have a copy – and a mythology grew. Certainly, the private sector felt the Ryrie rules were being interpreted in an unhelpful way. Two features are worthy of special note. The first is that the Treasury was reluctant to concede that private-sector funding would be allowed to make a net additional contribution to physical investment: it could only substitute for existing planned public expenditure. This interpretation became known as the 'lack of additionality' of private-sector investment and caused much adverse comment. The second noteworthy feature is that the Treasury would insist that all risks should be shifted to the private sector; and there was to be no element of government guarantee.

In November 1993 Kenneth Clarke, Chancellor of the Exchequer, published an important consultation document, *Breaking New Ground: The Private Finance Initiative* (HM Treasury, 1993).

Its particular value was that it represented a definitive, easily-available statement of Treasury policy. It is significantly more positive in tone towards the idea of *joint* ventures between government and the private sector:

> We aim to promote efficiency, to improve services and to stimulate fresh flows of investment. We want to harness the private sector's efficiency and management expertise, just as much as its resources, bringing a new approach to investment in a whole range of activities and services traditionally regarded as the exclusive domain of the public sector.... The obvious answer is to take many of these projects into the private sector, where they can be managed by people able to raise substantial amounts of risk capital in the markets. This would create a more focused and disciplined handling of risk. But the Government recognizes that it would be impossible to transfer *all* risks to the private sector.

Risk transfer

The proponents of private-sector finance say that risks should be and will be transferred from the public sector to the private sector. As the Association of British Chambers of Commerce said to the Commons Transport Committee (*Roads for the Future*, session 1988–89):

> Where commercial risk is genuinely in the hands of the private sector, one can expect the private sector to be a better judge of that commercial risk – and therefore, in commercial terms, of priorities – than the public sector would be. This is because risk, so galvanizing in the commercial world, is essentially a misnomer in the public sphere. 'Mistakes' may be made but, so long as the correct internal procedures were followed, the participants will not greatly suffer.

While government can raise money relatively cheaply because it is a large low-risk borrower, account must be taken of the benefits that tend to go with private finance and management, such as improved efficiency, lower costs, and reduction in the risks falling on the taxpayer. Annex D of the DoT consultation paper, *Paying for Better Motorways*, identifies the following risks: design risk, construction costs risk, opening date risk, traffic risk, maintenance risk and operational risk. A 1997 case study by the Highways Agency (DoT, 1997) also identifies protestor risk and latent defect risk. Most of these risks have been transferred to the private sector on the DBFO schemes reported in the case study. The exceptions are costs or delays caused by the Highways Agency and planning risks – because all the schemes had already been through public inquiry.

At least some of the risk must be transferred. Otherwise there would be no incentive for the private sector to increase efficiency in order to reduce the risk or mitigate its consequences. However, many risks will be present under either conventional public-financing or private-financing systems. The issue is whether the *costs* associated with the risks are greater or less if they are borne by the private sector. The literature suggests two distinct reasons why governments can bear risks at lower social cost than can the private sector: its superior ability to pool the risks of a large number of projects and its superior ability to spread any one risk over a large number of 'shareholders' (Layard and Glaister, 1994). These reasons explain in part the higher interest costs of financing a project from the private sector rather than from the public sector. There is, therefore, a trade-off between shifting risk onto the private sector to sharpen the incentives to mitigate risk, and retaining it in the public sector to reduce its social cost.

There are actions the government could take to assist the private sector to manage the inherent risks in highways investment. For instance, it is harder to forecast the future traffic on any one new link in a road network than to forecast 'average' national traffic. Thus a commercial risk associated with traffic flows on a link road will be both high and difficult to appraise. The private sector could do much to manage this risk if it were free to build up substantial portfolios of schemes – in effect pooling some risks. They can do this pooling only if a sufficiently large number of schemes is made available at one time. That strategy is not consistent with the recent procedure of offering a small number of schemes, one at a time. The private sector occasionally seeks guarantees that competing roads will not be built or improved in the vicinity of their scheme, though this has not been conceded. Several other techniques are available to reduce risks on traffic flows to a level tolerable to the private sector, many of which have been used in the privately-financed bridges – especially the Skye Bridge scheme (Moles and Williams, 1993). These techniques include the use of a contract in which the date of reversion of the asset to the state is not fixed, but will be delayed until a defined return has been earned, and various other devices to circumscribe the 'downside' risks to the promoters. The private sector seems confident it is possible to generate some secure and good lending opportunities.

Private-sector financing of toll motorways

The direct approach to using private-sector funding to build transport infrastructure is to encourage private companies to finance, build and manage routes themselves. In 1990 central government named several toll road schemes it hoped could be built with private finance but there was not much enthusiasm from contractors. Two bridges have been built (Dartford Crossing and the second Severn Bridge), though they may not be a true test of the financial ability of the private sector to build from scratch since in both cases existing crossings provided part-built infrastructure and the topography created a captive market. The first wholly privately-funded and operated overland motorway in the UK is expected to be the Birmingham Northern Relief Road, for which a 53-year concession was granted in February 1992 to Midlands Expressway (a consortium of Trafalgar House and Iritecna of Italy).

Tolls and shadow tolls

In principle electronic road-user charging offers an ideal system. Electronic techniques are developing fast and costs fall daily. The successful demonstration of contactless 'smart cards' by London Transport in 1994 on buses in Harrow illustrates what could be achieved with technology then available. Considerable sums are being spent on research to bring electronics to the aid of management of the road infrastructure, notably by European bodies, such as in the DRIVE programme. One such experiment, jointly funded by the EU and the DETR, on one of the main roads into Leicester from August 1997 was designed to test what level of charge is necessary to persuade people to transfer from car to bus (*Guardian*, 23 July 1997).

However, at the national level there are several obstacles. First, the DETR has accepted that the methods likely to be feasible within the next few years would consist of a relatively small number of large, expensive pieces of equipment in fixed roadside locations that would interact with vehicles. Given the dense network of roads in the UK and the high proportion of motorized trips that are for short distances, the implication is that electronic charging would be sensible only on a minority of specialized roads; that is, motorways. *Paying for Better Motorways* argued that new sources of funding would be required to keep pace with the growing use of fast roads. It proposed that direct charges might be made for the use of existing motorways and suggested various ways of charging. An electronic toll of about 1.5p per mile for cars and about 4.5p per mile for heavy goods vehicles would raise £700m a year. Alternatively an annual permit of £50 per year for cars and up to £500 for the heaviest goods vehicles would raise about £500m a year. The government ruled out the use of conventional toll booths and barriers; they cause congestion and pollution in addition to costing 10 per cent of gross revenue (OECD, 1987: 78). An additional disadvantage of any tolling mechanism – not highlighted by the government – would be the likely diversion of some traffic from motorways to less safe local roads. The Secretary of State for Transport, John MacGregor, presented the discussion on motorway tolling as seeing 'whether private finance can augment public finance' in road construction so as 'to get the road programme completed as quickly as we can' to reduce the congestion expected 'by the end of the century' (*HC Debs*, 8 February 1993: 699). Motorway tolls in the UK could be used to provide increased expenditure on public transport within a steady transport budget. However, the Green Paper stressed that toll proceeds would be used only for constructing and operating roads, a political gesture to reduce opposition from the road transport lobby. This strategy could not be guaranteed unless the Treasury could be persuaded that toll income could be hypothecated to a particular service; that is, it need not be treated as revenue for general expenditure. There were soon suggestions that ministers had in mind the offering of franchises to private-sector companies to maintain certain public roads and to collect tolls, much as the turnpike trusts did in the eighteenth century, and indeed DBFO contracts (see below) routinely make provision for real tolls to take the place of shadow tolls.

It is possible that satellite-location systems and geographic-information systems could change the position in the near future. The government has sponsored research on electronic techniques for collecting tolls. Although these have reached the stage of trials at the Transport Research Laboratory, progress has been much slower than was first envisaged. This may be due in part to the unexpected technical difficulties of the problem but it is also due to a lack of enthusiasm on the part of the industry because they are unconvinced of the commitment of government actually to introduce any tolling system. The advantages would have to be weighed against the costs of equipping all the vehicles in the country, the problems of diversion and the costs of enforcement, bearing in mind the long-established existence of fuel and other taxes that provide a crude proxy and that are cheap and easy to collect. They may perceive that whatever the experts' arguments about the merits of explicit road-user charges, people generally have yet to appreciate them and they are likely to be resistant to the idea. This comment applies equally to urban and to non-urban road pricing. The Labour government's August 1997 Consultation Document, *Developing an Integrated Transport Policy*, is cautious and only mentions the possibility of charging for roads use in the following terms:

> 17. Is there, as suggested in the previous Government's paper 'Transport The Way Forward', a role for making greater use of economic instruments to influence how people choose to travel, such as increasing the price of public parking, possibly taxing companies' car parking provision, and charging for the use of roads? How should the receipts from such sources be used?

Until 1993 the government had rejected the road construction industry's proposals to use 'shadow tolls' as distinct from the real tolls envisaged in *Paying for Better Motorways*. Then the Treasury issued a statement in which the government recognized the potential offered by shadow tolls:

The Government intends to introduce contracts under which the private sector will design, build, finance and operate roads. Promoters will receive payments from the government in relation to the level of traffic using roads constructed or improved in this way. The Department of Transport will hold early discussions with the construction industry and others to identify appropriate schemes. The aim will be to secure substantial transfer of risk to the private sector. The first contract should be let in about eighteen months (HM Treasury, 1993)

The Highways Agency and Private Finance Panel case study of March 1997 notes that 'One of the objectives of the DBFO programme was to foster a private sector, domestic road operating industry' (DoT, 1997b: ch.6). This strategy appears to have been highly successful. As the case study (and a subsequent summary of progress) reports, by summer 1997 DBFO schemes already involved 385 miles with a capital value of £750m. Contracts were being prepared for a further 293 miles with an estimated capital value of £393m which, if confirmed following the new government's review of the roads programme, would raise the proportion of the national road network transferred to the private sector to over 10 per cent.

There is now considerable flexibility evident in the arrangements for privately-funded road schemes. Public expenditure is being reduced in the short term without having to inflict a correspondingly deep cut on the roads programme. The shadow toll system has been successful in bringing the perceived benefits of private-sector involvement. The Highways Agency claimed that the first eight DBFO contracts have beaten 'the public sector comparator by an average value of 15%' (ibid. foreword).

If this method of funding roads investment is continued it would not be many years before a majority of the national roads network was in private hands. However, with shadow tolling, the availability of public-sector funding over a long period remains the critical issue. When the government lets contracts for shadow-tolled schemes it commits itself to a legally-binding contract. This longer-term commitment is what critics of short-termism have been seeking. At the same time, various parts of government are beginning to realize, somewhat belatedly, that substantial volumes of many future years' public expenditure are being pre-empted. The government is moving from a one-off lump sum payment to a stream of annual payments. More physical infrastructure can be procured in the early years within a given total expenditure in any one year, which reassures the public in a climate of public expenditure cuts. But unless shadow tolls are eventually replaced by user-charges paid direct by the motorist to the contractors, which would fall outside public expenditure altogether, the growing burden of the shadow tolls will ultimately squeeze out other procurement or force the government to accept a net increase in public expenditure on roads. The Commons Treasury Select Committee commented on these new problems in public-sector accounting and control (Treasury Committee, 1996).

Urban road pricing or congestion charging

The Highways Agency and Private Finance Panel study says that 'One of the main reasons for using shadow tolls was that they offered a workable method of acclimatising the private sector to the concept of payment per vehicle as a precursor to the introduction of user paid toll roads' (DoT, 1997b: para. 5.1). The difficulties with proposals to raise revenues by charging tolls on motorways were noted above. The case for charging road users in *congested urban areas* is stronger. If there is congestion the decision by an individual to make a road trip imposes an additional cost on others, by slowing them marginally or by adding to pollution, that he or she will not generally take into account (Newbery, 1990). The various responses to this problem include doing nothing, and enforcing some kind of physical restraint on the volume of vehicle use. The economics and traffic engineering professions have long been attracted by the possibility of introducing a system of charging money to users to make them face the true costs of their decision to use road space. It would give the use of roads to those vehicles that most benefit from that use. Vehicles, such as full buses, which benefited most from time savings would be given a quicker journey. Road space would be used more efficiently. Moreover, the charges would produce revenue.

In July 1995 the Department of Transport published the outcome of a major, four-year feasibility study into congestion charging in the London area. The study concluded:

There would be significant economic saving to London as a whole, principally from reduced journey times and increased travel time reliability . . . Bus users would benefit considerably from better traffic conditions . . . travellers in the higher income category, who are most likely to be car drivers, would be most affected, with the benefits in time saving and reliability improvements they would obtain being outweighed by the charges they would pay. Travellers from the medium and low income categories would benefit in aggregate . . . Tests of congestion charging combined with strategies for improved public transport showed that such improvements could offset some of the adverse effects of congestion charging alone . . . The net revenue would be sufficient to pay for extensive investments in public transport which could provide net economic benefits to each of the three income groups (1995a: paras 3.14, 3.19–20, 3.33).

One of the many policy packages analysed would, it was estimated, reduce traffic in Central London by 17 per cent, increase traffic speeds by 26 per cent, revolutionize bus speeds and service reliability, reduce accidents by 5 per cent and reduce emissions from traffic by between 10 per cent and 20 per cent. About £6bn of new money would become available that could be used to fund public transport investment. Some object that those who have to use cars would be penalized. But these car-users are generally people who stand to gain most by clearer roads. It would be possible to organize exemptions and rebates. Charges would not apply at off-peak times and weekends. It is also claimed that commerce would be damaged. Yet commercial vehicles lose the most from congestion and stand to gain the most through its reduction. Taxis would benefit and could take over many of the private car's functions in central London. The general quality of life in the centre would be significantly improved to commerce's advantage.

Having considered the report, the government decided it would not attempt to implement a congestion-charging scheme in London in the immediate future. First, introducing charges for roads that people have come to regard as 'free' would not be acceptable to the public unless the revenues were guaranteed to be available for reinvestment in improvements to public transport and similar, local purposes: once again, the hypothecation battle would have to be won with the Treasury. Second, it was sceptical of the electronic high-tech charging mechanisms that tempt traffic engineers: investment in equipment would be costly and the technological risks were judged unacceptable. Third, whatever the merits of road pricing, it is peculiarly difficult to explain to politicians and the public.

Attitude surveys suggest that the general public may be starting to appreciate the case for urban road pricing. In 1989 the Metropolitan Transport Research Unit in association with Gallup found that over half of regular drivers in Central London supported the idea of imposing a fixed charge for each journey into or through Central London. The level of support rose to almost two-thirds if exemption would be made for certain users. Research carried out for London Transport by the Harris Research Centre in late 1990 showed 38 per cent of Londoners positively in favour of making car and van drivers pay to drive into Central London and 44 per cent positively against. Opposition was substantially lower among those living closer to the centre, those who usually travelled by bus or Underground and those in lower income groups. It is possible that attitudes might change quickly if some pioneering urban scheme were demonstrated to be beneficial or if concern about traffic growth and its attendant disadvantages led to a perception that charging for road use was a sensible way to address the problem. London is one of the places where the benefits of congestion charging would be greatest, but it is also the place where the consequences of a failure would be the most serious. The first experimental schemes might therefore be best carried out in a smaller city; several cities are considering the possibility.

Financing or funding?

It is useful to draw a sharp distinction between financing and funding a project. This differentiation is at the heart of some of the confusion surrounding the topic of public-sector funding. *Financing* refers to the activity undertaken by an institution or group of institutions when they assume responsibility for lending financial capital to purchase an asset, or undertake a construction project, in return for a future flow of cash payments.

Funding is the provision of cash payments, now or in the future, which correspond to the resources devoted to the manufacture of an asset or construction of a project. Many politicians from the leading parties would like to see the private sector taking the burden of *funding* infrastructure from the state. But many of the actual proposals are about changing *financing* arrangements, or about changing the method of procuring assets or services. Beneficial incentives for efficient management can be created, but it is not private-sector funding.

Procurement through private-sector finance

The deal announced in late 1994 by which London Underground would procure new trains for the Northern Line illustrates well the benefits of competition in procurement. It is an exact parallel of the pre-1994 system of London bus tendering (which is detailed in Chapter 9), except that the public sector will provide the drivers (Kennedy, Glaister and Travers, 1995). The private sector borrows money, builds and maintains the vehicles, and it services the debt and operating costs through contractual payments from the public sector. There are penalties for poor quality of service, so the private sector bears the cost risks and performance failure risks. The efficiency gains from private-sector management, and proper matching of risks with incentives, is traded against the higher economic cost of capital. Similar arrangements had already been used to procure additional automatic ticket gates at some heavily used stations outside the central area (they pay for themselves by reducing fare evasion) and there is no reason in principle why many other procurements could not follow these precedents.

But the Northern Line deal is a new way of *financing* and *procuring* public infrastructure. It is not a new source of *funding*. It could have been financed in the traditional way by grant; that is, public debt, which would have been serviced in full in the form of reduced public subsidy in the future. The replacement of Northern Line trains was self-financing because the cost-savings from one-person operation and lower maintenance costs justified the capital outlay. In old-fashioned, nationalized industry terms the scheme would have obtained the 8 per cent real rate of return that public investment is expected to show. Executing the deal would have *reduced* the call on public funds over the long term. The PFI-assisted deal contributed the management efficiency and gains from making risks congruent with incentives, net of the increased cost of borrowing by the private sector rather than by the public sector. The involvement of the private sector did not add the capital and maintenance costs of the trains to the resources available to London Underground over the long term, but it did mean that those costs (financed in the private sector) could be incurred without adding to the public sector borrowing requirement.

There is little evidence to suggest that any genuine ways will be found to share the revenue risks of investments in the Underground. First, in the absence of sophisticated ticketing systems there is the complexity of such a highly integrated transport system and the consequent difficulties in defining revenue risks and rewards. Second, it would be difficult for the private sector to sign contracts involving revenues with an organization such as London Underground, so long as it is subject to detailed political intervention. At any moment the government could change fares policy, or investment levels, or some other crucial factor. However, the government is committed to using private finance more fully in the funding of the Underground within the context of new arrangements for London governance.

Private funding of loss-making activities

In the case of a proposition which would remain non-commercial (that is, loss-making) even after any efficiency benefits due to private sector involvement, the decision to execute such projects must by definition increase the public-sector commitment in the long run, no matter how it is financed. It is a simple point: the private sector will not provide resources for something they perceive to be loss-making – though they will help with *financing* it for an appropriate return.

CrossRail provides a good illustration. Even if this scheme would create sufficient *economic* value to balance both its construction and operating costs, so long as there is a political commitment to maintaining standard, zonal pricing for the London Underground system including the new line, there is little chance the revenues attributable to the opening of the new line would be sufficient to cover much more than the new operating costs. This outcome would leave the capital costs to be found. The government's declared commitment to carry out the scheme cannot be reconciled with its insistence there must be a considerable proportion of private-sector funding. Proposals to secure private finance against future revenues are ill-conceived, because most of the margin above operating costs would be ticket revenues lost from other Underground lines. These other lines would be unable to make offsetting cost savings so, unless they could generate additional revenue, the revenue lost to CrossRail would have to be replaced by subsidy from the taxpayer. The proposition is public-sector funding in disguise. Therefore, the scheme may well be worthwhile but only capable of being financed with the help of public-sector funding, given the institutional realities.

Conclusion: the limitation of private-sector funding

Where charging systems exist that allow the conversion of sufficient of the economic benefits into cash to fund a scheme, there is no fundamental difficulty in securing full private-sector funding. Examples include toll bridges and tunnels crossing estuaries. However, there is considerable confusion about what can realistically be achieved from introducing private finance into public infrastructure projects. In his November 1994 Budget speech announcing cuts in future government funding for transport, the Chancellor appeared to be stating that future reductions in state *funding* would be made good by private finance. The introduction of genuine competition in procurement, and the greater involvement of private-sector management, offer considerable benefit, allowing existing funding to go further. The PFI (or PPP) can assist in this process. These benefits may well be sufficient to offset the additional costs stemming from the competitive bidding process and the higher cost of borrowing in the private sector. But proposals to produce large quantities of new net and long-term *funding* from the private sector in inherently loss-making activities are over-optimistic.

The effect of the structure chosen for rail privatization was to create legally enforceable commitments by the Treasury to pay subsidy to train operating companies for periods of between seven and 15 years. The capitalized value of these contracts was reflected in the lump sum for which Railtrack was floated as a privatized company – which appeared in the public accounts as negative expenditure for the one year in which it occurred. Essentially, this was a form of government borrowing from the new shareholders of Railtrack. From the point of view of those attempting to manage the industry this stability of funding was exactly what they had been seeking for many years. However, it does mean that substantial annual public spending is now pre-empted in future years.

The spectacular growth in roads capital spending funded through shadow tolls has had a similar effect. It has been possible to protect the rate of physical investment in roads even though current annual spending on the old basis has been cut. At the same time the government have been able to claim that gains in value for money have been realized, as predicted, from the greater involvement of the private sector in designing, building, financing and operating roads and by enabling the private sector to manage risks in a more efficient way. Taken together with the apparent intention to introduce user-paid tolls in due course and the contractorization of roads maintenance programmes by the Highways Agency which has taken the place of the old agency agreements with local authorities, this begins to look like a thoroughgoing privatization programme launched in the last year of the Conservative government – though it was never described as such. Moreover, it is being continued by Labour who are under the same financial pressures as their predecessors and who are keen to use their PPPs to transfer financing to the private sector.

But, in the absence of full-scale tolling, the Exchequer must pay sooner or later for shadow-tolled schemes. Since these are contractual liabilities the cash will take priority over other items of annual spending. It will be many years before the full implications for public expenditure and for the quantum of physical investment in railways and roads can be assessed. In the meantime the general public – and ministers – may be surprised to discover just how far the Major government went towards 'privatizing' national roads, and the extent to which public spending plans are pre-empted by the long-term funding liabilities.

Unwillingness to face the basic economics of most transport systems has allowed people to delay facing up to an uncomfortable fact: if new funds on a large scale are to be found then it will have to be done in some way that does not rely on private-sector funding. This conclusion applies to many public transport schemes because the capital costs cannot be recovered through fares, and to many road schemes because there is no satisfactory system in place for charging road users. Unless and until fundamental changes are made to the way both roads and public transport systems are financed – particularly in congested areas where the functions may be complementary – central government will continue to bear a responsibility for formulating and executing policies which supplement the fares and user charges for both road and rail transport systems. Meanwhile, private *finance* will have a role to play. There needs to be greater clarity about what private finance can and cannot be expected to achieve, and new systems of accounting and control within government need to be developed to deal with the way the Private Finance Initiative has altered the balance between capital expenditure and recurrent funding.

9 Competition and Investment

The policy of the Conservative governments between 1979 and 1997 was to use market forces to improve the delivery of transport services – driving down fares, costs, charges and subsidies and increasing the quantity and quality of investment – by releasing it from the restraints of public-sector control. Competition has been increased in the provision of air, bus, rail and road freight services. The regulatory arrangements have been adjusted accordingly to secure the public interest within the new structures. This chapter assesses the extent to which these goals have been attained, particularly in road and rail transport.

Though government's formally expressed aims for transport are expressed in generalities, they express clearly the ideology of the political executive. Transport infrastructure choices are not decisions made purely on technical grounds. Under the Major government the strategic aim in transport policy was: 'an efficient and competitive transport market to serve the interests of the economy and community, with maximum emphasis on safety and the environment'. Political direction is apparent in the list of ways this aim was to be achieved:

- opening up new ways to make best use of private sector skills, initiative and funds;
- substantial public-sector investment, where appropriate;
- getting better value for money from public expenditure on transport;
- increasing competitiveness;
- sustaining and improving both the environment and road safety;
- using the price mechanism to give users and providers the right signals about the real costs of transport;
- advancing UK transport interests in world markets. (DoT, 1993a: 2)

These aims are predominantly economic in character, which is unsurprising since the underlying purpose of the Conservative reforms was to improve the economic performance of the transport industries by moving as much as possible into the private sector. More decisions were supposed to be taken on economic grounds in the context of a competitive market, and fewer by politicians and bureaucrats on grounds presumed less likely to produce a desirable distribution of resources. An additional objective, consistent with moving decisions into the private sector, has been to reduce public expenditure whilst at the same time raising both the quantity of investment and its quality.

In its August 1997 consultation document the new Labour government had its own list. Transport policy should play its part in:

- promoting environmental objectives;
- promoting economic development, across all parts of the country;
- promoting greater efficiency in the use of scarce resources, including road and rail capacity;
- enhancing the vitality of town and city centres;
- meeting the needs of rural areas;
- reducing social exclusion and taking account of the basic accessibility needs of all sectors of society, including disabled people;
- ensuring a high standard of safety across all modes, and promoting a travelling environment in which personal security is not compromised; and, crucially,
- promoting greater awareness of the issues throughout society. (DETR, 1997: para. 10)

This chapter will examine how successful government policies were between 1979 and 1997 in shifting the balance in transport decision-making from politicians to private-sector businesses working within the disciplines of the market. It then examines their impact on the quality and quantity of transport investment. The legislation that created the former nationalized industries exempted them from normal competition law. They are now subject to it, so we start with a description of the basic provisions of UK and European competition law.

The relevant competition legislation

The three pieces of domestic legislation relating to competition are the Fair Trading Act 1973, the Restrictive Trade Practices Act 1976 and the Competition Act 1980. This legislation is enforced by the Director General of Fair Trading (DGFT), the Monopolies and Mergers Commission (MMC) and the Secretary of State for Trade and Industry. Most of the sectoral regulators – including the Rail Regulator – have concurrent jurisdiction with the DGFT under both the Fair Trading Act and the Competition Act. The procedures these bodies follow in working together are set out in the guide, *Monopolies and Anti-Competitive Practices*, issued by the Office of Fair Trading (OFT, 1995).

The test is whether some action can be shown to be against the public interest. In the case of the Fair Trading Act and the Competition Act any action is presumed not to be against the public interest until it has been shown to be so. If the technological circumstances create a natural monopoly, then, by definition, it will be cheaper for a single enterprise to produce than for several. Monopoly may then be in the public interest, providing there is sufficient control over prices, quantity and quality of output to prevent abuse of the dominant position. This logic lay behind the creation of some of the newly privatized network-based utilities as monopolists under the control of a specialist regulator. In the case of the Restrictive Trade Practices Act any registrable agreement is presumed to be against the public interest; it is an offence to fail to register it and it must be approved by the DGFT or the Restrictive Trade Practices Court. In all cases, if an action has been determined to have been against the public interest there is no penalty in respect of the action before the determination. Either it will become prohibited under an order issued by the Secretary of State, or it will be condoned, or agreement to moderate the behaviour will be reached with the offender. Unlike US anti-trust law there is no system of fines or damages to be paid to parties injured by the offending behaviour before the decision of the Secretary of State. To qualify for investigation the alleged offender must have a turnover above a threshold (£10m a year) and supply a significant portion of the relevant market (in many cases at least 25 per cent).

The UK is subject to the competition provisions of the Treaty of Rome (see Chapter 4), in particular to Articles 85 (prevention, restriction or distortion of competition) and 86 (abuse of dominant position), and these are important where international services are concerned, for example in aviation and shipping. However, they are of little direct relevance in the case of local passenger transport markets because Community law applies only where practices may have an effect on trade between member states. The new Labour government has indicated that it intends to reform competition law generally. It has proposed a Competition Commission to take on the functions of the MMC and also to hear appeals against decisions of the DGFT, under a tough competition regime to be introduced in 1998. The legislation will introduce a ban on anti-competitive agreements and anti-competitive behaviour. Companies that offend will risk fines of up to 10 per cent of worldwide turn-over. Customers and competitors which suffer damages would be able to sue for compensation in the High Court. These reforms will have the incidental effect of bringing the UK more nearly into line with the position under the Treaty of Rome and in other EU countries (*Financial Times*, 1 August 1997).

In practice there is no such thing as perfect or optimum regulation. The relevant question is always whether an imperfect system of regulation will achieve a better outcome than an imperfect, less-regulated market over a long period of time. Regulation usually has outcomes different from those originally intended. In particular, administrative barriers to entry risk creating the opportunity for the very exploitation of monopoly positions that worries some commentators about the current situation in the bus industry.

Competition and deregulation of bus services

The White Paper, *Buses* (DoT, 1984), took a simple line on competition. Regulation itself was seen as the important barrier which prevented competition. It was thought that significant barriers to entry to the industry could not be sustained by incumbent operators if the regulation was abolished: economies of scale, network effects, and problems of imperfect information were not considered sufficiently important to cause concern. It was acknowledged that predatory practices had been observed in the past, but it was argued that it would not be commercially sensible, or even possible, for an incumbent to ward off competition on many fronts simultaneously without the sustenance provided by a protected, regulated sector. It was also acknowledged that before 1930, under competition, there had been a tendency towards territorial companies and that operators in the dense urban areas had formed anti-competitive associations.

The lack of concern about these matters was founded on several observations. There is now pro-competitive legislation; corruption and criminal enforcement of cartels is not likely to be as much of a problem in Britain as it is in some other parts of the world; and any combines, associations and territorial monopolies would be so constrained in their behaviour by the threat of competitive entry by new operators seeking to undercut existing firms that they would have to behave almost as if the industry were perfectly competitive – the market would be contestable, to use the modern terminology. These propositions were strongly questioned at the time by opponents of bus deregulation (see, for example, Gwilliam, Nash and Mackie, 1985a and 1985b).

The 1985 Transport Act made the local bus industry subject to UK and EC competition law, like any other industry. The Labour government has promised further reform: the 1997 election manifesto said 'the key to efficient bus services is proper regulation at local level, with partnerships between local councils and bus operators an essential component'. And in its August 1997 consultation document, *Developing an Integrated Transport Policy* (para. 21), it said: 'Regulation will help achieve efficient, high quality bus services at the local level, providing an adequate framework and real choice.' Relevant questions in considering further reform are:

- Is general competition law deficient and will the proposed new competition regime solve the problems?
- Is there some feature of local passenger transport markets which means either that the law should be applied in a special way, or that the law should be changed in some way to suit?
- If the present system is deficient, how damaging are the deficiencies and will a proposed new bus regulation regime be less damaging than the current one?

Barriers to entry

In the bus industry, exploitation of monopoly power may involve raising fares, reducing the quantum of service, or reducing other dimensions of service quality, either to make excess profits or to feather-bed inefficiency. If barriers to entry are negligible then this exploitation cannot happen because sooner or later a competitor will enter, taking advantage of the opportunity created. By the mid-1990s the MMC had ruled on several cases. It established that two geographically contiguous companies could form a 'substantial part' of the UK within the meaning of the legislation and that such mergers would be viewed with concern. On the other hand, mergers involving bus companies that were not contiguous – of which there have been several – were regarded as being of little concern. However, the 1989 MMC ruling on the Badger Line merger case established a precedent that non-contiguous local territory occupied by two bus companies could also constitute a substantial part of the UK, even though it is much less than 25 per cent of the UK bus market. Thus small bus companies may be caught by one or other of these thresholds.

Some attempts to erect barriers have been detected and prevented after intervention by the competition authorities; for instance the attempt to restrict the use of bus terminals by the bus companies which control them. Other barriers are alleged to have appeared since deregulation. Beesley (1992: chapter 11) suggests that the existence of payments for concessionary fares, the rule that forces operators to declare their intentions to enter or withdraw from a route six weeks in advance, the underdevelopment of the leasing market for vehicles, and the prohibition on self-employed drivers from hiring themselves out to an operator unless they themselves hold operator's licences: all constitute secondary barriers to entry.

Predatory behaviour

Predatory behaviour has been alleged in the bus industry. The tactics may involve one operator reducing fares or increasing capacity in the hope of driving another operator out of business. Although what looks like predatory behaviour is not uncommon, it is notoriously difficult to demonstrate objectively that it has occurred. The OFT's test has three components:

- whether it is feasible for an alleged predator to recover his lost profit after dispatching the prey (and that must imply some source of super-competitive profit);
- whether the alleged predator actually incurs short-term losses as a result of his conduct; and
- that there was an intent to predate.

A number of the allegations of predation dealt with by the OFT have involved the bus industry (see OFT, 1995: 20). Typically, either an offender has simply agreed to desist, or no action is required because by the time the decision has been taken the prey has disappeared from the scene and market circumstances are quite different. It has been alleged that large companies have worked to establish the presumption that they would behave aggressively towards an entrant, even to the extent of damaging their own long-term profitability – in other words to behave irrationally. A barrier would thus be created because potential entrants give credence to this threat.

It has been argued that there are special features of the local passenger transport market which either imply a different interpretation of the existing laws or amendments to them. The leading argument is that transport markets need to be coordinated and integrated. In drafting the 1985 Act the government took the view that private, for-profit operators would recognize the need to inform passengers of their services, to market them and to relate them in a sensible way to those of others. Otherwise they would lose business. But many commentators attribute the disappointing failure of the increase in the total number of bus miles to generate a commensurate amount of new patronage (see Chapter 2) to a failure of the system to deliver the information, service stability and timetable coordination which passengers require. It is possible there is simply a shortage of the right kind of entrepreneurial skill in the bus industry, an enduring result of a regulated system in which marketing skills were less important. If this view is correct then there may be a positive advantage in agglomeration of companies because the rare, specialist skills in short supply can be used to advantage over a larger market.

There are some sophisticated technical arguments which carry some weight to suggest that in these kinds of markets price competition will not work as it should, and that this will lead to excessive provision of services. This is one rigorous interpretation of the old, but much-abused notion of 'wasteful competition'. But a theoretical demonstration of a tendency to over-supply the market, compared with a theoretical optimum, does not of itself demonstrate a case for restriction of output by regulation. That would imply that, in practice, an omniscient regulator could determine what the optimum actually was, and could enforce it without sacrificing other important benefits of competition or falling foul of the classic dangers associated with regulation – especially regulation which restricts the quantity offered. In other words, proposed new regulation (such as the systems currently in operation in London, Holland and Sweden) would have to do better than the system abolished under the 1985 Act.

It has also been pointed out that there are revenue benefits from service regularity which are external to the individual operator but internal to the market as a whole. That is, it may be to the individual's short-term commercial advantage to disrupt service regularity, but it is against passengers' interests and in the long run it damages the industry as a whole. If so there will be an inadequate incentive on the individual firm to cooperate for the benefit of the passenger.

The emergence of local monopoly in the bus industry is not, in itself, a bad thing, and it could offer some advantages in terms of making service coordination and integration easier. In dense urban areas transport users make complicated trips often involving several changes from one operator to another: car to train; train to bus; bus to bus ... Local monopoly may facilitate making the physical layout of interchange points convenient, ensuring that different services run to timetables which minimize waiting times for interchanging passengers, ensuring that information is readily available in one place (for example, that rail stations carry bus timetables) or that there is a central and comprehensive enquiry point, or a common ticket. These benefits to passengers may be delivered spontaneously by a local monopoly operator. But these possible advantages must be set against the usual public-interest concerns which surround monopoly.

Even if the requisite degree of coordination is achieved in the open market there is a risk that scheduling and timetabling agreements, which would be registrable under the Restrictive Trades Practices Act, would be judged to be anti-competitive and against the public interest. Worse, a fear of this outcome may discourage operators from even considering attempting to come to sensible arrangements. A similar problem may arise concerning market-driven attempts to cooperate over the acceptance of a competitor's tickets and travel cards. The development of rail privatization has emphasized this problem as we note below.

Is there a sufficient case for change?

One weakness of the existing procedures is general, but seems to be particularly serious in the case of the bus industry because entry and exit of firms can happen so quickly. This factor is the slowness of the processes, coupled with the lack of penalty on a party judged to have offended before the judgment: no fine and no payment of damages to an injured party. All that is required is an agreement to desist. Bus markets can change so quickly that serious or fatal damage can be inflicted upon complainants before their complaint is upheld. Equally, an aggressive operator can 'try on' a dubious practice knowing that, at worst, he or she will be told to stop it after a substantial delay. One response to this practice has been to suggest something on the lines of the US system of triple damages (see Beesley and Lipworth, 1994), though there are obvious difficulties in the assessment of such damage in a context where, for instance, it has proved difficult to demonstrate that alleged predators have been incurring losses. As we have noted, the Labour government has its own proposals for reform which would involve penalties and damages.

A possibility would be the creation of a specialist regulator with powers and duties similar to those of the Rail Regulator. An overriding duty to promote competition would help to prevent a slide into the undesirable state of affairs which the 1985 Act abolished. Another possibility would be to combine the function with that of the Rail Regulator, though this combination might create an unmanageable span of responsibilities. In addition the regulator could be given duties to collect and publish consistent information about timetables, possibly also proactively to coordinate timetables, enforce interchangeable ticketing and enforce regularity and predictability of services. To avoid the disadvantages of the pre-1985 regulated regime the Regulator would not be given powers to control fares or limit total quantity offered, except in special circumstances, or where he or she judges the public interest to be at risk by the normal criteria of competition law. In 1995 the House of Commons Transport Select Committee, reviewing 'the consequences of bus deregulation', recommended a similar course of action. An alternative would be to move to something close to the London model, in which a planning authority would determine all services and fares, and would procure these services under competitive tendering.

There are some indications that the bus industry is beginning to grow in the way that the White Paper originally envisaged. Patronage is not falling as fast as it was and it is increasing in some places. There is considerable active trading of bus companies, including purchases of companies by overseas capital. Some of the larger companies are now publicly quoted on the Stock Exchange and their share prices have been buoyant. The *Buses* White Paper underestimated the importance of potential failures of competition, and UK competition law is at present not ideally suited to dealing with problems that may occur. However, so far it is unclear how important competitive failures have been in practice. It seems unlikely that a great deal of damage has been done. It is particularly difficult to avoid framing legislation and its administration which will unintentionally hinder desirable, market-led integration and coordination.

Impact on costs, charges, fares and subsidies

A major reason for adopting the policy of bus deregulation was that it was the method most likely to succeed in meeting the timetable for subsidy reduction set by the public expenditure requirements. The aim was to introduce genuine competition into bus labour markets by creating a competitive industrial structure – that is, to both deregulate and privatize. However, the tendering alternative was adopted in London and the ways in which the two systems have turned out are compared below.

Outside London, deregulation proper occurred in January 1987, although a transitional arrangement started in October 1986. In terms of the objective of bringing revenue support back to the public expenditure plan levels, the policy worked well. It was made possible by the predicted fall in bus operating-costs per vehicle-kilometre. The real fall from 1983 to 1993 was 87 per cent in the former metropolitan counties, 58 per cent in the shire counties and 54 per cent in London. One source of these savings is a deterioration in terms and conditions of employment, with real weekly and hourly earnings in the industry falling, against an increase in other industries. Another source of savings was the fall in numbers employed which, together with increases in output, suggests considerable increases in output per employee. These are superficial comparisons, but several authors have made careful analyses to understand what has happened in detail; they confirm the general impression given by the aggregate statistics (see Gomez-Ibanez and Meyer, 1989; Gwilliam, 1989; Tyson, 1989; White, 1990; White and Turner, 1990). White and Turner note there was a 'windfall' reduction in costs due to the substantial reduction in fuel prices – worth 2 to 3 percentage points in cost saving. On the other hand, real labour costs have gone up so that, relative to general male weekly earnings, costs per bus mile have fallen by much more than the 30 per cent predicted in the White Paper. The predictions in the White Paper were relative to the earnings levels then ruling, not to present real levels. This outcome was consistent with the general strategy of the administration at the time: to weaken the power of the labour unions and break up nationally-negotiated agreements on terms and conditions.

In the English metropolitan areas, fares rose by an average of 33 per cent more than retail prices, 1983 to 1993. They rose by only 10 per cent in the English shire counties. There has been a remarkable increase in output where a decrease might have been expected: a 20 per cent increase in total vehicle-kilometres, 1983 to 1993 (but the average vehicle size has fallen, see below). As many vehicle-kilometres are now operated as commercial service as the total service in 1985–6; outside the big metropolitan areas there are more. The proportion of the routes extant before deregulation that carried on afterwards as commercial propositions – well over 80 per cent – was more than anybody had predicted (see Gomez-Ibanez and Meyer, 1989).

The cost reduction must be counted as the success of the 1985 Act. Public expenditure has been reduced in the face of rising real costs of labour in a labour-intensive industry. Yet physical output increased, fares rose only moderately and fares concessions were protected.

Patronage

So far, the official statistics indicate that patronage has not increased. Gomez-Ibanez and Meyer (1989) and White and Turner (1990) argued that, after standardizing for the fares increases the decline in patronage is much as it would have been on the basis of secular trends, so the increase in vehicle-kilometres does not appear to have generated more patronage. We have seen that costs per vehicle-kilometre have fallen considerably. But vehicle-kilometres have increased whilst passenger-kilometres have remained stagnant – so load factors have fallen and costs per passenger kilometre have fallen little. The explanation given by White (1990) is that the potential benefit of the extra vehicle-kilometreage was not converted into better service quality, because of irregular running, or vehicle bunching, lack of service coordination, or confusion amongst passengers because of frequent changes, or some other factor.

There can be no doubt that some of these factors played a part. However, it is not at all clear that it is a complete explanation. In most detailed case studies bus output increase was accompanied by an improvement in observed or estimated service quality. Banister and Mackett (1990) documented the favourable small-vehicle experience in terms of patronage (although they can find little direct evidence on delivered service quality) and note that the full market potential for minibus operations had not yet been identified. Evans (1987) estimated 'scheduling efficiency' in two case studies, defined as the theoretical average passenger waiting-time if buses had regular headway on every route as a percentage of the corresponding figure with bus times as they were. He estimated a 5 or 6 percentage point fall in efficiency since competition started which is not enough to vitiate the considerable increase in bus kilometres – yet measured patronage did not respond. He surveys other examples and notes: 'This gap between estimated and expected patronage is a puzzle, both at the national level and at the level of the case-study towns.' Evans finds the most convincing explanation of the unexpected patronage results, and the one accepted by other commentators, is that a known infrequent service has been replaced by an unknown frequent one, so that effective waiting times have not been reduced. White in 1997 gave an assessment of the most recent statistics. He says: 'The publication of *Bus and Coach Statistics* 1994/5 indicated a more positive picture than in earlier years . . . The flattening out of trend decline may indicate a return to 'normal' conditions, as a more stable network emerges . . . Real total revenue from users also increased, for the second year in succession. Bus-kilometres continued to grow . . .'

Tendering for bus services: the London alternative

In London, buses were not deregulated, but they were progressively put out to competitive tender, which is an alternative way of creating competition in the labour markets.

The cost saving from putting a given route out to tender was estimated to be 20 per cent on average (Kennedy, Glaister, Travers, 1995). It is of the same order as those previously estimated in the contexts of refuse collection and ancillary hospital services. After allowing for costs of administration the estimated cost saving was 16 per cent, on a like-for-like basis. But the tendering process often resulted in old buses being replaced by more expensive new ones. The estimated cost saving, net of administration costs after taking this factor into account, is 14 per cent, to which should be added any passenger benefits associated with new vehicles.

For several years the government declared an intention to deregulate bus services in London, as in the rest of the country. However, this intention was subordinated to privatization in 1993 and by 1994 London Buses had been privatized in ten separate companies, so London Regional Transport (LRT) could at least compare performance standards and aim to raise standards towards the upper range. The proposal for deregulation lapsed with the change of government in 1997.

Deregulation in 1985 would have reduced London bus costs more rapidly, but after several years of tendering this advantage has been attenuated – though it may still be the case that unit operating costs in the regulated London system are higher than they would have been under deregulation. However, the policy of route tendering and privatization in London has been highly successful. Whilst efficiency improved, the reliability of service to passengers also improved, partly because of enforceable quality clauses in the contracts with the service providers (Kennedy,

Glaister, Travers, 1995, give estimates of the revenue benefits attributable to this). It was easy for the regulatory authority – in this case LRT – to implement policies for protecting integrated ticketing and coordinated service planning. The London model is bound to be a leading candidate when the Labour government undertakes the review of the bus industry outside London presaged in the August 1997 Consultation Document.

Competition and privatization of rail services

The railways White Paper, *New Opportunities for the Railways* (1992a), originally envisaged that in due course there would be competing passenger services on significant sections of the network. This objective was one of the main reasons for separating ownership of the fixed infrastructure from the operation of trains: it would avoid the problems of achieving fair competition which have arisen in other regulated industries such as telecommunications, where the infrastructure owner is also a service-provider.

However, there has been a long tradition of using cross-subsidy to finance public-service obligations, especially in the non-commercial sectors: Network South East and Regional Railways. Even within the commercial, InterCity sector there has been cross-subsidy. The wish to introduce competition creates a problem: profits will be competed away in the form of lower fares and higher service levels. This is elimination of monopoly profit (to the benefit of consumers) on profitable routes. So if the public-service obligations to provide unremunerative services are to be preserved, these internally-generated profits must be replaced by an increase in external support. This problem was clearly illustrated by the privatization and deregulation of the bus industry outside London and may well have been a factor in the decision not to deregulate buses in London.

There has been no sign of a willingness on the part of the government to fund any such increase in external support – for instance in the official public expenditure plans. The first Franchising Director felt this problem keenly, being aware that the budget he expected to win was unlikely to be generous enough to keep all services going, in addition to replacing the lost monopoly profits. He therefore argued strongly that the Rail

Regulator should grant exclusive rights of access to franchised train operators in order to help him sell the franchises with the least possible financial support. The Regulator has a duty to take into account the financial position of the Franchising Director but he or she has to balance this against duties to promote competition and to promote the use of the network. This conflict had to be resolved before the franchises could be offered for sale. After consultation, the Regulator made his policy statement (ORR, 1994). It is a complex policy – understandably so in the circumstances. For the immediate future there will be no new competitive services allowed – although it is implicit that much of the competition (which is considerable) that exists in the inherited service patterns will continue. There will be scope for increased competition here in terms of the marketing of the services.

In line with the general Conservative philosophy the structure was designed with great emphasis on creating competition. But, as in the bus industry, common ownership is developing and, as we have noted, many people argue that competition is not appropriate in the transport industries, preferring instead notions of 'integration' and 'coordination'. Many of the Rail Regulator's duties are concerned with securing so-called 'network benefits'. The policy question is the extent to which they will be secured under competition, and the acceptability of any economic power which may derive from monopolies which evolve or are deliberately created in order to secure integration. An example is offered by the Central and Scotrail franchises: they were awarded to National Express, but that company also has a large portion of the local bus market (80 per cent in the case of Central). On 22 May 1997, the new government referred both cases to the MMC for review.

The Midland Main Line case was determined by the MMC in late 1996. Five National Express London-based inter-city coach services compete directly with the rail franchise taken by National Express. The Commission was asked whether the ownership of both coach services and rail franchise should be permitted. There was almost no coach competition against National Express on these routes. A critical question was whether there are barriers to entry of coach services: if not, then it could not exploit any dominance. The Commission concluded that National Express does have significant competitive strengths which are likely to discourage entry. These include a network both of services and of sales agents. The OFT (who carry out a preliminary investigation) had wanted National Express to withdraw from the coach market, but the MMC disagreed. The Commission judged that to insist on divestment would have been disproportionate and inappropriate for other reasons. Instead it recommends a set of behavioral undertakings relating to coach fares and levels of service.

In another case the large bus operator, Stagecoach, was warned that the OFT would be concerned if they were to purchase the Scotrail franchise: Stagecoach has 20 per cent of the Scottish bus market. Stagecoach was involved in another important competition case when it bought Porterbrook, one of the rolling-stock companies, which leases equipment to the Stagecoach-owned South West Trains and to franchises owned by other operators. The responsible department of state, the Department of Trade and Industry, decided not to refer the case to the MMC. It was content with undertakings on non-discrimination, confidentiality, provision of information, cross-subsidy, cooperation with Train Operating Companies and separate reporting and accounting.

Whilst there may be some arguments in favour of bus and rail mergers if there is adequate competition from other sources, as in the Scotrail and Central cases, the Regulator has made it clear that he would be reluctant to approve any further merger between the owners of rail operating franchises. An important reason is his ability to judge relative performance through 'yardstick competition'. Good examples of the usefulness of this ability were provided in mid-1997: judging the reliability of train service performance, and of accuracy in selling the correct tickets to passengers. It may be difficult to specify a reasonable absolute standard, but it is much easier to point to unexplained differences between companies and expect the worst performers to improve towards the average.

Charges for passenger access to Railtrack

One of the major tasks the Rail Regulator has is to approve charges for the use of the network: access charges. There were no market-derived prices to use as a starting point. However, there were some administered prices created by the Department of Transport in the period before the Regulator took his powers and they were in force for the first year, 1994–5. The Regulator took these prices as a starting point for the review during that year. The charges levied by Railtrack and set by the government for 1994–5 had three principal components: operating costs, current cost depreciation and a return on capital.

The approach is cost-based. The government sought to answer the question: 'What is the cost to the economy of keeping the railway running whilst in the public sector?' That, they argued, is what the charges should be. The relevant concept is economic opportunity-cost. The capital expenditure spent on railways each year is capital that would have an alternative use in some other, public-sector investment, where, by assumption, it would yield a real return of 8 per cent a year. In determining charges for 1995–6 the Regulator did not express a view of what an appropriate capital value for Railtrack might be. He simply determined that all charges should be rebased by reducing them by 8 per cent from the department's starting point, and that they should be reduced by a further 2 per cent each year below the Retail Price Index between 1996–7 and 2000–1, when the next periodic review will take effect. The next periodic review of access charges will take place in 2000, to be implemented from 1 April 2001. A parallel review of competition will take longer and be implemented one year later.

In July 1997 the new Labour government announced the implementation of the once-off 'windfall tax' on the privatized utilities which they had promised in their election campaign. As far as Railtrack was concerned the bill of £160m was smaller than the markets had anticipated and the share price rose by about 15 per cent on the announcement. The general opinion was that Railtrack would be able to absorb this figure within its efficiency gains without disturbing the planned programme of periodic review of charges.

By construction the access charges contain sufficient revenues to fund the investment Railtrack must make in order to be able to deliver an adequate service. There has been some public comment about the rate at which Railtrack has been spending, and a concern that funds intended for investment might ultimately end up in the pockets of shareholders. The Regulator expressed his own concern about Railtrack's spending early in 1997 and he pressed Railtrack to produce improved long-term investment plans. In the summer of 1997 he reached agreement with Railtrack that, after consultation, he would modify its licence 'to strengthen Railtrack's accountability to the Rail Regulator for the delivery of its stewardship obligations, and to give the Regulator greater enforcement powers in the event that Railtrack fails to deliver the programme to which it has committed itself' (ORR press notice of 29 July 1997). The sanctions include unlimited fines. By late 1997 Railtrack would have to publish details of how it planned to comply with its obligations, including the priority it attached to work on different parts of the network. If Railtrack found it could meet its obligations without spending the full amount allocated the Regulator would want the option of passing on some of the costs savings to the train operators and ultimately to passengers. On publication of these proposals Railtrack's share price again rose on the exchanges, indicating that they were no more severe than the markets had been anticipating.

Passenger fares

The Franchising Director decided he would regulate franchised passenger service fares only 'to the extent necessary'. He set a safety net of national price regulation of a 'saver' fare and weekly season ticket. In addition a 'tariff basket' has been introduced in particular areas (RPI minus 0 per cent for four years, then minus 1 per cent for the next four), and no fare is to rise faster than 2 per cent a year. (In some metropolitan areas the Passenger Transport Executives are setting fares.)

Caps on tariff baskets are tied to service performance, and extraordinary fares increases are permitted if they fund investment to improve quality of the railway. The Franchising Director has yet to declare his criteria for distributing subsidy: he has begun a consultation on the subject. So far he has essentially replicated the old services. But as franchises come up for renewal and the system develops it will become essential to develop some formal criteria.

Freight access charges

The most important principle is that freight operators should not be a financial burden on passenger operations and that Railtrack should not unreasonably exploit its monopoly position. Given the view that the costs attributable to freight movements are relatively low – especially in cases where the infrastructure is not provided for freight alone – but that there are substantial invariant costs to be recovered, one immediately thinks of some form of cost recovery where price margins above avoidable cost are higher in markets where there is greater monopoly power (as it is in the classical 'Ramsey pricing' solution). Then charges vary according to willingness to pay: each traffic is required to contribute towards the non-variable costs in such a way that the charges reduce their traffic by a similar amount. So a traffic which is only just viable at variable cost will be charged variable cost, whereas one which is profitable will be asked to bear a higher proportion of the non-variable costs.

In his policy statement the Regulator, endorsing the policy originated by the DoT, decided he would not attempt to specify detailed regulated tariffs (ORR, 1995). Rather, he adopted the principle that the operators and Railtrack will have the best information and that the most practical solution is simply to allow the parties to negotiate their own rates – as has happened in the past. Once agreed the rates must be approved by the Regulator as part of the access contract. The Regulator will apply several tests. He will require to be satisfied that the rate is not below avoidable cost. And it must not be above a cost ceiling which is the 'standalone cost' that would be incurred by a notional efficient competitor. This last condition is the interpretation of prevention of exploitation of monopoly power. Allowing negotiated charges implies a degree of price discrimination between operators (but not cross-subsidy). But the Regulator will not permit undue discrimination, nor prices which significantly distort competition between freight users in the final markets in which they themselves compete.

In recent years the freight businesses have been given the objective of avoiding losses, on the old accounting basis. However, they have failed in this. It is therefore quite possible that the Regulator's prohibition on cross-subsidy from the passenger side, together with the changes in costing, will lead to a substantial increase in average charges to rail freight. The government has made some direct subsidies available, but the amounts appear to be relatively small. They may have to be increased if the government's declared aim of reversing the dramatic historical shift of freight from rail to road is to be achieved.

The near-monopoly of rail-borne freight now held by English, Welsh and Scottish (EWS) has brought its own regulatory problems. For instance, EWS and Railtrack proposed to make an access agreement covering track access and pricing as a way of avoiding the need to carry out detailed negotiations over every service provided (subject to the Regulator's approval). Under this agreement EWS would have been allowed to put in a block bid to run trains between two points on the network without giving precise timings until it is closer to the actual running of the service. Smaller operators were concerned that this arrangement would make competition harder for them and it would make their own timetabling more difficult.

In his consultation the Regulator proposed that Railtrack should allocate notional timings to the services in its timetable. He also named 14 key points on the network where capacity is limited and where the number of EWS trains would be restricted to make space for competitors. He expects more disclosure of information on its contracts to enable him to judge whether it is discriminating against smaller companies. The Regulator's objective is to preserve the benefits of a single comprehensive contract between EWS and Railtrack without creating barriers to other rail freight operators.

The outcome of rail privatization

The May 1997 election provides a good moment to review the development of the railways policy. In addition to the fact that there was a fundamental change in government, it marks the point at which the sale of the industry was complete and the regulatory regime was settled.

The purchasers　Table 9.1 shows the number of companies of each type which were sold, the number of new owners and the sale proceeds. The table shows that the spread of ownership was

TABLE 9.1 The new types of rail companies

Type of company	Number of companies	Number of new owners	Total sale price (£ million)
Freight and parcels	7	5	246
Train catering	1	1	12
Rolling stock	3	3	1700
Train engineering services	3	3	2
Government owned	2	1	0
Maintenance workshops	7	4	33
Signalling and telecoms	4	4	200
Infrastructure design offices	7	5	5
Infrastructure (Railtrack)	1	1	1950
Infrastructure maintenance	7	7	125
Track renewals	6	6	44
Equipment supplies	6	5	38
Central services	14	12	45
Still to be sold	4	—	—
Closed as unsaleable	9	—	—
Totals	81		4400

initially quite wide, though mergers and takeovers – if they are permitted – may reduce the spread. Table 9.2 concentrates on the identity of the purchasers of the 25 train-operating franchises. Bus companies bought many of the franchises, in some cases in their own bus territory, a factor which creates significant issues for competition policy. Interestingly, one-third of all subsidy now goes to National Express because they won five of the franchises – some, as in the case of Scotrail and Central, the last to be franchised and the biggest loss-makers. The company will thus be in receipt of subsidy the same order of magnitude as had some of the old nationalized industries like British Leyland and British Steel. As we have noted, this company is the major long-distance coach operator.

Future subsidy Figure 9.1 shows a summary of the financial terms that have been agreed for the 25 train operating franchises. All the franchise agreements are for at least seven years. Those which will be renegotiated after seven years disappear from the diagram after 2003, and others drop out before the full 15-year term.

TABLE 9.2   The purchasers of train operating franchises

Company	Established activity	Franchise-operation
Passenger		
Stagecoach	buses	SW Trains, Island Line
First Bus	buses	Great Western, Great Eastern, NW Regional
Sea Containers	ferries, container leasing, hotels, Orient Express	Great North Eastern (East Coast Mainline)
National Express	coaches, buses, airports	Gatwick Express, Scotrail, North London Railways, Central, Midland Main Line
CGEA (France)	water management, industrial cleaning, buses, trains	Network South Central, South Eastern
Prism Rail	buses	London Tilbury & Southend, Cardiff Railway, S Wales and West, West Anglia Great Northern
John Laing	construction	Chiltern
Go-Ahead	buses	Thames Trains, Thameslink (with Via GTI)
Via GTI (France)	buses, trains, metros	Thameslink (with Go-Ahead)
Virgin Group	airlines, financial services, music, retail, radio	Cross Country, West Coast Main Line
MTL Trust Holdings	buses	Merseyrail Electrics, Regional Railways NE
GB Railways	(new company)	Anglia Railways
Freight		
Wisconsin Central Transportation	rail freight	Trainload freight, Rail Express systems, Railfreight Distribution
Freightliner	management buy-out	Freightliner

The fall in subsidy over the years is dramatic, and if it is delivered it will be a triumph in improving the performance of an important utility whilst preserving the quality and quantity of service. There are concerns that franchisees may not be able to deliver: that this may turn out to be an example of the 'winner's curse', whereby bidders who happen to have the most favourable estimates of future returns discover that they have been too optimistic only by the very fact that they are the winners of the auction. This problem is more likely to affect the franchises let later in the programme because bidding became very aggressive towards the end. Franchisees have taken two big risks. First, they are assuming that they can significantly reduce costs. Second, they are hoping to generate new, profitable traffic.

FIGURE 9.1   Rail franchise payments

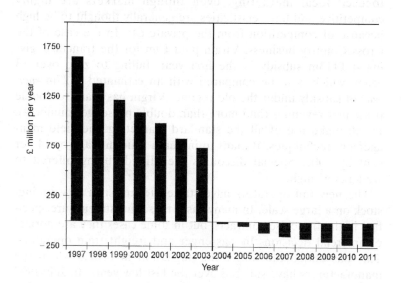

Costs   It seems likely that large-scale cost savings can be made if competition is successfully introduced into train operators' labour markets, just as they were in the bus and other industries. In 1992–3 the industry had 138 000 workers but only 1500 part-timers. Work patterns were inflexible in an industry which is subject to great peaks in demand. There were few split shifts. New labour contracts are already emerging. Great Western's train drivers now have a guaranteed salary of £20 200 in place of a basic wage of £11 700 plus many allowances. They have a shorter working week, more rest days and holidays. Drivers will drive single-manned up to 125 mph instead of 100 mph. On the Midland Main Line National Express have cut the workforce by 23 per cent and on Gatwick express by 17 per cent. CGEA is importing much more flexible working practices from rural French lines into Network South Eastern and South Central. In July 1997 National Express made an offer to 800 Scotrail drivers which would increase their average earnings by 23 per cent to £21 500 and cut their basic working week from 39 to 37 hours per week. The new management is reported as hoping to finance the improvement by reducing administration costs.

Revenues   New owners see scope for increasing revenues by more focused local marketing, even though markets are highly competitive and fares elasticities are generally thought to be high because of competition from the private car. In the case of the Cross Country business, Virgin paid £9m for the franchise, giving it £113m subsidy in the first year, falling to zero over 13 years, which is to be compared with an estimated £127m *each year* of subsidy under the old regime. Virgin has plans to double passenger revenues (and more than double passenger numbers). It will make use of all the standard marketing and yield management techniques. It plans to increase train mileage by 14 per cent by 2002. Special discounts are already being offered to students at night.

The new rail operators have started to invest in new rolling-stock on a large scale. In many cases these investments are specified in the franchise contracts, but in some cases they are normal commercial decisions by passenger and freight train operators. This has ended the long-term stagnation in orders which the manufacturers have suffered over the last few years. In July 1997 North Western Trains placed an order bringing the total value of rolling-stock orders over the previous months to £526m. On one set of estimates, by Save Our Railways, five franchises look like running into difficulty. (*Daily Telegraph*, 7 April 1997). But the predicted losses are relatively small and eight other franchises are expected to make big profits: the profits far outweigh the losses. In July 1996 the Association of Train Operating Companies (to which all 25 train operating companies belong) announced that during the year passenger journeys had increased by 45 million – 7.5 per cent – over the previous year. This figure is more than one would expect on basis of the rate of growth of economic activity over that period and the normal response of rail travel to it.

A real threat of bankruptcy is essential if cost savings are to be realized and it follows that some franchises may, indeed, go bankrupt. This is an important discipline and one that is lacking in a state-owned enterprise. It is likely that franchisees will attempt to persuade the Labour government to make concessions, believing it to be more likely to respond than the previous government would have been. Indeed, one of the major companies has already claimed that its franchise period should be extended in order to allow it to defray the costs of new rolling-stock to cope with growth in patronage. If the government fails to take a firm stand against these pressures then the commercial failings of the old system will be quickly re-established. If the threat that government will not bail out failing firms is to be credible it is necessary that there be proper provision to step in and keep the services of a failed company going. Such provisions are set out in the legislation: it would be up to the Regulator to implement them.

Freight   One of the greatest challenges of the new railways policy is to revitalize the rail freight business. It had been the government's intention to create three competing rail freight companies. In the event the market appeared to be weak and Wisconsin Central persuaded the government to sell them the freight business as a single company (which now trades as English, Welsh and Scottish Railways, mentioned earlier). Wisconsin asserted that the costs of running the trainload freight operation in three parts would have been 20 per cent higher than those of a single undertaking. Wisconsin expect to move costs closer to those obtaining in the USA. They say they will reduce the workforce from 7500 to 4000. Projecting a three-fold increase in rail freight traffic over ten years, it has ordered 250 new locomotives from North America and a large number of freight vehicles from manufacturers in York (*Lloyd's List*, 1 August 1997).

Conclusion on rail privatization

Full rail privatization was completed only just before the change of government in May 1997. Yet change in the performance of the industry is already rapid. Whilst it will take some years experience before meaningful conclusions can be drawn, the early signs were promising. Costs to the Exchequer were set to fall, reliability of service was improving (with the exception of some incidents which achieved considerable notoriety) and train operators were beginning to achieve their aspirations for substantial expansion of the passenger rail market. There is now greater transparency in costs and subsidies. For the first time changes are becoming apparent to passengers and taxpayers (local and national) which are clearly attributable to the railways policy. The long-term access contracts between Railtrack and the train operators are set to achieve an increased and much more secure level of investment in the railway infrastructure.

The Labour government has promised reform, involving the restoration of a measure of more direct state control. There is a risk that the new structure, so expensively created, will be prevented from functioning as effectively as it might, by the kind of direct intervention which proved so destructive to the performance of the industry throughout much of the twentieth century. Whatever the government decides is to be the nature of its direct control over the railway, the issues of policy on competition between bus and rail, and the relationship between any rail regulator and a new bus regulator, will have to be resolved. These decisions will be made in the context of the Labour government's wish to develop a 'coordinated and integrated' transport policy. In their turn, all these matters will be subject to the reforms in competition law and of the general system of utilities regulation the Labour government has promised.

Roads

Central government's aims for roads spending, including its contribution to local government roads expenditure, are stated in the Department of Transport's Annual Report. Its four objectives in the 1993 report express well the conflicting pressures on the department:

- assist economic recovery by reducing transport costs;
- conserve and improve the environment by trying to strike a balance between any environmental loss associated with the construction of new roads and the benefits and by removing through traffic from unsuitable roads in towns and villages;
- enhance road safety by building safer roads, securing improvement in the safety of vehicles, and encouraging better behaviour both by drivers and other road users;
- maintain and manage the existing network in a cost-effective manner while making the best use of the existing network. (DoT, 1993a: 39)

The roads investment appraisal process

DETR's Central Highways Policy Directorate has the responsibility for drawing up the roads programme. An initial sort is made of proposals coming from regional offices and elsewhere, based on rough estimates of traffic flows and economic costs and benefits.

> Proposals for national road schemes are scrutinised carefully to ensure that they represent good value for money, taking account of economic and environmental effects... The costs and benefits are discounted at 8 per cent, the same rate used in the appraisal of other transport investments. The results of this analysis are considered with the environmental assessment (DoT, 1993a: 52).

The procedure for deciding the details of a particular scheme combines a technical examination of the options with a consultation process involving bodies outside the department. The technical examination comprises three different types of analyses: a traffic study; an economic analysis; and an environmental appraisal. The three strands to the assessment process mirror the Secretary of State's three different types of objectives for new construction or improvement: 'assist... economic recovery...; conserve and improve the environment...; enhance road ssfety...' (DoT, 1993a: 39).

The DETR priorities on schemes for new roads take account of both environmental and economic objectives and do not depend solely on the rate of economic return (DoT, 1991a: 4). Yet cost–benefit figures are of great importance. DoT's reports systematically note: the roads programme shows 'an economic return overall of about 11 per cent in real terms', or the 'ratio of benefits to costs... is 2: 1 on average' and 'represents a real rate of return of around 20% per annum', or 'the average benefit: cost ratio... is... 2.3: 1' (DoT, 1985: 3; DoT, 1991a: 6; DoT, 1993a: 52). Similarly, when announcing in 1993 how much it had been spending each year on local road safety schemes, DoT added a rider that the average cost of such a scheme was £15 000 and saved on average annually one injury-accident, whose estimated costs were then about £26 000. 'These schemes pay for themselves nearly twice over in the first year alone' (DoT, 1993a: 63).

Officials and official reports increasingly demonstrate their willingness to take environmental gains into consideration: 'In some cases schemes which have negative Net Present Values [the measure of national economic benefits] on the economic assessment proceed because they produce environmental benefits which are judged sufficient to outweigh the negative NPV' (DoT, 1991b: 7).

Traffic study

The traffic study is one of the three strands to the analysis both in its own right (for instance, forecast dates for congestion) and as an input to the other two strands. From traffic surveys, trends in traffic growth and any known planned developments likely to attract extra vehicle activity, forecasts are made of current and future traffic flows on both the existing roads and the possible alternative routes once the improvement is made. Consideration may be given to traffic management schemes, road improvements and new roads. The forecasts include both high growth-rate and low growth-rate scenarios. Local trends in traffic growth take into account local forecasts of population or employment change but build on the National Road Traffic Forecasts, themselves based on assumptions that traffic demand is related to growth in GDP (see Figure 1.1 in Chapter 1), and, to a lesser extent, to changes in fuel prices.

Economic analysis

The results of the traffic study become the input to COBA, a computer programme first developed by the Road Research Laboratory in about 1960. It compares the costs of constructing and maintaining a road scheme over 30 years with the benefits gained by road users and others. It compares the cost-effectiveness of a project with a do-nothing/do-minimum proposal. The techniques are described in DoT's COBA, QUADRO and URECA manuals (QUADRO is a computer programme using the same principles as COBA to take into account queuing and delays at road works; URECA evaluates urban projects). Benefits are calculated in money terms from the expected changes to traffic volumes and traffic conditions both on the new or improved road itself and on the network of roads nearby. COBA then estimates the savings in vehicle operating costs, savings in journey times and reductions in the number and severity of accidents and balances them against construction and maintenance costs.

The basis for calculating the benefit arising from each factor is the price people would be willing to pay for that benefit. The principles and some of the empirical evidence are set out in detail in Layard and Glaister (1994). Vehicle operating costs are the costs to road users less the tax element, since the Exchequer would have to make up that tax loss through raising revenue elsewhere. Saving in journey times considers the benefit to people travelling both on business and for leisure. Working time is valued at the cost to the employer. Leisure and shopping trips and other personal journeys are regarded as 'non-working time' and valued at 40 per cent of working-time DoT (1987c). The same values are used for schemes throughout the country (1991b). Accident costs are mostly valued as the medical, police and material damage caused, the loss of output from people injured, and includes an element for 'pain, grief and suffering'. The valuation of a life saved is estimated on a 'willingness to pay for a reduction in the risk of death' basis – £0.5m in 1988 prices, and £0.75m in 1996 prices. DETR has recently been investigating how this 'willingness to pay' principle of valuation could be extended to non-fatal injuries.

COBA does not include any explicit element for gains made to individual regions, firms or people which would be offset by losses made by other regions, firms or people. To do so would be to count some economic effects twice over. COBA in effect evaluates the net gain to the nation of savings made by road users, which may be reflected in extra profit or lower charges to customers, or simply in saving users their own time. DETR estimates that one pound spent on their road improvement schemes results in approximately 86p in time and vehicle operating-cost benefits for business users (£1.06 for private users), plus 38p in accident benefits. In 1993 the average benefit: cost ratio of DETR schemes was 2.3: 1. It was higher for motorway schemes (2.6: 1) and lower for all-purpose roads (2.2: 1) (1993a: 52).

Environmental assessment

The third strand of the preparatory analysis for a scheme is a non-quantitative assessment of its impact on the environment, both positive (such as the removal of heavy vehicles from the proximity of mediaeval foundations) and negative (such as the destruction of rare types of natural habitat) and the costs of mitigating adverse effects. The 'environment' here includes the landscape, nature conservation, buildings-townscapes and air quality.

Environmental appraisal has been a part of the department's procedures since the mid-1970s. The EU Environmental Impact Assessment Directive 85/337 extended principles already generally adopted for roads in the UK. The regulatory framework is changed since large projects may now come to the attention of the European Commission and the European Court of Justice. The procedures set out in the directive must be applied to all motorways, and to most other transport projects if they are likely to have significant effects on the environment. Lines for long-distance rail traffic (including the Channel Tunnel Rail Link) are also required to have an environmental appraisal.

The department published a Manual of Environmental Appraisal in 1983, and an updated volume was issued in July 1993; the Scottish Office issued the similar Scottish Traffic and Environmental Appraisal Manual in 1986. The methods were originally developed for inter-urban routes and adapted for urban roads from 1987 on the basis of advice from the Standing Advisory Committee on Trunk Road Assessment (SACTRA). The techniques set out in the manual assist department officials to assess in a structured way the impact of changes in traffic noise, visual intrusion, accidents, effects on the ecology, development potential, conservation areas and so on. Traffic flow data is used in the assessment of road safety, driver stress, pedestrian delay, traffic noise and pollution caused by vehicles. Environmental effects are not valued in monetary terms. DoT accepted in 1992 SACTRA's recommendation to add water quality and drainage, vibration, night-time noise and the effects of blight.

The assessment process also tries to weigh up the effect on the various categories of users of the town or area involved. For instance if there are large numbers of tourists, or if there is a regional policy to encourage tourists, the assessment will include a section describing the potential changes to the quality of their environment. The COBA system can accommodate some conservation costs by, for example, including the capital cost of providing land of equal amenity value to the public or buying land to replace a natural habitat destroyed by new building. But the value of a Site of Special Scientific Interest may go beyond the short-term economic cost of providing an alternative site. It is more difficult to measure the costs of losing an ecosystem.

SACTRA's examination of DoT's procedures for assessing environmental impact found faults in this third strand to project evaluation. It recommended DoT improve its environmental assessment by putting monetary value on those environmental effects which could be so valued and that the government should carry out research and tests to this end. In addition 'the value judgements and technical assumptions made, and the methods used, should be explicit, open to scrutiny, challenge and possible revision'. DoT agreed with the principles but noted SACTRA's own comment that not all environmental effects could be valued and that judgment would still have to play a part (SACTRA, 1992: paras 16.43 and 16.12; DoT, 1992b: 4). Noise nuisance seems to be the most likely factor to yield monetary evaluation techniques in the near future.

SACTRA recommended too that the assessment framework be widened over space and time. DoT replied it would carry out case studies to examine regional and strategic effects of particular schemes and their environmental impact over varying timescales. The department also accepted that the present scheme-level appraisal was insufficient to capture the total and cumulative effect of the programme and said it would examine the feasibility of developing relevant assessment procedures in conjunction with the Department of the Environment. It rejected SACTRA's suggestion that directive 85/337/EEC expected significant environmental effects to be examined at every appropriate scale, not just scheme level (SACTRA, 1992, paras 16.03–06).

DoT continued to consider road improvements in a piecemeal manner; for example, it decided in July 1993 to submit to public inquiry its plan to provide feeder roads either side of the Heathrow section of the M25 ('widening the M25 to 14 lanes'), a procedure which seemed not to require the redevelopment of the M25 as a whole to be the subject of an environmental appraisal. It appears as though DoT only realized slowly that assessing the environmental impact of its schemes at project level but also at route level was not just a worthy if difficult thing to do, but something it was required to do. Because of EU requirements, environmental appraisal will now have to be more detailed and take place at an earlier stage. A fuller environmental study will need to be made at the time a scheme becomes public knowledge; that is, when it enters the road programme.

Consideration of options

Weighing up the priorities between two projects of equal cost–benefit ratio but where, for instance, the benefit in one derives mostly from the relief of congestion, and in the other from a reduction in accidents, is a matter of judgment exercised by the Secretary of State. Political judgment – implying ministerial judgment – governs the choice made between competing policy objectives and even within competing elements of one objective. Examples of investment decisions in which political judgment has played an important part include the motorway road-widening programme. Widening carriageways has a very high cost compared with the cost of building a road from scratch. Dualling is relatively cheap; widening very expensive. On the other hand where there is already a motorway, widening may take less land than building another carriageway alongside. It may therefore be preferred to dualling on environmental grounds, but it often avoids the need for a public inquiry which would require the issues to be brought into the open. If the European Commission were to succeed in persuading the EU Council of Transport Ministers to adopt its proposed directive on strategic environmental assessments, it would oblige DETR to provide the resources to evaluate the whole roads programme. The department's alternative approach has been that of the centrally directed widening-scheme which increases capacity on existing roads, but makes no evaluation of its total impact.

The investment process as described by DETR is mainly a spontaneous generation of schemes coming forward as proposals from regional offices and working their way through the appraisal system on individual merit. The maps in the Roads Programme show that a rough network is being formed over the decades from schemes which achieve entry to the national programme on individual COBA-based merit (or are built by local authorities, with TSG or EU-funding). But there is no published requirement for a project to derive from, or contribute to, some larger strategic plan for roads or for transport, let alone one whose environmental impact has been assessed.

Comparisons between road and local rail assessment procedures

The department rarely makes a direct comparison between the advantages of road and rail in solving a local transport problem. In 1993, Labour's Shadow Transport Minister, Joan Whalley, asked what assessment had been made of the economic and employment benefits from public funding of CrossRail, Orbital Rail and improving Thameslink, by comparison with proposed road schemes. The Minister, Steven Norris, replied: 'Assessment of road and rail projects in London is based on consistent planning assumptions and methodology. We make direct comparisons between road and rail schemes only where they offer alternative means of meeting specific transport objectives' (*HC Debs*, 22 March 1993: 482).

Cost–benefit analysis is routinely used for evaluating new public transport schemes in urban areas (such as light-rail, and rail extensions). The benefits to 'non-users' from the relief of roads congestion, and to both users and non-users in savings in journey times are exact equivalents of a road's COBA or URECA assessment. Similar environmental comparisons are made, for example, of the disturbances and costs of alleviating noise. Technical evaluations do not take account of employment benefits either in direct job provision or in providing better access to labour markets. It is possible ministers bear these factors in mind when exercising their political judgment on which options to pursue. The less tangible benefits are taken into some account. Section 56 of the 1968 Transport Act was introduced to enable local authorities to invest in passenger transport schemes provided the costs were fully covered by income from users (sales revenue) and by non-user benefits (reduction of congestion, noise, visual intrusion). In 1992 the DoT said it would take non-user or external benefits into account when assessing investment proposals for urban rail services. The value of the costs–benefit ratio is less a criterion for funding than an extra guide which ministers might use in establishing priorities between competing projects (but the same is true for roads).

There are some minor inconsistencies between similar elements of the appraisal methods for road and rail. The differences in safety expenditure and in the monetary value put upon a life is often questioned. A life is valued at about £2m at 1996 prices on the Underground and rail systems, whereas it is about £0.75m on roads. The methodology includes an element for the physical damage associated with an accident – and that costs more on average for rail than for road. However, the main difference between the two values may be that people are willing to pay more to achieve a higher level of safety when they are entrusting themselves to others on public transport than when they are themselves responsible. The disparity is recognized by the department, but 'the methodology is respectable', reflecting what people say they are willing to spend on safety when travelling by the two modes.

A more significant debate is on whether road and rail spending on safety is treated equally. It would be politically difficult to reduce the monetary value of safety on rail. Some expenditure consequent on the Fennell and Hidden Reports (on the King's Cross fire and Clapham Junction accidents) was regarded by professionals as being wasted, in the sense that more could have been done for safety by spending the same amount of money differently (Evans, 1995). A more positive approach could be obtained by valuing road safety more highly, or by according higher priority to road projects which provide safety gains.

That calculations of economic benefit is only one of many factors in determining government decisions was illustrated by the Jubilee Line Extension, being constructed at a cost of more than £2.5bn. Olympia and York, the developer of the Canary Wharf commercial offices scheme, had agreed that it would make a contribution of a series of cash payments over a period of more than 20 years. It totalled a nominal, cash sum of £400m, though its real value was somewhere between £150m and £200m, depending upon assumptions about future rates of inflation and rates of discount: in other words, not more than 10 per cent of the cost. The standard cost–benefit appraisal of the project, using comparable procedures to those employed in the Central London Rail Study, showed benefits as being 95 per cent of the costs. That is, transport benefits fell short of the costs by 5 per cent. (This calculation was carried out before the business demise of Olympia and York, when the construction costs were expected to be £1000m and before the severe over-supply of London commercial office space became fully apparent.)

Before the Jubilee Line Extension was proposed, the Central London Rail Study had estimated that benefits would exceed costs by about 30 per cent for two other new rail schemes serving substantial parts of London: CrossRail and the Chelsea–Hackney line. However, it was the Jubilee Line Extension which was first given the authority to deposit a private bill (a key decision) as a result of the contribution offered by the developers and their effective lobbying of senior ministers. The success of the Canary Wharf development was seen as a potent symbol of the financial services revolution and the move down-river from the City. The subsequent need to rescue the development from bankruptcy became the final spur to the second key decision, once the bill had cleared Parliament, to commit resources to construction. Meanwhile, the other two schemes have neither parliamentary powers nor funding.

Roads investment

Just as DETR's budget each year is primarily determined by the previous year's budget, so the roads investment programme is governed by history, being based on an existing programme of road schemes. The programme would take 20 years to complete and new schemes are continually being added. Being added to the programme does not guarantee a scheme's construction; it may be dropped from the programme at one of the various stages of examination, or as the consequence of a subsequent review of all schemes. The most usual identification of a potential scheme stems from a traffic problem raised by the public, local MPs, the police, local authorities and other interested parties. Since 1919 the ministry's central services have considered schemes submitted by its regional offices or county surveyors. Thus most national road schemes originate at local level and in an ad hoc way, stimulated by a record of congestion or accidents or some environmental problem, and the programme grows incrementally.

The opposite approach – 'a thorough examination of the transport problems in each area by using a combination of technical information-gathering and analysis and widespread consultations with interested parties' – was introduced by DoT in 1987 for a limited geographical area, with the London Assessment Studies. It was an innovative approach by the department in the way it identified and assessed transport problems. The studies looked at the effects of a set of road schemes and a set of rail schemes (Central London Rail Studies, such as CrossRail, Orbital Rail, and improving Thames Link). However, these studies were seen as a 'top-down' approach. The roads proposals were rejected by the local authority associations and the anti-roads lobby, and ministers saw people were not prepared to vote for them. Some of the rail schemes are to be implemented, after some delay – for example, Thames Link. Others have been deferred, in some cases for want of funding – for example, CrossRail.

An intermediate procedure is the general review of the roads programme by the Central Highways Policy Directorate, such as that which produced *Roads for Prosperity*. The National Traffic Forecasts published in 1989 indicated that growth in demand would bring major problems for the highways system as a whole. The DoT carried out a joint review with the Treasury, looking at forecast traffic demand and its effect on the roads programme. Some ideas went in centrally (that is, not from regional offices), including the £6bn motorway-widening programme. The same procedure has been used since then to cut the programme back again as political considerations related to concerns about the environment and about public expenditure have made cuts more popular than increases.

It is unclear how schemes are placed in order of priority within the programme. The National Audit Office criticized the DoT in November 1993 for not having prioritized the schemes within the motorway-widening programme, as it had said it would, according to the date at which they were forecast to become congested. Prioritizing schemes within the roads programme would not be easy. Technical considerations, themselves changing as traffic patterns change, have to be balanced with pragmatic considerations (adjusting the programme to the amounts of money flowing in, ensuring a reasonable stability in workloads in each region) and political considerations (change in emphasis by a new minister or a new cabinet, or a by-election). Given these factors, it is not surprising that priorities are not published in the national roads programme.

Party-political factors undoubtedly add weight to more technical criteria both in individual cases and in making strategic choices. There have been some well-publicized cases where urgent electoral priorities have stopped road projects (major London road schemes twice) or brought forward long-delayed projects. For example, construction of the Newbury bypass, an important but controversial link on the road between the Midlands and the port of Southampton which had been programmed for 15 years, was announced through a timely parliamentary question just before a crucial by-election in 1993; and the Humber bridge is the under-used product of a parliamentary by-election in Hull North in January 1966 (when the Wilson government had a small parliamentary majority). More generally, NEDC's road construction specialists noted in the mid-1980s that priority had been given to increasing the size of the motorway system by building comparatively cheaply at the expense of higher maintenance bills that outweighed the initial savings. Although DoT's general principle had been to search for the most economic design over the expected life-cycle of the road, this principle had not been applied since the mid-1960s, probably 'for presentational reasons' (NEDC, 1985: 12). The recent rapid expansion of the programme of procuring privately financed roads under DBFO schemes has the advantage of allowing managers of schemes with normal commercial incentives to take proper account of the whole-life costs of roads in making their designs, because they bear the risks on maintenance costs.

Conclusions

In Chapter 8 we noted how the aspiration of the late 1980s to increase public spending on the roads network was frustrated in the early 1990s by the greater force of the aspiration to cut public expenditure in total. However, more recently it became possible to increase investment in railways through long-term contracts for subsidy with train operators and to protect investment in national roads through shadow tolling contracts with private roads financiers. This policy has brought a much greater and more direct involvement of the private sector in the planning and execution of investment in transport. The private sector already provide the bus services in London, and both provide and plan them outside London.

It is clear that value for money has increased markedly in the London bus system. Costs fell and service quality improved. There are already signs that there will be cost reductions in the privatized railway, and the system of regulation is intended, as a minimum, to preserve the quantum and quality of service. Train operators are confident that they can expand both passenger and freight markets. Managers now have a more predictable financial regime and they work under normal commercial regimes. This is likely to contribute towards greater efficiency. On the other hand rail privatization included an element of rather expensive borrowing: servicing the capital sum represented by the sale proceeds of the public assets will be a burden on future taxpayers (one of the reasons that 'subsidy' appeared to increase).

In the case of deregulated buses out of London unit costs were certainly greatly reduced as was taxpayer support. It is not self-evident that value for money increased, because service quality did not unambiguously improve in all cases. The industry is responding surprisingly slowly to its new circumstances and there are some outstanding competition questions to be resolved. The Labour government promised to introduce some degree of regulation and this change will further complicate the assessment.

It will be several years before it becomes possible to assess the value for money improvements – if any – from the new, and surprisingly large-scale, involvement of the private sector in the financing and execution of roads construction and maintenance. In March 1997 the Highways Agency claimed an average saving of 15 per cent on the first eight DBFO schemes relative to the public-sector comparator, though no detail or references were given in support of the claim. In particular it is not clear to what extent the improved design and efficiency in operations have been set against higher borrowing costs. It remains to be seen whether the temporary relief to public finance has not simply mortgaged and hence reduced the resources available to finance future expenditure.

Part V

Conclusions

10 Towards a Transport Policy for the Twenty-First Century

This book has explored the financial and economic constraints within which transport policy is made (Part IV), as well as the planning systems at local and national level which allow both environmental and economic considerations to be assessed and given proper weight in the taking of decisions about particular schemes (Part III). The networks of policy-makers and those who seek to influence them at local, national and supranational levels of government have been identified (Part II). These complex structures and institutional arrangements reflect the complexity of the pressures and influences which have to be reconciled in the formulation of transport policy. Having laid out the pitch, explained the rules of the game, and provided notes on the players, it is now time to return to a review of the key issues and policy options which need to be addressed, as transport policy, shaped by these actors and limited by these constraints, moves into a third millennium in which more people and more goods will want to travel further and faster than ever before.

Transport and the environment

In the debate about transport and the environment which began in the late 1980s, the main issues have been identified and brought into increasingly sharp relief. But they have not yet been resolved. Transport projects are controversial and arouse strong passions in their advocates and their opponents. In the past people have sat down in the street to demand much-needed bypasses, and new transport ministers are always surprised by the constant stream of delegations led by constituency MPs who come to make the case for particular new roads or road improvements. But the same schemes may well prompt others to climb into trees and barricade themselves into houses and even tunnels under the ground to protest against the destruction of the urban and the rural environment. The physical obstruction of road-building activity became larger in scale during the 1990s and the techniques used more sophisticated, winning more media coverage and increasing the cost to the authorities and therefore to the taxpayer. But such scenes were not new; they were only the latest in a long line of protests which have focused public attention on the cost to local communities of new structures cutting a swathe through city neighbourhoods or attractive countryside. The history of such protests dates back to the Westway extension of the A40 through North Kensington in the 1960s or the Third London Airport proposals in the 1970s – and even to the objections which were raised to the building of the railways in the nineteenth century.

As recently as the early 1980s it was possible to dismiss most such objectors as belonging to the 'not in my back yard' tendency, but the increasing importance which needed to be attached to the environmental implications of transport policy began to come to the fore as a national concern following publication of the White Paper *Roads for Prosperity* (DoT, 1989a). Responding to the rapidly-worsening road congestion which accompanied the economic boom of the late 1980s – traffic increased by 7 per cent in 1989 alone – and a new national road traffic forecast which predicted further increases of between 87 per cent and 142 per cent by 2025, *Roads for Prosperity* proposed a substantial increase in the road-building programme to keep traffic moving. The new programme was welcomed by the Freight Transport Association and the Confederation of British Industry, which pointed to the heavy economic costs associated with congestion, but the climate of public opinion was changing. New doubts were beginning to be expressed by those who argued that providing for increased road transport on the scale proposed would do unacceptable damage to the environment.

Such views had been heard before, and ignored, but when the Green Party won 15 per cent of the votes in the 1989 elections for the European Parliament, all the major political parties were obliged to review their policies and give themselves a greener image. The Department of the Environment published *This Common Inheritance* (DoE, 1990) which was followed in July 1991 by the Department of Transport's own report *Transport and the Environment* (DoT, 1991b). The DoT report acknowledged the importance of environmental concerns, and explained what the department was already doing to address them, but it also drew attention to the requirements of a growing economy, making the point that 'we must accept that preserving the environment has a cost and be prepared to bear it'. (ibid. 3). Treasury ministers were not slow to spot the opportunity which this presented. The pre-election budget of November 1991 had been generous to transport, but a year later, following the Earth Summit at Rio de Janeiro with its high-profile focus on climate change and global warming, the Chancellor of the Exchequer, who by then urgently wanted to redress the balance between taxation and public expenditure, found it irresistibly convenient to increase fuel duty immediately by 10 per cent, and to announce a commitment to further annual increases of a minimum of five per cent above the rate of inflation, which he could justify as being required to encourage consumers to demand and manufacturers to design cars whose emissions would cause less of the pollution which is believed to contribute so much to global warming.

Raising fuel duties was a significant practical move, but it was only one aspect of the commitment to 'sustainable development' which was the central feature of the Earth Summit. Sustainable development had been defined by the 1987 World Commission on Environment and Development as 'development which meets the needs of the present without compromising the ability of future generations to meet their own needs'. In 1994, as a direct response to its Earth Summit commitments, the government published a White Paper setting out a wide-ranging strategy for sustainable development (DoE, 1994). The transport chapter of that document (chapter 26), stronger on analysis than on prescription, noted the commitment to annual fuel duty increases as the main means of reducing transport emissions of carbon dioxide, and EU plans to tighten up on other standards governing exhaust emissions. It drew attention to the forthcoming planning guidance (PPG13) as a longer-term means of reducing the demand for transport, but it also included a justification of the road-building programme on the grounds that a smooth flow of traffic causes less pollution than stop–start conditions on heavily congested roads. Looking to a future in which it might be 'no longer acceptable to build some roads', in which case 'prices and physical management measures would be the best way to ration the limited resource', the White Paper (paras 26.33–4) confirmed the government's intention, already announced in 1993 (DoT, 1993b), 'of introducing electronic tolling on the motorway network when the technology is available. Motorway charging will help to address congestion from rising demands for road capacity as the economy grows. It will improve the competitive position of rail and other forms of transport'.

Further work has followed from the 1994 White Paper. The Department of the Environment and the Government Statistical Services (1996) published a set of some 120 indicators of sustainable development for the United Kingdom. (The four transport use indicators are in section b, the eight energy use indicators in section e.) The indicators for energy use and for transport use since 1970 showed that, whereas there had been dramatic increases in the fuel efficiency of the industrial and commercial sectors, there had been little change in the fuel efficiency of road transport. Passenger mileage by car had doubled while rail mileage had remained about the same, and bus mileage had fallen by a quarter. As a result transport was burning twice as much fuel in 1995 as it had done 25 years before, with obvious consequences not only for the depletion of energy reserves but for the volume of exhaust emission gases.

Meanwhile, the Royal Commission on Environmental Pollution (1994) had published a major report on *Transport and the Environment*, which advocated a wide range of policies to reduce the impact of transport on the environment, and proposed demanding targets for the reduction of transport-related sources of pollution to be backed up by severe measures to achieve them. Shortly afterwards the Standing Advisory Committee on Trunk Road Assessment (SACTRA) published evidence that new roads intended to alleviate congestion may themselves be responsible for generating significant volumes of additional traffic. For 30 years traffic generation had been ignored in the economic appraisal of road schemes, because it was harder to evaluate than the benefits to existing traffic, and not regarded as significant for decision-making – if it occurred it was probably a bonus, suggesting that the new road link had increased economic activity – but following SACTRA's 1994 report, the government accepted that the likely significance of traffic generation should in future be assessed in the case of every scheme in the national roads programme (DoT, 1996b: paras 11.54–5).

The transport debate

Faced with this growing body of weighty advice calling into question many of the fundamental tenets of transport policy, the then Secretary of State, Dr Brian Mawhinney, used a series of speeches in 1995 to air the many issues which needed to be addressed in what he called a national debate on transport policy. His speeches, published as a consultation document (DoT, 1996b), covered all the main issues – a competitive economy, impact on the environment, the special features of freight transport and of urban transport, and not least the thorny issues associated with freedom and personal choice. Echoing the position which Malcolm Rifkind had taken five years earlier in his foreword to *Transport and the Environment*, Dr Mawhinney concluded his speech on transport choices with these words:

> We must be realistic in our debate. It is not the role of Government – certainly not a Conservative Government – to limit people's choices unnecessarily. Our instinct is to extend choice and to allow individuals to make decisions that best suit them. By the same token, people must not feel that there is little that they can do as individuals. On the contrary, there is a great deal they can do. I would like those who put forward calls for great national strategies to recognize this (DoT, 1995b: 51).

More than 260 organizations and individuals set out their views in response to the invitation to participate, and in April 1996 the government published its response, *Transport: The Way Forward* (DoT, 1996b), taking the same opportunity to respond formally to the 1994 report of the Royal Commission on Environmental Pollution. After such an extensive and serious re-examination of transport policy over several years, culminating in more than a year of a national debate, there were hopes that this new statement would attempt to answer the many important questions which had been raised. In the event, the Green Paper was little more than a skilful restatement of the problem with some limited development of current policies, such as the constructive suggestion that national trunk road planning might be adjusted to take more account of regional priorities and local needs (ibid. chapter 11 and annex 1), as the newspapers were quick to recognize (*Guardian*, 26 April 1996: 'Transport policy going nowhere'; and *Independent*, the same day: 'Transport paper opts for the easy route'.)

The numerous targets proposed by the Royal Commission were largely dismissed on the grounds that no-one knew what measures might be needed to attain them or what such measures might cost. The government preferred to wait and see how local authorities got on with achieving the targets some of them had set. Comparisons with other countries (particularly those which suggested that the UK could aim for a higher proportion of passengers and freight to be carried by public transport) were dismissed on the grounds that circumstances in other countries are different, which is no doubt true but scarcely a sufficient response. Although the government seemed to have come close to recognizing in the course of the debate that restraining traffic would require some combination of the stick and the carrot, the only carrot on offer was the expectation that privatized public transport would be more attractive than it was in the public sector.

Transport: The Way Forward shied away from using regulation or charging to discourage further growth in the use of the car, and the Annexes contained much detail about the difficulties surrounding any evaluation of the environmental costs which the motorist ought to be asked to bear (DoT, 1996b: paras 8.16, 9.3 and annexes 4 and 5). There were plans to start trials 'to explore whether it is technologically feasible to introduce electronic tolling on motorways', but any positive commitment to charging was limited to the use of the existing economic instruments, namely vehicle excise duty and fuel duty. Progress seems to have been slow since November 1993 when the government first announced its intention to introduce motorway tolling when the technology was available.

The indecision which characterized the Conservative government's response to the transport debate was perhaps no more than could be expected of an end-of-term government, reluctant to make policy commitments which could threaten an already fragile parliamentary majority. Whatever the cause, the Green Paper took refuge in worthy generalities, insisting that transport policy must reconcile the desire for a healthy, sustainable environment with the aim for a prosperous, competitive economy under conditions of careful control over public spending. The summary concluded with becoming modesty that:

> It is not a prescription for all time. Public attitudes on what measures are acceptable is bound to continue to evolve [sic]. But we need to change the way we think about transport; and this paper is intended as an important milestone on the way ahead (DoT, 1996b: 12, 14).

At this point the debate was taken up by the Labour Party. In May 1996, within weeks of the Conservative government's Green Paper, the Labour Party issued its own document, *Consensus for Change*. It declared that a consensus had now emerged to the effect that we 'should not try to build roads to keep up with projected traffic growth' and 'we need better public transport in order to keep the roads moving'. Within this new consensus Labour looked forward to working with Public–Private Partnerships (the Labour successor to the Private Finance Initiative, see Chapter 9) and local–national partnerships 'to create the long-term thinking, combined with urgent action, that our transport needs require'. In contrast to the fragmentation and lack of direction which was perceived as characteristic of Conservative transport policy, *Consensus for Change* advocated an integrated transport policy – integration between different areas of policy, different levels of government, different areas of the country and different transport modes and operators. But despite a foreword which claimed for these thoughts the status more of a 'White' than a 'Green' Paper, there was very little indication of what a Labour government would actually do to put it into effect.

There was a pause in the debate during the remainder of 1996, but it resumed with the election campaign in the spring of 1997. *The Economist* observed in its election briefing that there was not much to choose between Tory, Labour and Liberal Democrat routes to better transport, but the Labour Party's election manifesto stated that 'a sustainable environment requires above all an effective and integrated transport policy at national, regional and local level that will provide genuine choice to meet people's transport needs'. It was barely a month before a Secretary of State in the new Labour government, who was also Deputy Prime Minister and head of a reunited Department of the Environment, Transport and the Regions, had promised a White Paper on an integrated transport policy, to be published in 1998. Separate reviews were announced of the roads programme, the deregulated bus industry and the regulatory framework governing the privatized railways, and yet another public consultation exercise was launched to invite comments on some 27 questions related to an integrated transport policy (DETR, 1997). There was little that was new, but it was noticeable that the objectives of the review placed the environment ahead of the economy, and included 'reducing social exclusion and taking account of the basic accessibility needs of all sectors of society, including disabled people'.

The current transport debate has deep roots. It is about applying to transport policy the principles of sustainable development 'which meets the needs of the present without compromising the ability of future generations to meet their own needs'. This definition, drawn from the World Conference on Environment and Development (see above), has been redefined for British policy as 'reconciling two basic aspirations of society: to achieve economic development to secure rising standards of living both now and for future generations; and to protect and enhance the environment now and for the future' (DoE and Government Statistical Services, 1996: 1). Reconciling such conflicting aspirations is the stuff of high politics. It will have to extend to every mode of transport, not just cars and roads, but cyclists and pedestrians, public transport as well as private mobility. It will entail painful trade-offs between the rights of the individual, who would like to feel free to go wherever he or she pleases quickly and conveniently, and the rights of society to impose limits on that freedom where it impinges too heavily on the rights of others to the tranquil enjoyment of their environment in peace and safety. It will affect the company trying to get its goods to market quickly and cheaply as well as the private motorist trying to get to work or to visit a friend.

With so much at stake, and no easy answers in sight, transport has moved up the political agenda and is likely to remain there for some time to come. Because transport policy affects people so directly it will be fiercely contested, and the leadership required to build support for a new transport policy will require an unusual degree of political skill, courage and conviction. The Labour government of 1997 seems to have recognized this challenge. When he announced the review leading to the integrated transport policy John Prescott accepted that 'some policies needed to protect the environment would be unpopular with voters, and promised to lead the battle to win over public opinion. Politicians had special talents for communicating with and persuading ordinary people on difficult issues' (*Independent*, 6 June 1997). The point was not forgotten when the consultation document, *Developing an Integrated Transport Policy* emphasized 'promoting greater awareness of the issues throughout society' as a crucial objective of the review itself.

It is beyond the ambitions of this book to set out what the ultimate content of a new transport policy should be, but it may be appropriate to conclude with a survey of the key issues which policy-makers, be they politicians, officials in central or local government, leaders of businesses in the transport industry or interest groups seeking to influence them, will all have to address with urgency and determination over the next few years if transport policy in Britain is to respond to the challenges and opportunities of the twenty-first century.

The key issues

Rising demand

There are those who, seizing enthusiastically on the acknowledgment that new roads can generate additional traffic, would like to believe that the problem could be solved by consigning all the bulldozers to the scrapyard. However, most commentators accept that growing demand cannot be so airily dismissed. The 1989 National Road Traffic Forecast, which expected increases of between 87 per cent and 142 per cent by 2025, has been replaced by a new forecast which, against a somewhat higher

1996 baseline, expects the increase up to 2025 to lie between 53 per cent and 83 per cent (DoT, 1996b: para. 11.25). Even if the actual increase turns out to be at the lower end of this range, there is no getting away from the challenging prospect of a very large increase in demand. The link between economic growth and transport demand is strong and well attested and there are several other social and economic factors which will continue to drive it up. As the economy continues to expand, and people have more disposable income, they tend to spend more on travel. As the size of households falls and the number of households increases, people have to travel more to maintain their relationships. People are living longer, and the proportion of older people (especially women) with a driving licence will continue to rise. The opening up of the British economy to European and global competition has contributed to increased demand for the transport of both goods and services.

Another factor which influences transport demand is the trend towards larger schools and hospitals as well as shops. Larger units are often able to deliver a higher standard of service at an acceptable cost or a competitive price, but a smaller number of larger units serving larger catchment areas must mean that on average both staff and customers have to travel further. There are limits to efficiencies of scale, but it is not clear that these have yet been reached in all cases, for example in the optimum distribution of hospital services, where the rising cost of new specialist technologies makes it expensive and inefficient to provide them at more than a few of the largest hospitals.

There are powerful economic forces at work here, associated with changing lifestyles (Royal Commission on Environmental Pollution, 1994: paras 2.17–27), and much as people might like to see a levelling off in the rate of growth of demand for transport, it is not realistic to plan on the basis that growth will cease. A prudent assumption that demand for travel will continue to grow broadly in line with GDP would have important consequences for transport policy. In particular it is no good placing too much reliance on cutting the road-building programme. It may well be right to do that, but even if the reduction in demand growth attributable to removing from the road programme the traffic-generating effect of some new roads is significant locally, it will be marginal in terms of any national effect. Overall, cutting the roads programme will have very little effect on the inexorable growth of demand for transport. In the absence of other policy changes, it will mean more congestion and more pollution as stop–start conditions become ever more widespread. What is needed is a clearer focus on the other steps which could be taken to reduce both congestion and pollution on the assumption that transport demand will continue to increase with or without a large road construction programme.

Safety

Safety is the first of two factors which is likely to make it more expensive to devise an acceptable transport policy for conditions of growing demand and congestion. Public transport operators are expected to make the provision of a safe service their first priority. The government is also expected to give the highest priority to safety in any aspect of transport policy for which it is responsible. Changing technologies, increasing speeds and increasing congestion all carry risks. Many of these are successfully anticipated at the design stage, but centuries of experience suggest that accidents will continue to occur and that many advances in transport safety will flow from their rigorous and impartial investigation and the application by regulators and operators alike of the lessons drawn from them. No-one disputes the need to take steps to prevent the recurrence of avoidable accidents, but almost invariably the recommendations which flow from accident enquiries lead to increases in the capital or ongoing costs of transport provision.

Although people are prepared to take calculated risks with their own lives, for example in crossing the street or in driving too fast on a foggy motorway, they like to regard safety as an absolute requirement when they travel by public transport. But absolute safety is unattainable and the quest for it is unrealistically expensive. For example, automatic train protection (ATP) could reduce the risk of collisions, but it has been calculated that to install it across the whole railway network would imply expenditure in the region of £10m for every life which might be saved (Evans, 1996), expenditure which would displace or at least delay other projects which could make a more cost-effective contribution to passenger safety. In future the terms of reference for public inquiries following major transport accidents are likely to be required to take into account the costs as well as the benefits of any new safety measures which may be recommended. This proviso should enable a more rational debate to take place, but there will in practice be strong pressure to take steps which could prevent the recurrence of accidents on public transport, even if the cost is high. To the extent that additional expenditure may fall on transport industries in the private sector, and so have no direct impact on public expenditure, governments may prove more rather than less inclined to accept and impose such recommendations.

Environment

The second factor which is pushing up the costs of transport as we move towards the twenty-first century is our growing concern for the environment. The impact of transport on the environment takes many forms, and may well have to be countered in different ways. For example, transport contributes significantly to the increasing concentrations of carbon dioxide in the atmosphere which with other so-called greenhouse gases is held responsible for global warming; but since the UK produces only three per cent of all carbon dioxide emissions from human activities, and transport generates less than a quarter of UK emissions of carbon dioxide, reducing UK transport emissions will not on its own solve the problem, even if the causes have been correctly diagnosed, which is open to some doubt. So far as global warming is concerned, Britain must make its contribution within an international context if there is to be any significant effect (figures drawn from Royal Commission on Environmental Pollution, 1994: paras 3.58 and 3.73).

Many other pollutants have much more immediate effects on the local environment. In 1992 transport (mainly road transport) accounted for 90 per cent of UK carbon monoxide pollution, 57 per cent of nitrogen oxides, 48 per cent of particulates and 38 per cent of volatile organic compounds (ibid. paras 3.7–11, and tables 3.2–3.3). Regulations setting ever-stricter conditions on vehicle exhaust emissions may initially impose higher costs on manufacturers and purchasers, and even depress the market for new vehicles, though the potential impact is likely to be exaggerated by industry sources. Yet estimates of the costs imposed on society by such emissions, and hence the benefits which could be attained by suppressing them, are also high (see Small and Kazimi, 1995; Eyre *et al.*, 1997). Similar considerations apply to much noise pollution both from road vehicles and from aircraft. Pitching the regulatory requirements at the right level will be both difficult and controversial, and agreement will have to be reached at least within the European Union, if British manufacturers and users are not to be placed at a serious competitive disadvantage. However, the environmental benefits of less noisy vehicles, lower fuel consumption and less noxious emissions could well justify the initial cost of such regulations.

Carbon dioxide emissions from transport will be reduced mainly by improving the efficiency of the combustion process so that less fuel has to be burned to go the same distance, or by persuading people to make fewer journeys by car. Following the dramatic fuel price increases which were imposed on the motor industry by the oil crises of the 1970s, manufacturers competed very effectively to improve fuel consumption levels. More recently, with fuel prices falling in real terms, and cars becoming up to 30 per cent heavier because of extra safety requirements, fuel efficiency has stagnated or even declined. But Greenpeace Germany demonstrated in 1996 that a lighter Renault Twingo fitted with a re-designed engine could use 43 per cent less fuel than the commercial model, and could be built at an additional cost which might be around 12 per cent (or £870 per car) if it went into mass production (*Independent*, 14 August 1996). It would appear that major improvements in fuel efficiency and reduced pollution are available if the right regulatory or taxation mechanisms can be put in place to make them economically attractive.

Another major concern is the protection of the urban and rural environment, which is the continuing task of the planning system at both local and national levels, discussed in Chapters 6 and 7. It may initially be much easier and cheaper to allow major new developments to take place on greenfield sites, relying on most people to get there by car, but if traffic growth is to be discouraged wherever possible, it will become increasingly important to site schools, hospitals, leisure centres, shops and offices where a high proportion of staff and customers can use public transport. Judgments about this will have to continue to be made case by case, but if some new roads or railways or airports still have to be built or extended, it seems likely that the conflict between economic necessity and environmental concerns will often have to be resolved by accepting higher costs in the public sector, or by imposing them on the private sector – for example, by requiring more tunnelling, or by imposing more stringent requirements for access by public transport to reduce the need for road access.

The policy options

Technology

Given these inexorable pressures to provide more transport whilst raising safety standards and protecting the environment, the first priority must be to make the best possible use of existing transport infrastructure. On all forms of transport the ingenuity of engineers and computer experts has been widely used to optimize the capacity of the network and it is to be expected that further advances in technology will continue to make a helpful contribution. Simple concepts such as longer trains and platforms, as well as more advanced systems such as state-of-the-art signalling, can increase the frequency and capacity of trains on congested commuter networks. The humble traffic light increases the volume of traffic which can negotiate junctions safely, while reserved lanes and transponders on buses can give public transport priority. Integrated systems such as SCOOT can link traffic lights to respond to changing traffic conditions and optimize traffic flows over a large urban area. Similar systems can be used on the motorway network to detect the build-up of congestion and use variable message signs to slow traffic down or direct it onto alternative routes. In-car computers linked to networks of roadside sensors can already select the most efficient route for some journeys depending on actual traffic conditions, and their use will spread as system coverage becomes more complete. Engines that are more efficient and catalytic converters to reduce harmful emissions do not increase the capacity of the network, but they do hold out the prospect of accommodating a significant increase in traffic without making air pollution any worse.

All these measures are worthwhile, and many of them succeed in increasing capacity and improving safety without doing any significant further damage to the environment but, with the possible exception of the scope for technology to reduce air pollution, they can make only a tiny impression on the scale of the problem.

Public transport

Faced with the limitations of technology, the old answer was to build still more roads, but this option is now perceived as having such serious financial and environmental drawbacks that it is difficult to envisage circumstances in which it could once again be regarded as the appropriate response, at least on its own. Among those who are opposed to an extensive road construction programme but recognize that increasing congestion is not acceptable either, the most popular solution to rising demand for travel is probably to cut the cost and improve the provision of public transport. Good public transport has an important role to play where large numbers of people are making separate journeys which could at no great inconvenience be made together. When the Deputy Prime Minister, John Prescott, made a speech on World Environment Day to launch a review leading to an integrated transport policy he vowed that within five years more people would be using public transport and driving their cars less and invited the public to judge him against that commitment (*Independent*, 6 June 1997). Since only 12 per cent of journeys are made by public transport in the United Kingdom, compared to a European average of 16.5 per cent, a shift towards greater use of public transport may well be a reasonable objective of policy, but a shift of the share to the European average would still only account for a small proportion of the forecast growth in car travel, and difficult questions remain about the most cost-effective means of achieving such an outcome.

Reducing fares on public transport is one option. But this policy, which was popular under some Labour councils in the early 1980s, led to heavy demands for extra subsidy without having much impact on traffic congestion. Low fares tended to generate additional journeys by those who might otherwise not have travelled so much; they did not induce large numbers of people to leave their cars at home; and the increased subsidies made it harder than ever to find the money to invest in improvements to transport infrastructure. Investment is another way to attract more passengers, but 1994 studies of both the trans-Pennine route and the A1–M1 corridor between London and Sheffield suggested that the corresponding reduction in car traffic would be less than 3 per cent. Many of the advocates of a public transport solution would prefer not to believe such disappointing research results. Yet, where major public transport investment went ahead on the highly successful Manchester Metrolink, the number of vehicles entering the city centre on the major routes served by Metrolink fell by only 4 to 6 per cent in the morning peak, or about two per cent of all cars entering the city centre (see Chapter 7). Part of the explanation may lie in the public attitude surveys conducted in the context of the transport debate. These suggest that whilst there is strong support for improvements to public transport, 'few people indicated that they would actually use it if improvements did occur; it seemed that the advantage for many of improved public transport would lie in attracting other car users off the road' (DoT, 1996b: para. 13.12 and annex 2). The conclusion has to be that improved public transport, popular as it is, could absorb very large amounts of expenditure without – on its own – persuading more than a small minority of travellers to leave their cars at home.

Control by regulation or by market forces

If the 'carrot' of improved public transport is not enough on its own to get people out of their cars, it is hard to resist the conclusion that the 'stick' of less popular measures may be needed as well, designed either to raise the cost of motoring or to impose restrictions on car use. At national level, fuel taxes are already being raised year by year. New cars have to meet ever higher emission standards, which makes them more expensive to manufacture. The taxation benefits of company cars are being reduced. So far these measures have been applied gradually, and manufacturers have been able to mitigate their impact through offsetting efficiency savings; they may have to be stepped up if they are to have a significant effect. For example, the Royal Commission recommended that fuel taxes should be used to double the price of fuel relative to other goods by 2005 (1994: para.

7.58), which would imply doubling the rate of increase to which governments have been committed in recent years. In fact increases would need to even steeper, because falling world oil prices have meant that the real increase experienced by motorists over the three years 1994–6 has been no more than 1.5 per cent per annum (*Economist*, 23 August 1997). Charges may have to be levied for the use of congested roads at peak times. Access to city centres may have to be further restricted, parking spaces taxed and parking charges raised.

The five-cities study conducted by the Transport Research Laboratory in 1994 suggested strongly that parking restrictions or charging would be much more effective in reducing traffic levels than halving public transport fares (DoT, 1996b: para. 10.20; TRL, 1994). Halving the number of city centre parking spaces was expected to reduce the number of car journeys within the city centres by about one third; doubling parking charges would reduce them by one-sixth; whereas the effect of halving fares on public transport would be negligible. Parking restrictions, parking meters, traffic wardens and wheel clamps have all been unpopular when first introduced, but the evidence suggests that such measures are effective and in practice widely if unenthusiastically accepted as necessary. Their use will continue to spread, and new forms of restriction and charging will no doubt be tried. Privately owned parking spaces at businesses within restricted parking zones could be a likely target. Some European cities have experimented with systems which exclude half the cars every day, but this tends to favour those who can afford two cars, or at least two registration plates. France bans lorries on Sundays. In Britain lorries are banned from some areas during the night, and road engineering has been widely used to discourage the use by through traffic of unsuitable roads, to improve the safety of pedestrians and cyclists and to give priority to public transport.

The value of regulations depends partly on whether the authorities (mainly the police – see Chapter 3) have the will and the resources to enforce them, and critically on whether there is public support for their doing so. A large proportion of local atmospheric pollution is caused by a small number of badly maintained vehicles, many of them behaving illegally with impunity. Many bus lanes are rendered useless by illegal parking, often by commercial vans which impose a heavy cost on the urban economy when they cause delays by stopping, for their own convenience and economic advantage, where they should not do so. Effective road capacity could be significantly increased by redirecting parking enforcement towards preventing selfish parking which greatly reduces capacity at junctions. More effective enforcement might require that the police give it higher priority, or that the responsibility be given to others, but it would also require a greater willingness on the part of the public to accept that the regulations really do apply to them, and not just to everyone else.

A key role in regulation is played by decisions not about transport itself, but about land use. Developers may have to be refused permission to build facilities which generate large amounts of traffic at locations which cannot be well served by public transport – and such restrictions may have to apply to the siting of new schools and hospitals as well as shops and offices. But many of these decisions will have to be taken at local level. Acquiring an adequate site convenient to public transport may be much more expensive than approving a planning application for a spacious greenfield site on the edge of town which most people will have to reach by car. Where private-sector development is concerned, acute financial pressures may lead a council to make concessions to developers in exchange for contributions to much-needed community projects. It is tempting to approve the construction of an attractive and lucrative out-of-town shopping complex on the derelict industrial site beside the ring road if much of the business will be attracted away from neighbouring town centres which are not your responsibility, and the developer is offering to provide the leisure centre you cannot otherwise afford. A hard-pressed council is even more likely to grant permission if it has reason to believe that development will be allowed by another council nearby, or by the Secretary of State for the Environment on appeal.

How far governments are prepared to go in imposing regulations is a politically controversial matter. Traditionally left-wing governments have been more willing to impose regulations than right-wing governments. The importance of the connection between transport and land-use planning has been recognized by bringing environment and transport policy together in one department. It was a Labour government which in 1968 made the fitting of seat-belts compulsory and introduced breath tests for alcohol. John Prescott has made it clear that the Labour government of 1997 will favour road rationing to give buses priority over cars in congested streets. But if there is to be more regulation in favour of bus lanes, there may also be more regulation of the competitive conditions which have prevailed in some parts of the bus industry under deregulation, which have themselves contributed to city congestion.

The main alternative to administrative regulation is regulation by price and market forces. This approach is usually associated with right-wing governments, which like to emphasize the benefits of competition in the provision of public services and maximum freedom of choice for the customer, as Brian Mawhinney did in his contributions to the transport debate (see above). These considerations tend to favour methods of control which rely on pricing signals, such as parking charges or tolling and road charging, which may be at least as effective as administrative regulation, but a less comfortable instrument of policy for a government which wants its transport policy to reduce social exclusion. Regulation by price allows people to make more choices depending on what they can afford.

Although people say, when exposed to the facts (see summary of survey findings in DoT, 1996b: 127, annex 2), that they can be persuaded to accept that measures need to be taken to constrain growth in road traffic, for example by increasing costs of use, they are not usually enthusiastic, when such measures are introduced, about being charged for things which used to be free (such as parking space), or charged heavily for things which used to be relatively cheap (such as petrol). As a result, ministers with an eye on the opinion polls are understandably reluctant to impose such measures unless they are very sure that they will work and that they will at least be widely accepted even if it is too much to hope that they will be welcomed. There is a risk that draconian charges and restrictions will be angrily resisted if the benefits are not obvious and there is no reasonably convenient alternative, but there is also a risk that small cost increases, such as the gradual increase in fuel taxes, will have little or no effect other than to raise additional revenue.

Cecil Parkinson explains in his memoirs why he backed away from an initial market-driven enthusiasm for road-charging:

Adding £1 to the price of driving in London would make little or no difference to car numbers. Small price rises are never successful in persuading people to change their habits. An extra twenty pence on the price of cigarettes has very little effect on the numbers who smoke. I have similar doubts about European Community proposals for a carbon tax which will add only about five pence to the price of petrol. As a tax it will produce additional revenues, but as a means of discouraging consumption of fuel it will have only a minimal impact. Much more severe price rises would be necessary if consumption levels were to be radically cut (1992: 294).

In practice, once the public have got used to being regulated, right-wing governments seldom rush to remove those regulations that are seen to serve a useful function; and similarly, once people have got used to paying, left-wing governments can seldom afford to abolish the charges. Indeed, given tight constraints on public expenditure and the reluctance of any government to increase direct taxation, the money-raising capacity of road charging may well make it attractive to any government as an alternative to more regulation.

Targets

Targets are controversial. The government has had a road safety target since 1985, and is making good progress towards achieving the objective, which was to reduce the level of road casualties by one-third compared to the average level in the early 1980s (DoT, 1996b: para. 6.4). A well-conceived target may have played its part in giving the UK one of the lowest death and serious accident rates in Europe. The Royal Commission on Environmental Pollution recommended further road safety targets and new targets on noise, exhaust emissions, fuel efficiency, the shares of passengers and freight to be carried by public transport, and the proportion of urban journeys to be undertaken by car and by cycle. Targets in general, and the Royal Commission's targets for passenger travel in particular, were rejected in *Transport: The Way Forward* on the grounds that it was not clear how they could be achieved, or at what cost, or how effective they would be in reducing traffic (DoT, 1996b: paras 13.10–14). Targets may have some educational value, but unless they are carefully set and seriously monitored they risk creating the illusion of decisive policy-making whilst actually absolving leaders from taking more painful decisions with real consequences.

The setting of targets was the principal objective of the Road Traffic Reduction Act 1997, a private member's bill sponsored by Friends of the Earth, which was passed in the dying days of the Conservative government. The scramble to get it onto the statute book resulted in the elimination of all national targets, and local authorities were given a very wide range of discretion to select targets for all or part of their local road network. Cynog Dafis, MP, who secured a high place in the ballot for private members' bills in the new parliament, promptly introduced the Road Traffic Reduction (National Targets) Bill 1997 which proposed targets for national traffic five per cent and ten per cent below 1990 levels in 2005 and 2010 respectively, requiring the Secretary of State to draw up a national road traffic reduction plan to achieve them. Private members' bills seldom reach the statute book without some degree of government support or at least acquiescence, which Ministers, who had so recently supported the concept of targets in opposition, were reluctant to withhold. The price of their support was once again the deletion of all specific targets, but the bill kept targetry on the agenda as one possible element in an integrated transport policy.

Some local authorities have already established targets for road traffic volumes or for the shares of transport to be carried by buses and by cycling, and it may well be that the attractions of targets will be increasingly recognized as more and more responsibility is shifted onto local authorities, who are in the best position to identify relevant targets for local circumstances.

The package approach or an integrated transport policy

Transport policy has a major national dimension, but its effects are experienced locally. Much traffic congestion is local, even if it affects the motorways and major trunk routes which carry traffic into and around major towns and cities. About 60 per cent of car journeys are under five miles, a quarter under two miles. School trips account for nearly 20 per cent of all car journeys in the height of the weekday morning peak in urban areas, and the proportion of children driven to school by car increased from 12 per cent to 23 per cent between 1989 and 1994 (DoT, 1996b: paras 1.12 and 14.48). Local problems are best solved at local level, where local representatives are best placed to put together the combination of measures which they judge best suited to their particular circumstances. Local rail and bus services, parking charges and restrictions, tougher enforcement, park and ride facilities, planning and land use policies which take seriously the need to reduce dependence on the car, improved provisions for cycling and walking including pedestrianization schemes and some road engineering or even some new construction may all have a part to play within a local transport policy. Whether such policies are called a package approach or an integrated transport policy may have more to do with differences of political style than content. It is common ground that a successful local transport policy has to be a blend of many different features. But whatever the combination of features, there will almost certainly be considerable costs to face, and that is perhaps the biggest challenge of all, for governments at national and at local level.

Finding the money

If it is accepted that demand will continue to grow, and that safety and environmental pressures will tend to increase the cost of both building the infrastructure and operating the transport services needed to ease levels of congestion which would otherwise become intolerable, it is necessary to consider where the resources are going to come from. Since there is unlikely to be any easing of those pressures to reduce public expenditure which led to the new reliance on private sources of finance discussed in Chapter 8, it seems prudent to assume that public expenditure will continue to be tightly constrained, and when difficult choices have to be made, capital expenditure on transport will not have a particularly high priority across the range of government expenditure.

The recent emphasis on private finance has provided a temporary breathing space. But it remains to be seen whether the privatized railway companies can deliver the services agreed with the Office of Rail Franchising at the controlled fares and steeply declining subsidy levels envisaged in their contracts. Under these constraints on their ability to raise fare-box revenue, much will depend on their ability to cut costs if they are to make sufficient profits to invest in the new equipment which is needed if services are to improve and have any chance of attracting new freight or passenger business. Cutting costs is often a painful business entailing the introduction of new working practices, for which the companies can no longer rely on government support against union resistance. On the contrary, under the new Labour government, the Franchising Director quickly showed South West Trains and Regional Railways that cutting costs could lead to the threat of heavy fines if too many redundancies led to service cancellations. In the early years of the contracts the companies have had the benefit of considerable subsidies and, as it has turned out, increased revenues related to a growing economy, but the situation may look very different in a few years' time if shrinking subsidies happen to coincide with a downturn in the economy. If the sums do not then add up, investment will suffer, or the government will come under strong pressure to increase the operating subsidy (which will be firmly resisted) or to allow fares to rise.

Meanwhile, on the roads side, it has been found difficult to extend private construction remunerated by real tolls, beyond major estuarial crossings such as the Thames at Dartford or the second Severn crossing where drivers have no reasonable toll-free alternative. The only exception so far is the Birmingham Northern Relief Road, which will enable through traffic to by-pass a major congestion black spot where the M6 passes through Birmingham. The new wave of DBFO (Design, Build, Finance, Operate) contracts financed by shadow tolling (see Chapter 8) may represent good value for money as the department maintains, but shadow tolls will generate a growing stream of payments to the contractors from the departmental budget once the roads are open to traffic. Privately-financed construction remunerated by shadow tolling gets around the constraint on public expenditure at the time of construction, but pre-empts the budget in future years when the contractor has to be paid.

It seems probable that public expenditure on transport will come under severe pressure over the next few years. Pressures from safety and the environment will drive costs up. Shadow tolling will pre-empt the future budget. Planned reductions in the rail budget are at risk if the privatized companies find it more difficult than they expected to deliver the cost savings on which the performance of their contracts depends. If it is unrealistic to look to public expenditure to finance the additional capital investment which will be needed to meet the growth in demand which can be foreseen, logic suggests that new ways will have to be found to raise money from users. Private motorists are likely to be a prime target, particularly if one of the objectives is to persuade at least some of them to make more use of attractive public transport alternatives.

It is not so easy to devise acceptable means of raising more money from car-users. Parking charges are already commonplace, and if commuting by car is to be discouraged, it may become necessary to make provision for local authorities to levy a charge or tax for the use of parking spaces on private land. The easiest way to charge moving vehicles for road use is to increase fuel duties. This tax has the advantage of being cheap and easy to collect, and those who travel most are hit the hardest; but it is not at all well focused. It is particularly unfair on those who live in rural areas, where congestion and some forms of air pollution are less of a problem and there is little or no public transport. Tolls and shadow tolls are another way of charging the moving vehicle, but neither shadow tolling nor increased fuel duties remove capital investment from the constraints of the annual public expenditure round. Only real tolls or some other form of direct charging within the private sector can do that.

The economic arguments in favour of more direct charging have long been persuasive. The car is often more convenient than public transport, and that will always count in its favour, but more people would leave their cars at home if the perceived cost of each journey were not confined to the cost of the fuel used. The argument against toll booths on motorways is that they would require too much additional land, cause increased congestion and delay, and divert traffic onto less suitable roads. However, this is an area where technology is coming to the rescue. Charges could be levied electronically without causing delay, and they could be varied to persuade people to avoid travelling at times of peak congestion, where possible. They could more readily be levied, perhaps at different rates, on alternative routes to discourage through traffic diversion, and they could in appropriate circumstances be levied on congested routes to raise money in advance for the planned construction of relief works. One disadvantage of electronic systems is that the charges are not collected at the point of use, where they would be most effective, but this difficulty and the risk of evasion might be largely overcome if the account had to be settled with every purchase of fuel. A pay-at-the-pump scheme has already been suggested by the Royal Commission on Environmental Pollution (1994: para. 7.49 and Box 7C).

The government has been studying the feasibility of electronic tolling for some time, and by 1997 had reached the stage of trials at the Transport Research Laboratory. *Transport: The Way Forward* noted the opportunities which a successful trial would open up both to make motorists more aware of the real costs of each journey, and to transfer more investment to the private sector; but the Green Paper also noted that introduction was still some way off since primary legislation would be required (DoT, 1996b: para. 8.16). A form of city congestion charging was also being tested on one route into Leicester, but this too would require new legislative powers (DoT, 1996b: para. 17.40). Such powers will not be popular, but a government which takes transport policy seriously will need to face the challenge of taking legislation through Parliament within the next few years if charging is to play the rational part it could in a transport policy for the twenty-first century.

Conclusion

There are no simple answers. The pressures are very great. Transport demand will continue to grow, and meeting that demand will be more expensive if money has to be spent on higher safety standards, higher levels of environment protection and better public transport. Eighteen years of Conservative governments have been markedly successful in improving the efficiency of Britain's transport industries in the narrow sense of reducing unit costs. But they chose to take virtually all the benefit in the form of reduced public expenditure.

The Labour government of 1997 therefore inherited a structure of transport industries, now very largely in the private sector, which is probably healthier and less dependent on government subsidy than at any time since the First World War. There is more competition between air and sea, rail, coach and bus travel in a range of different markets than there has ever been. But the public mood has changed. Public opinion has been aroused but is still torn between an urge to build more roads born of impatience with the almost daily experience of traffic congestion and a realization that, while that may appear to be the answer to the immediate problems, there are limits to the amount of traffic which can be accommodated without doing unacceptable damage to the environment. There is an increased understanding of the problems posed by the seemingly inexorable growth of car travel, implying some adjustment to the balance between market determination and public regulation. Every town and city will have to find its own solutions within the broad framework of policies and resources determined centrally, but the government must play its part, too, in carrying any necessary legislation through Parliament, in determining the level of resources to be provided, in setting and using the regulatory framework within which public transport operates, and in carrying out its own direct responsibilities for the national networks.

Given the conflicting pressures arising from growing demand, tight resource constraints and the requirements of both safety and the environment, together with the direct impact which transport policy decisions have on the quality of life, there can be little doubt that transport policy will be vigorously contested as Britain prepares to meet the challenges of the twenty-first century. The continuing debate will focus around the Labour government's promised White Paper on an integrated transport policy, and the measures taken to implement those policies. It has said it expects to be judged by the results, and particularly by its success in getting more people out of their cars and onto public transport. It remains to be seen whether it will have the courage to adopt a long-term strategy and stick to it, or whether policy will continue to drift while one review succeeds another and individual decisions are dictated by political expediency and the short time-horizons inherent in the political process.

Further Reading

Each chapter in the book has references to works that will be useful for following up an issue. Here we suggest a few texts for each chapter that we think are specially helpful on the topic of that chapter, whether by providing more background, or in giving more detail. However, we start with a list of official reports – not all produced by the government – that are relevant to the debate underlying the whole book and especially to its introduction and conclusion.

Official reports (in date order)

Department of the Environment (1990) *This Common Inheritance: Britain's Environmental Strategy*, Cm 1200 (London: HMSO).

SACTRA (1992) *Assessing the Environmental Impact of Road Schemes* (London: HMSO).

Royal Commission on Environmental Pollution (1994) 18th Report [the Houghton Report] *Transport and the Environment*, Cm 2674 (London: HMSO).

Department of the Environment (1994) *Sustainable Development: The UK Strategy,* Cm 2426 (London: HMSO).

SACTRA (1994) *Trunk Roads and the Generation of Traffic* (London: HMSO).

Department of Transport (1996) *Transport: The Way Forward: the Government's response to the Transport Debate*, Cm 3234 (London: HMSO).

Department of the Environment, Transport and the Regions (1997) *Developing an Integrated Transport Policy* (London: DETR).

2 The evolution of transport policy

British Railways Board (1963) *The Reshaping of British Railways* [the Beeching Report] (London: HMSO).

Buchanan, C. (1963) *Traffic in Towns: Reports of Steering Group and Working Group* (London: Department of Transport).

Gwilliam, K.M. (1964) *Transport and Public Policy* (London: George Allen & Unwin).

Royal Commission on Transport (1930) *Final Report*, Cmnd 3751 (London: HMSO).
Savage, C. (1966) *An Economic History of Transport*, 2nd edn (London: Hutchinson, 1966).

3 Making Transport Policy in Britain

On the decision-makers
Cabinet Office (various years), *Civil Service Yearbook* (London: HMSO).
Department of Transport (various years) [Annual Report] *Transport: The Government's Expenditure Plans . . . . . .* (London: HMSO).
James, S. (1992) *British Cabinet Government* (London: Routledge).
Stoker, G. (1991) *The Politics of Local Government*, 2nd edn (London: Macmillan).
On transport decision-making:
Banister, D. (1994) *Transport Planning in the UK, USA and Europe* (London: Spon).
Truelove, P. (1972) *Decision Making in Transport Planning* (Harlow: Longman).
Wistrich, E. (1983) *The Politics of Transport* (Harlow: Longman).
On transport decision-making in London:
Transport Committee (1982), Fifth Report [session 1981–82], *Transport in London*, HC 127-I (London: HMSO).
Travers, T. and Jones, G. (1997) *The New Government of London* (York: Joseph Rowntree Foundation).
Glaister, S. and Travers, T. (1997) *Governing the Underground: Funding, Management and Democracy for London's Tube* (Centre for Regulated Industries, June).

4 Making Transport Policy in the EU

European Commission (1992) White Paper: COM (92) 494, *The Future Development of the Common Transport Policy: A global approach to the contribution of a Community framework for sustainable mobility.*

On EU transport policies:

Abbati, C. degli (1987) *Transport and European Integration* (Luxembourg: OOPEC).
Aspinwall, M.D.(1995) *Moveable Feast* (Aldershot: Avebury, 1995) – on EU shipping policy.
Despicht, N.S. (1964) *Policies for Transport in the Common Market* (Sidcup, Kent: Lambarde Press).
Whitelegg, J. (1988) *Transport Policy in the EEC* (London: Routledge).

On EU policy-making:

Nugent, N. (1994) *The Government and Politics of the European Union*, 3rd edn (London: Macmillan).
Richardson, J.J. (ed.) (1996) *European Union: Power and Policy-making* (London: Routledge).
Wallace, H. and Wallace, W. (1996) *Policy-Making in the European Union*, 3rd edn (Oxford: OUP).

5 Interest groups

On the place of interest groups in policy-making:

Alderman, G. (1984) *Pressure Groups and Government in Britain* (Harlow: Longman) – with many examples on transport.
Grant, W. (1995) *Pressure Groups: Politics and Democracy*, 2nd edn (Hemel Hempstead: Harvester Wheatsheaf).
Lukes, S. (1974) *Power: A Radical View* (London: Macmillan).
Marsh, D. and Rhodes, R.A.W. (1992) *Policy Networks in British Government* (Oxford: OUP).

On transport interest groups:

Bryant, B. (1996) *Twyford Down: Roads, Campaigning and Environmental Law* (London: Spon) – an informed, clear analysis of how a road project was decided from the point of view of its opponents.
Wistrich, E. (1983) *The Politics of Transport* (Harlow: Longman).
Hamer, M. (1987) *Wheels within Wheels* (London: Routledge & Kegan Paul) – a polemical account of the pro-roads lobby.

6 Local Planning

On the local planning system:

Brindley, T., Rydin, Y. and Stoker, G. (1996) *Remaking Planning: The Politics of Urban Change*, 2nd edn (London: Routledge).
Rydin, Y. (1993) *The British Planning System: An Introduction* (London: Macmillan).

On local transport planning:

Truelove, P. (1992) *Decision Making in Transport Planning* (Harlow: Longman).
Department of the Environment and Department of Transport (1994) *Planning Policy Guidance: Transport* (PPG13) (London: Department of the Environment and Department of Transport).

Steer Davies Gleave (1995) *Alternatives to Traffic Growth: The Role of Public Transport and the Future for Freight* (London: Transport 2000)

7 National Planning

In addition to the official reports listed at the beginning of this section:
Banister, D. (1994) *Transport Planning in the UK, USA and Europe* (London: Spon).
Bryant, B. (1996) *Twyford Down: Roads, Campaigning and Environmental law* (London: Spon).
Rydin, Y. (1993) *The British Planning System: An Introduction* (London: Macmillan).

8 Sources of Finance

Eyre, N.J. *et al.* (1997) 'Fuel and Location Effects on Damage Costs of Transport Emissions', *Journal of Transport Economics and Policy*, January.
Glaister, S. and Travers, T. (1994) *Tolls and Shadow Tolls* (London: Automobile Association).
Small, K. and Kazimi, C. (1995) 'On the costs of air pollution from motor vehicles', *Journal of Transport Economics and Policy*, January.
Sterner, T. *et al.* (1992) 'Gasoline tax policy, carbon emissions and the global environment, *Journal of Transport Economics and Policy*, May.
Treasury Committee (1996), Sixth Report [session 1995–96], *The Private Finance Initiative*, HC 146 (London: HMSO).

9 Competition and Investment

Beesley, M.E. (1997) *Privatisation, Regulation and Deregulation*, 2nd edn (London: Routledge).
Beesley, M.E. (1997) 'Rail: The role of subsidy in privatisation', in M.E. Beesley (ed.), 'Regulating the Utilities: Broadening the Debate', *IEA Readings*, 46.
Bishop, M., Kay, J. and Mayer, C. (1995) *Privatisation and Economic Performance* (OUP).
Bishop, M., Kay, J. and Mayer, C (eds) (1995) *The Regulatory Challenge* (OUP).
Kay, J.A. (1996) 'The future of UK utility regulation', in M.E. Beesley (ed.), 'Regulating Utilities: A Time for Change?', *IEA Readings*, 44.
Monopolies and Mergers Commission (1996) *Report on the Midland Main Line–National Express Group Merger*, December.
Nash, C. (1994) 'Rail Transport Regulation', in Gilland and Vass (eds), *Regulatory Review 1994* (Centre for Regulated Industries).

Bibliography

Abbati, C. degli (1987) *Transport and European Integration* (Luxembourg: OOPEC).

Adonis, A. (1993) *Parliament Today* (Manchester University Press).

Alderman, G. (1984) *Pressure Groups and Government in Britain* (Harlow: Longman).

Aspinwall, M.D. (1995) *Moveable Feast* (Aldershot: Avebury).

Bachrach, P. and Baratz, M.S. (1962) 'Two faces of power', *American Political Science Review*, 56, pp. 949–52.

Banister, D.J. (1994) *Transport Planning in the UK, USA and Europe* (London: Spon).

Banister, D.J. and Mackett, R.L. (1990) 'The minibus: theory and experience and their implications', *Transport Reviews*, 10/2.

Barker, T. and Robbins, M. (1974) *The History of London Transport* (London: George Allen & Unwin).

Bayliss, D. and Tyson, W.J. (1988) *Competition for local bus services in Great Britain* (Paris: International Commission on Transport Economics, UITP).

Beesley, M.E. (1985) 'Deregulating the bus industry in Britain: A Reply', *Transport Reviews*, 5/3.

Beesley, M.E. (1989) *The Role of Government in a Deregulated Market* (Paris: ECMT).

Beesley, M.E. (1990) 'Collusion, Predation and Merger in the UK Bus Industry', *Journal of Transport Economics and Policy*, special issue, September.

Beesley, M.E. (1992) *Privatisation, Regulation and Deregulation* (London: IEA).

Beesley, M.E. (ed.) (1994) 'Regulating Utilities: the way forward', *IEA Readings*, 41.

Beesley, M.E. (1997a) *Privatisation, Regulation and Deregulation*, 2nd edn (London: Routledge).

Beesley, M.E. (1997b) 'Rail: The role of subsidy in privatisation', in M.E. Beesley (ed.), 'Regulating the Utilities: Broadening the Debate', *IEA Readings*, 46.

Beesley, M.E. (ed.) (1997c) 'Regulating the Utilities: Broadening the Debate', *IEA Readings*, 46.

Beesley, M.E. and Lipworth, S. (1994) 'Abuse of monopoly power', in M.E. Beesley (ed.), 'Regulating Utilities: the way forward', *IEA Readings*, 41.

Beesley, M.E. and Littlechild, S.C. (1983) 'Privatisation: principles, problems and priorities', *Lloyds Bank Review*, 149.

Bennathan, E., Escobar, L. and Panagakos, G. (1989) 'Deregulation of Shipping: What is to Be Learned from Chile', *World Bank Discussion Papers*, 67.

Bishop, M., Kay, J. and Mayer, C. (1995) *Privatisation and Economic Performance* (OUP).

Bishop, M., Kay, J. and Mayer, C. (eds) (1995) *The Regulatory Challenge* (OUP).

Bös, D. (1993) 'Privatisation in Europe: a comparison of approaches', *Oxford Review of Economic Policy*, 9/1.

Brindley, T., Rydin, Y. and Stoker, G. (1989) *Remaking Planning: The Politics of Urban Change*, 1st edn (London: Unwin Hyman).

Brindley, T., Rydin, Y. and Stoker, G. (1996) *Remaking Planning: The Politics of Urban Change*, 2nd edn (London: Routledge).

British Railways Board (1963) *The Reshaping of British Railways* [the Beeching Report] (London: HMSO).

Brunner, C. (1929) *Road versus Rail: The Case for Motor Transport* (London: Benn).

Bryant, B. (1996) *Twyford Down: Roads, Campaigning and Environmental Law* (London: Spon).

Buchanan, C. (1963) *Traffic in Towns: Reports of Steering Group and Working Group* (London: Department of Transport).

Burnham, J., Jones, G. and Travers, T. (1992) 'The Government of London: Transport', *Greater London Paper*, 19 (London: LSE).

Cabinet Office (1996) *Civil Service Yearbook 1996* (London: HMSO).

Cawson, A. (1986) *Corporatism and Political Theory* (Oxford: Blackwell).

Cawson, A. and Saunders, P. (1983) 'Corporatism, Competitive Politics and Class Struggle', in R. King (ed.), *Capital and Profits* (London: Routledge).

Chester, D.N. (1936) *Public Control of Road Passenger Transport* (Manchester University Press).

Corry, D., Le Grand, J. and Radcliffe, R. (1997) *Public–Private Partnerships* (London: IPPR).

Cross, A.K. and Kilvington, R.P. (1985) 'Deregulation of inter-city coach services in Britain', *Transport Reviews*, 5/35.

Dahl, R. (1956) *Preface to Democratic Theory* (Chicago: University of Chicago Press).

Despicht, N.S. (1964) *Policies for Transport in the Common Market* (Sidcup, Kent: Lambarde).

Department of the Environment, Transport and the Regions (DETR) (1997) *Developing an Integrated Transport Policy* (London: DETR).

Dodgson, J.S. and Katsoulacos, Y. (1990) 'Competition, Contestability and Predation; the Economics of Competition in Deregulated Bus Markets', in D. Hensher (ed.), *Transportation Planning and Technology* (London: Gordon and Breach).

Dodgson, J.S. and Topham, N. (1987) 'Shadow Price of Public Funds: a Survey', in *Transport Subsidy* (Hermitage: Policy Journals).

Department of the Environment (hereafter DoE) (1976) *Transport Policy: A consultation document* (London: HMSO).

DoE (1989) *Strategic Planning Guidance for London* (London: HMSO).

DoE (1990) *This Common Inheritance: Britain's Environmental Strategy*, Cm 1200 (London: HMSO).

DoE (1994) *Sustainable Development: The UK Strategy*, Cm 2426 (London: HMSO).

DoE (1995a) *PPG13: A Guide to Better Practice* (London: HMSO).

DoE (1995b) *Town Centres and Retail Developments* (London: HMSO).

DoE (1995c) *Rural England: A Nation Committed to a Living Countryside*, Cm 3016 (London: HMSO).

DoE (1995d) *Planning for Rural Diversification: A Good Practice Guide* (London: HMSO).

DoE (1996) *Indicators of Sustainable Development for the United Kingdom* (London: HMSO).

Department of Environment and Department of Transport (DoE and DoT) (1992) *Transport and the Environment Study*. Joint memorandum to the Royal Commission on Environmental Pollution (November 1992).

DoE and DoT (1994) *Planning Policy Guidance: Transport* (PPG13) (London: Department of the Environment and Department of Transport).

DoE and Government Statistical Services (1996) *Indicators of Sustainable Development for the United Kingdom* (London: HMSO).

Domberger, S. (1987) 'Franchising in Competitive Tendering', in S. Estrin and C. Whitehead (eds), *Privatisation and the Nationalised Industries* (London: Sticerd, London School of Economics).

Department of Transport (hereafter DoT) (1984) *Buses*, Cmnd 9300 (London: HMSO).

DoT (1985) *National Roads 1985: England* (London: HMSO).

DoT (1987a) *Traffic and Parking: Tapwork Report* (London: Department of Transport).

DoT (1987b) *mv Herald of Free Enterprise* [Sheen Report] (London: HMSO).

DoT (1987c) *Policy for Roads in England* (London: HMSO).

DoT (1989a) *Roads for Prosperity*, Cm 293 (London: HMSO).

DoT (1989b) *New Roads by New Means*, Cm 698 (London: HMSO).

DoT (1991a) *The Role of Investment Appraisal in Road and Rail Transport* (London: Department of Transport).

DoT (1991b) *Transport and the Environment* (London: Department of Transport).

DoT (1992a) *New Opportunities for the Railways: The Privatisation of British Rail*, Cm 2012 (London: HMSO).

DoT (1992b) *Assessing the Environmental Impact of Schemes: Response to SACTRA Report* (London: Department of Transport).

DoT (1992c) *Transport and Works Act 1992: A Guide to Procedures . . .* (London: HMSO).

DoT (1993a) *The Government's Expenditure Plans for Transport 1993–94 to 1995–96*, Cm 2006 (London: HMSO).

DoT (1993b) *Paying for Better Motorways: Issues for Discussion*, Cm 2200 (London: HMSO).

DoT (1994) *Britain's Railways: a New Era* (March).

DoT (1995a) *Congestion Charging Research Programme* (London: HMSO).

DoT (1995b) *Transport: The Way Ahead* (London: Department of Transport).

DoT (1996a) *Transport: The Government's Expenditure Plans 1996–97 to 1998–99*, Cm 3206 (London: HMSO).

DoT (1996b) *Transport: The Way Forward: the Government's response to the Transport Debate*, Cm 3234 (London: HMSO).

DoT (1997a) *Transport: the Government's Expenditure Plans 1997–98 to 1999–2000*, Cm 3606 (London: HMSO).

DoT (1997b) [Department of Transport Highways Agency and Private Finance Panel], *DBFO value in roads*, March 1997; and subsequent (undated) notices of 1997.

DoT and DoE (1978) *Report on the Review of Highway Inquiry Procedures*, Cmnd 7133 (London: HMSO).

Dowding, K. (1995) 'Model or Metaphor? A Critical Review of the Policy Network Approach', *Political Studies*, 43/1, pp. 136–58.

Dunnett, J. (1962) 'The Planning and Execution of Road Schemes', *Public Administration*, 40.

Evans, A.W. (1987) 'A Theoretical Comparison of Competition with the Economic Regimes for Bus Services', *Journal of Transport Economics and Policy*, January, pp. 7–36.

Evans, A.W. (1990a) 'Competition and the Structure of Local Bus Markets', *Journal of Transport Economics and Policy*, special issue, September.

Evans, A.W. (1990b) 'Bus Competition: Economic Theories and Empirical Evidence', in D. Hensher (ed.), *Transportation Planning and Technology* (London: Gordon and Breach).

Evans, A.W. (1995) 'Risk assessment by Transport organisations', mimeo (London: University College).

Evans, A.W. (1996) 'The economics of automatic train protection in Britain', *Transport Policy*, 3/3.

Eyre, N.J., Ozdumivoglu, E., Pearce, D.W. and Steele, P. (1997) 'Fuel and Location Effects on Damage Costs of Transport Emissions', *Journal of Transport Economics and Policy*, January.

Foster, C.D. (1971) *Politics, Finance and the Role of Economics* (London: Allen & Unwin).

Foster, C.D. (1985) 'The economics of bus deregulation in Britain', *Transport Reviews*, 5/3.

Foster, C.D. (1992) *Privatisation, Public Ownership and the Regulation of Natural Monopoly* (Oxford: Blackwell).

Glaister, S. (1985) 'Competition on an Urban Bus Route', *Journal of Transport Economics and Policy*, January, pp. 65–81.

Glaister, S. (1986) 'Bus Deregulation, Competition and Vehicle Size', *Journal of Transport Economics and Policy*, May, pp. 217–244.

Glaister, S. (1987) *Public Transport Subsidy* (Hermitage: Policy Journals).

Glaister, S. (1991) 'UK Bus Deregulation: the Reasons and the Experience', *Investigaciones Economicas*, May.

Glaister, S. (1995) 'The New Rail Industry 1994–95', *CRI Regulatory Review* (CRI).

Glaister, S. and Beesley, M.E. (1990) 'Bidding for Tendered Bus Routes in London', in D. Hensher (ed.), *Transportation Planning and Technology* (London: Gordon and Breach).

Glaister, S. and Mulley, C.M. (1983) *Public Control of the Bus and Coach Industry* (Aldershot: Gower).

Glaister, S. and Travers, T. (1994) *Tolls and Shadow Tolls* (London: Automobile Association).

Glaister, S. and Travers, T. (1997) *Governing the Underground: Funding, Management and Democracy for London's Tube* (London: Centre for Regulated Industries, June).

Gomez-Ibanez, J. and Meyer, J.R. with P. Kerin and L. Dean (1989) *Deregulating and Privatizing Urban Bus Services: Lessons from Britain*, Report for US Department of Transportation (Washington: Office of Private Sector Initiatives, DC 20590).

Government Office for London (1996) *Strategic Guidance for London Planning Authorities*, RPG3 (London: HMSO).

Grant, W. (1995) *Pressure Groups: Politics and Democracy*, 2nd edn (Hemel Hempstead: Harvester Wheatsheaf).

Groeben, von der, H. (1982) *The European Community: The Formative Years* (EEC: European Perspectives).

Gwilliam, K.M. (1964) *Transport and Public Policy* (London: George Allen & Unwin).

Gwilliam, K.M. (1989) 'Setting the market free: Deregulation of the Bus Industry', *Journal of Transport Economics and Policy*, January.

Gwilliam, K.M., Nash, C.A. and Mackie, P.J. (1985a) 'Deregulating the bus industry in Britain (B) The Case Against', *Transport Reviews*, 5/2.

Gwilliam, K.M., Nash, C.A. and Mackie, P.J. (1985b) 'Deregulating the bus industry in Britain: A Rejoinder', *Transport Reviews*, 5/5.

Hailsham, Lord (1976) 'Elective Dictatorship', *The Listener*, 21 October.

Hamer, M. (1987) *Wheels within Wheels* (London: Routledge & Kegan Paul).

Haskel, J. and Szymanski, S. (1993) 'Privatisation', *Economica*, pp. 161–81.

Hay, D. and Morris, D. (1991) *Industrial Economics and Organisation* (Oxford University Press).

Healey, P., Purdue, M. and Ennis, F. (1993) *Gains from Planning? Dealing with the Impacts of Development* (York: Joseph Rowntree Foundation).

Hensher, D. (ed.) (1990) *Transportation Planning and Technology* (London: Gordon & Breach).

Hillman, M., Adams, J. and Whitelegg, J. (1991) *One false move . . . A study of children's independent mobility* (London: Policy Studies Institute).

Hills, P. (1989) 'Early Consequences of the Deregulation of Services in Scotland', Conference on Competition and Ownership of Bus and Coach Services (Thredbo, Australia), May.

HM Treasury (1993) *Breaking New Ground: The Private Finance Initiative* (London: HM Treasury).

HM Treasury (1995) *Private Opportunity: Public Benefit: Progressing the Private Finance Initiative* (London: HM Treasury).

Houghton Report (1994) Royal Commission on Environmental Pollution, 18th Report, *Transport and the Environment*, Cm 2674 (London: HMSO).

Jones, G.W. and Stewart, J. (1985) *The Case for Local Government*, 2nd edn (London: Allen & Unwin).

Kay, J.A. (1996) 'The future of UK utility regulation', in M.E. Beesley (ed.), 'Regulating Utilities: A Time for Change?', *IEA Readings*, 44.

Kay, J.A. and Thompson, D.J. (1986) 'Privatisation: a policy in search of rationale', *Economic Journal* March, pp. 18–32.

Kennedy, D., Glaister, S. and Travers, T. (1995) *London Bus Tendering* (London: Greater London Group, LSE).

Layard, R. and Glaister, S. (eds) (1994) *Cost-Benefit Analysis* (Cambridge University Press).

Lindblom, C. (1977) *Politics and Markets* (New York: Basic Books).

London Pride Partnership (1994) *London Pride Prospectus* (London: London Pride Partnership).

London Pride Partnership (1996) *London's Action Programme for Transport: 1996–2010* (London: London Pride Partnership).

Lukes, S. (1974) *Power: A Radical View* (London: Macmillan).

Mackie, P. (1987) 'Transport' in M. Parkinson (ed.), *Reshaping Local Government* (Oxford: Policy Journals).

Marsh, D. and Rhodes, R.A.W. (1992) *Policy Networks in British Government* (Oxford: OUP).

Moles, P. and Williams, G. (1993) 'Privately funded infrastructure in the UK: an analysis of the Skye Bridge project', Working paper 93/3, Centre for Financial Markets Research, University of Edinburgh, May.

Monopolies and Mergers Commission (1991) *A Report on Passenger Services supplied by the Company* [London Underground Limited], Cm 1555 (London: HMSO).

Monopolies and Mergers Commission (1994) *Report on the Midland Main Line–National Express Group Merger*, December.

Morrison, H. (1933) *Socialisation and Transport* (London: Constable).

Nash, C. (1994) 'Rail Transport Regulation', in Gilland, T. and Vass, P. (eds), *Regulatory Review 1994* (London: Centre for Regulated Industries).

NEDC (1984) [Vaizey Committee], *A Fairer and Faster Route to Major Road Construction* (London: NEDO).

NEDC (1985) *Investment in the Public Built Infrastructure: Report A: Roads and Bridges* (London: NEDO).

NEDC (1992) Construction Industry Sector Group, *A New Approach to Road Planning: Improving the process of planning, consultation and compensation* (London: NEDO).

Newbery, D. (1990) 'Pricing and congestion: economic principles relevant to pricing roads', *Oxford Review of Economic Policy*, Summer.

Newbery, D. (1993) 'The case for a public road authority', paper to the Major Projects Association, October.

Newbery, D. (1995) *Reforming Road Taxation* (Automobile Association, September).

Newman, P. and Thornley A. (1996) *Urban Planning in Europe* (London: Routledge).

Niskanen, W. (1972) *Bureaucracy and Representative Government* (New York: Aldine-Atherton).

Northamptonshire Chamber of Commerce Training and Enterprise (CCTE) (1995) *Northamptonshire Economic and Labour Market Assessment 1995*.

Nugent, N. (1994) *The Government and Politics of the European Union*, 3rd edn (London: Macmillan).

OECD (1987) *Toll Financing and Private Sector Involvement in Road Infrastructure Development* (Paris: OECD).

Office of Fair Trading (OFT) (1995) *Monopolies and Anti-competitive Practices* (London: HMSO).

Office of Passenger Rail Franchising (OPRAF) (1995) *Passenger Rail Industry Overview*, May (London: HMSO).

Office of the Rail Regulator (ORR) (1994) *Competition for Railway Passenger Services: a policy statement*, December (London: ORR).

ORR (1995) *Framework for the approval of Railtrack's track access charges for freight services: a policy statement*, February (London: ORR).

Parkinson, C. (1992) *Right at the Centre* (London: Weidenfeld and Nicolson).

Pinsent & Co. (1995) *Rail Privatisation*, 5, January.

Plowden, W. (1971) *The Motor Car and Politics 1896–1970* (London: Bodley Head).

Potter, S. (1993) 'Transport, Environment and Fiscal Policies: On the Road to Change?', *Policy Studies*, 14/2.

Roth, G. (1988) 'Private ownership of roads: problems and opportunities', 67th Annual Meeting of the Transport Research Board.

Royal Commission on Environmental Pollution (1994) 18th Report [the Houghton Report] *Transport and the Environment*, Cm 2674 (London: HMSO).

Royal Commission on Transport (1930) *Final Report*, Cmnd 3751 (London: HMSO).

Rural Development Commission (1994) *Rural Service: challenges and opportunities* (London: HMSO).

Rural Development Commission (1996) *Country Lifelines: Good Practice in Rural Transport* (London: HMSO).

Rydin, Y. (1993) *The British Planning System: An Introduction* (London: Macmillan).

Standing Advisory Committee on Trunk Road Assessment (SACTRA) (1986) *Urban Road Appraisal*, Report for Department of Transport (London: HMSO).

SACTRA (1992) *Assessing the Environmental Impact of Road Schemes* (London: HMSO).

SACTRA (1994) *Trunk Roads and the Generation of Traffic* (London: HMSO).

Savage, C. (1966) *An Economic History of Transport*, 2nd edn (London: Hutchinson).

Small, K. and Kazimi, C. (1995) 'On the costs of air pollution from motor vehicles', *Journal of Transport Economics and Policy*, January.

Smith, M.S. (1997) 'The Commission Made Me Do It', in N. Nugent, *At the Heart of the Union* (London: Macmillan).

Starkie, D. (1982) *The Motorway Age* (Oxford: Pergamon).

Steer Davies Gleave (1995) *Alternatives to Traffic Growth: The Role of Public Transport and the Future for Freight* (London: Transport 2000).

Sterner, T., Dahl, C. and Franzén, M. (1992) 'Gasoline tax policy, carbon emissions and the global environment', *Journal of Transport Economics and Policy*, May.

Swift, J. (1995) 'The role of the Rail Regulator', Sir Robert Reid Memorial Lecture (Office of the Rail Regulator), January.

Transport Committee (1982) [session 1981–82] *Transport in London*, HC 127-I (London: HMSO).

Transport Committee (1993) [session 1992–93] *The Future of the Railways in the light of the Government's White Paper Proposals*, HC 375 (London: HMSO).

Transport Committee (1995a) [session 1994–95] *Cross-channel Safety*, HC 825 (London: HMSO).

Transport Committee (1995b) [session 1994–95] *UK Airport Capacity*, HC 790 (London: HMSO).

Travers, T., Biggs, S. and Jones, G. (1995) *Joint Working between Local Authorities: Experience from the Metropolitan Areas* (York: Joseph Rowntree Foundation).

Travers, T., Jones, G., Hebbert, M. and Burnham, J. (1991) *The Government of London* (York: Joseph Rowntree Foundation).

Travers, T. and Jones, G. (1997) *The New Government of London* (York: Joseph Rowntree Foundation).

Treasury Committee (1996) [session 1995–96] *The Private Finance Initiative*, HC 146 (London: HMSO).

Transport Research Laboratory (TRL) (1994) *Impact of Transport Policies in 5 Cities* (Crowthorns: TRL).

TRL (1997) *The Impact of the Okehampton Bypass*, July (Crowthorns: TRL).

Truelove, P. (1992) *Decision Making in Transport Planning* (Harlow: Longman).

Turner, R. and White, P. (1987) 'NBC's Urban Minibuses: A review and financial appraisal', TRRL Contractor Report CR42 (Crowthorne: TRRL).

Tyson, W.J. (1989) 'A Review of the Second Year of Bus Deregulation', Report to Association of Metropolitan Authorities and Passenger Transport Executive Group.

Tyson, W.J. (1990) 'Effects of Deregulation on Service Co-ordination in the Metropolitan Areas', *Journal of Transport Economics and Policy*, special issue, September.

West Sussex (1993a) West Sussex County Council, *Budget 1993–94*.

West Sussex (1993b) West Sussex County Council, *Transport Policy and Programme: 1994/95*.

White, J. (1993) *Fear of Voting: Local Democracy and its enemies 1894–1994* (Oxford: History Workshop and Joseph Rowntree Foundation).

White, P. (1990) 'Change Outside the Mets', Conference on 'Public Transport: the Second Year of Deregulation in the Metropolitan Areas', at Institute of Mechanical Engineers, London, March.

White, P. and Turner, R. (1990) in D. Hensher (ed.), *Transportation Planning and Technology* (London: Gordon and Breach).

Whitelegg, J. (1988) *Transport Policy in the EEC* (London: Routledge).

Winsor, T. (1995) 'The Strategic Aims of the Rail Regulator' (Office of the Rail Regulator, April).

Wistrich, E. (1983) *The Politics of Transport* (Harlow: Longman).

Index